How to use this book

 This symbol means that you will need to think carefully about a point. Your teacher may ask you to join in a discussion about it.

 This symbol next to a question means that you are allowed (and indeed expected) to use your calculator for this question.

 This symbol means exactly the opposite – you are not allowed to use your calculator for this question.

 This is a warning sign. It is used where a common mistake, or misunderstanding, is being described. It is also used to identify questions which are slightly more difficult or which require a little more thought.

It should be read as 'caution'.

 This is the ICT symbol. It should alert your teacher to the fact that there is some additional material in the accompanying Teacher's Resource using ICT for this unit of work.

Each chapter of work in this book is divided into a series of double page spreads – or units of work. The left-hand page is the teaching page, and the right-hand page involves an exercise and sometimes additional activities or investigations to do with that topic.

You will also come across the following features in the units of work:

 Task

The tasks give you the opportunity to work alone, in pairs or in small groups on an activity in the lesson. It gives you the chance to practise what you have just been taught, and to discuss ideas and raise questions about the topic.

 Do the right thing!

These boxes give you a set of step-by-step instructions on how to carry out a particular technique in maths, usually to do with shape work.

Contents

There are 100 000 000 000 stars in our galaxy.

 How do you say 100 000 000 000 in words?

The scientific or mathematical way of writing 100 000 000 000 is 10^{11}. 10^{11} means $10 \times 10 \times 10 \times 10 \times 10 \times 10 \times 10 \times 10 \times 10 \times 10 \times 10$.

Say this as '10 to the power of 11'.

 How many noughts are there in 100 000 000 000?
What is the connection between the power of ten and the number of noughts?

Task

Copy and complete the table below.

Name	Number	Power of ten	Example
ten	10	10^1	ten fingers
hundred	100	10^2	hundred years in a century
	1 000		
ten thousand			
	100 000		
million			
billion	1 000 000 000		
	1 000 000 000 000		

 Look at the powers of ten for the numbers thousand, million and billion.
What do you notice?

 How many noughts are there in ten billion?
Write the number 100 000 000 in words.

Look at the number 673 802.

673 802

This 6 represents 600 000. It is in the 100 000s column.

8 is in the 100s column. It represents 800.

 How do you say 673 802 in words?
In large numbers the digits are grouped in threes. Why?

Exercise

1　Write as a power of ten:
(a) 100　　　　　　　　　　　　　(b) 100 000
(c) 10 000 000 000　　　　　　　　(d) 10 000 000 000 000 000.

2　Write in figures:
(a) ten thousand　　　(b) one hundred thousand　　　(c) ten million.

3　Choose the largest number from each of the following pairs of numbers:
(a) 10^4 and one thousand　(b) 100 000 and 10^6　(c) ten billion and 10^9.

4　In 1352 the 3 is in the 100s column.
It represents 300.
The following numbers also contain the digit 3.
For each number say which column the 3 is in, and how much it represents.
(a) 732　　　　(b) 3 179　　　(c) 65 382　　　(d) 738 924
(e) 3 768 772　(f) 384 200 789　(g) 38 567 486　(h) 67 824 253

5　What does the 4 represent in each of these numbers?
(a) 564　　(b) 65 428　　(c) 146 593　　(d) 4 080 123 675

6　Write the following numbers in figures.

(a) Four thousand two hundred and sixty five.
(b) Five hundred thousand, six hundred and eighty seven.
(c) Eight million, two hundred and seven thousand, three hundred and ninety five.
(d) Seven billion, six hundred and twenty thousand, four hundred and nineteen.

7　Write these numbers in words.
(a) 6 574　　(b) 12 876　　(c) 675 004　　(d) 3 450 672　(e) 27 102 005

8　Add up:
(a) $1 + 20 + 300 + 4\,000 + 50\,000 + 600\,000$
(b) $700\,000 + 40\,000 + 8\,000 + 500 + 10 + 5$
(c) $7 + 300 + 400\,000$.

9　Write the number 123 456 789 as a sum like the ones in Question 8.

Activity　In a school there are 10 English teachers.
Each teacher has to mark 100 pupils' work.
Each pupil writes 10 essays. Each essay is 10 pages long.
Each page contains 1000 words.
How many words, in total, are read by all the English teachers?

Using large numbers

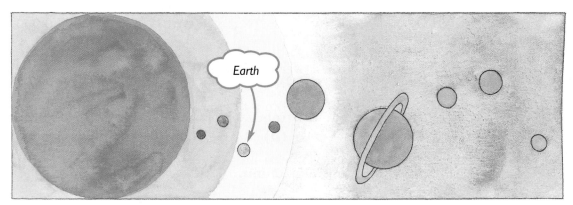

Light travels 300 000 000 metres every second.
It takes 500 seconds for light to travel from the sun to earth.

 What is the distance between the sun and the earth?

Calculations like this can be done easily when you know how to deal with numbers containing lots of noughts.

Task

Copy and complete the multiplication table given right.

×	10	100	20	30	200	300	1000	4000
2								
5								
7								
12								
20								
22								
200								

 Work out 330 × 200 000.
Explain how to do this in your head.

Dividing by numbers containing lots of noughts can often be done in your head.

$200 \div 10$
$20\cancel{0} \div 1\cancel{0} = 20$

To divide by 10, remove a nought.

$6\ 300 \div 300$
$6\ 30\cancel{0} \div 3\cancel{0}\cancel{0} = 21$

To divide 6 300 by 300, divide by 100 by removing 2 noughts. Then divide 63 by 3.

 Write down the answer to 4 800 000 ÷ 200.
Explain how you got your answer.

Exercise

You may need to know the following to work out some of the questions below.
1 Speed = distance ÷ time
2 Distance = speed × time
3 Time = distance ÷ speed

1. Write down the answers to the following:
   (a) 40 × 20   **(b)** 300 × 30   **(c)** 120 × 40
   (d) 60 × 700   **(e)** 340 × 200   **(f)** 700 × 8 000
   (g) 1 300 × 30 000   **(h)** 600 × 5 000.   **(i)** 1 300 × 40

2. Work these out in your head.
   (a) 500 ÷ 10   **(b)** 400 ÷ 20   **(c)** 360 ÷ 20
   (d) 360 ÷ 30   **(e)** 8 400 ÷ 40   **(f)** 1000 ÷ 50
   (g) 427 000 ÷ 700   **(h)** 7 800 ÷ 300   **(i)** 10 800 ÷ 900

3. The distance around the earth at the equator is about 24 000 miles. The earth turns round once every day (24 hours).

   (a) How fast is a person travelling when they stand on the equator?

   At latitude 60° north, the distance around the earth is about 12 000 miles. The Shetland Isles are at latitude 60° north.

   (b) How fast is somebody standing in the Shetlands travelling?

Shetland Isles

4. A light year is the distance that light travels in a year. The speed of light is 300 000 000 metres every second.
   (a) How far does light travel in 1 minute?
   (b) How far does light travel in 1 hour?
   (c) How far does light travel in a year? (This is the length of a light year.)

   You will get a good approximation if you use 400 for the number of days in a year and 20 for the number of hours in a day.

Activity

1 A red blood cell lives for 4 months.
It travels 1 metre every minute.
How far does it travel in its lifetime?

2 There are 126 million cells in the retina of the human eye.
A typical cell contains 1 billion molecules of fat.
How many molecules of fat in the retina of the human eye?

3 Venus is 110 million kilometres from the sun.
How many metres is this?
How long will it take for light from the sun to reach Venus?

The metric system

The best is yet to come...

**For just £23K on the road –
you get the car of your dreams and a lot more besides...**

GLOBAL

? How much does the car cost?

? The K stands for *kilo*. Where else have you seen the prefix *kilo*?

In the *metric system* of measures, length can be measured in *centi*metres.

? What does the prefix *centi* tell you?
Weight can be measured in *milligrams*. What does *milli* mean?

Task

Copy and complete the table below for the metric system of measures.

Prefix	Size	How the prefix is used
giga	$\times 10^9$ (or 1 000 000 000)	
mega		
kilo		1 kilogram = 1000 grams
hecto		1 hectare = 100 ares
deca		
Basic unit	$\times 1$	*Metre, litre, gram, are*
deci		
centi	$\times \frac{1}{100}$	1 centimetre = $\frac{1}{100}$ of a metre or 100 cm = 1 metre
milli		
micro		
nano		

1 are = 100 square metres

? What fraction of a second is a nanosecond?
How many decimetres in a metre?

Length is usually measured in kilometres (km), metres (m), centimetres (cm) and millimetres (mm).

? From the measurements below match any that are equal in length.

200 cm	5 km	1.5 m	2 m	0.65 m	5 000 m	1 500 cm	150 cm
6.5 cm	65 cm	0.002 km	500 000 cm	650 mm	1 500 mm	65 mm	

Exercise

1 The volume of bottles of liquid is given in litres, centilitres (cl) or millilitres (ml). From the measurements opposite, select any volumes that are equivalent.

> 330 ml   70 cl   20 cl   33 cl
> 200 cl   1.5 litre   50 cl
> 0.7 litre   2 litre   3 300 ml
> 0.5 litre   1 500 ml   3.3 litres
> 200 ml   500 ml

2 Fill in the blank spaces in the following sentences.
   (a) There are _____ centimetres in a metre.
   (b) A _____ metre is $\frac{1}{100}$th of a metre.
   (c) There are 1 000 _____ grams in a gram.
   (d) A kilolitre is _____ litres.
   (e) A megawatt is _____ watts.
   (f) There are 1 000 milliamps in _____.
   (g) To change from metres to millimetres multiply by _____.
   (h) A volume in centilitres can be changed into litres by _____ by 100.
   (i) The prefix _____ means 10 of the basic unit.
   (j) A gigaunit is _____ × the basic unit.

(Amps and watts are used when measuring electricity.)

3 3 litres is the same as 300 cl and 3000 ml.
   Write each of the measurements below in two different ways.
   (a) 5 grams   **(b)** 7 metres   **(c)** 35 centimetres
   (d) 70 centilitres   **(e)** 2 kilometres   **(f)** 0.8 kilograms

4 Write the following in order, smallest first.

   0.5 m,   35.9 cm, $\frac{1}{1000}$ of a kilometre,   512 mm

---

Activity The size of a computer's memory is measured in bytes.
A kilobyte is 1 024 bytes (not 1 000 bytes).
Find out why.

How many bytes are there in a megabyte?
How many in a gigabyte?

The answers are not 1 000 000 and 1 000 000 000 but they are near to these numbers.

Finishing off

Now that you have finished this chapter you should:

- be able to write large numbers in words and figures
- know how to write powers of ten
- know how big 1 million, 1 billion and 1 trillion are
- be able to multiply and divide large numbers that end in noughts
- understand the meaning of the prefixes used in the metric system of measures.

Review exercise

1. Write these numbers in words.
   (a) 25 467
   (b) 7 649 325
   (c) 564 744 853
   (d) 1 032 400 657.

2. Place the following numbers in ascending order of size:
   45 678   40 × 1 000 10^5 54 678 10^4 1 million.

3. Write in words the numbers contained in each of the sentences below.
   (a) Jupiter is 778 300 000 km from the sun.
   (b) Greenland has an area of 2 175 000 square kilometres.
   (c) Everest is 8 848 metres high.
   (d) The age of the dinosaurs lasted for 167 000 000 years.
   (e) There are 31 536 000 seconds in a year.
   (f) An accurate value for light speed is 299 792 500 metres per second.

4. Write these numbers in figures.
   (a) One million two hundred and fifty thousand, seven hundred and twenty six.
   (b) Ten billion three hundred and fifty three million, seven hundred and five thousand and twenty four.

5. Write down the answers to these addition sums.
   (a) 1 + 70 + 300 + 5 000 + 80 000
   (b) 5 + 200 + 4 000 + 700 000
   (c) 6 000 000 + 3 000 + 200 + 5

6. Work out:
   (a) 200 × 300
   (b) 32 000 × 200
   (c) 2 400 × 30
   (d) 800 ÷ 40
   (e) 24 000 ÷ 800
   (f) 36 000 000 ÷ 1 200.

7 For the millennium, an extra £200 million worth of bank notes were put into circulation in the United Kingdom.
This made the total value of bank notes in circulation about £30 billion.
The population of the country was about 60 million.
What value of notes is this for each person?

8 A square of dots is made like this:

(a) How many dots is this?

A larger square is made from smaller squares, like this:

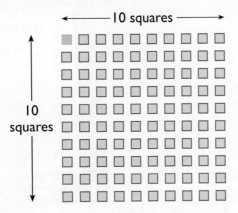

(b) What is the total number of dots in this square?

These new squares are now arranged to form an even larger square, like this:

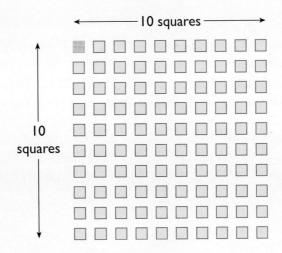

(c) How many dots are there now?

Your starship fleet is made up of
1 starport, 2 spaceships and 3 shuttles.
Place your fleet wisely!
You must also plot 2 black holes
before you begin.

KEY:

starport
(4 squares to hit)

spaceship
(3 squares to hit)

shuttle
(2 squares to hit)

black hole

Hassan's Board

Melinda's Board

❶ The aim of the game is
to eliminate all your opponent's
squares containing starports,
shuttles and spaceships.

❷ If you hit two black holes you
lose the game.

❸ You cannot see your opponent's board.

Hassan and Melinda are playing a game of Starships.

Hassan and Melinda take it in turns to name a square to eliminate on the other's board.

Hassan goes first and chooses square C5. He hits parts of a starport.

Go along to C

Then go up 5

To choose a square the letter is always given first, and then the number of squares up.

What other squares should Hassan hit to completely eliminate the starport?
Which 2 squares contain black holes on Melinda's board?
What is contained in square D6 on Hassan's board?

Task

Play your own game of Starships with a partner.

Exercise

1 The diagram shows part of a seating plan in an aeroplane.

(a) What colour hair has the person in seat B2?
(b) What is the man in seat D2 doing?
(c) Which seats are empty?
(d) In which seats are people wearing hats sitting?

2 Here is a map of Skull Island. Blackbeard and his pirate crew are using the map to try to find the buried treasure.

(a) The pirates want to land on the island. In which square should they leave their ship?
(b) In which squares are the dangerous rocks?
(c) What is in square B4?
(d) Where on the island is there quick sand?
(e) Where would you be if you were at the following squares:
    (i) E7   **(ii)** D5   **(iii)** A6?
(f) In which square is the treasure?
(g) Write down which squares the pirates should pass through to reach the treasure safely.

Activity   Make your own map of an island using a grid.
                      Draw a key to show which squares contain important features.

The National Grid

Many road atlases use the **National Grid** to describe positions of places.

This is a grid of squares over a map of Great Britain. The squares are 100 km across.

Each large square is divided into small squares. The position of Whitchurch is described as SJ54.

Task

1   Write down the positions of the following places:
    Northwich, Telford, Rhyl, Blackpool, Kidderminster.
2   Explain how the system works.

3   How wide is each small square?
4   How many small squares are there in each large square?
5   How *accurate* is a grid reference such as SJ54?

A two figure National Grid reference gives the approximate position of anywhere in Britain.

? **Can you give an approximate position for your school?**
Which large National Grid square is it in?

Exercise

Here is a map of part of Scotland showing National Grid squares.

1 Give the National Grid references of these places:
(a) Grantown-on-Spey   **(b)** Inverness   **(c)** Aberlour
(d) Dingwall   **(e)** Forfar   **(f)** Ballater

2 Write down the names of the places with these National Grid references:
(a) NH70   **(b)** NN68   **(c)** NJ15   **(d)** NO47   **(e)** NJ22

3 Write down the National Grid references of Kildrummy, Glenkindle and Mossat. (They are in square NJ.)
What is the problem?
What is the solution?

Finishing off

Now that you have finished this chapter you should be able to:

● describe the position of a square systematically
● use map referencing
● understand seating plans, etc.

Review exercise

1 Sally is rearranging her bedroom.
She draws a plan of her room.
Each square represents 1 square metre.

(a) What is in square B2?
(b) What is in square C3?
(c) In which squares is her bed?
(d) Where is Sally's desk?

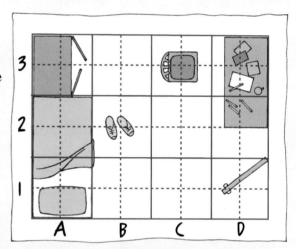

2 Here is the seating plan of a cinema.

(a) How many seats are there in row C?
(b) How many seats are there between the two aisles in row D?
(c) Jenny has seat E8. How many rows are there in front of her?

(d) Matt has seat F5. How many seats are there between him and the nearer aisle?
(e) Alison has seat A1. Charlie has seat A6. How many seats are there between them in that row?
(f) Write down the seats where you can sit with no-one next to you.
(g) Find the pairs of seats where two people can sit by themselves.

3 This map is part of the London A–Z. Underground stations are represented by black circles.

(a) Charing Cross underground station is given in the index as 2C 146. Explain how the referencing system works.

(b) Give the names and references of the other underground stations on this map.

(c) In which squares will you find:
  (i) Downing Street
  (ii) Pall Mall
  (iii) The Houses of Parliament.

4 Here is a **spreadsheet** from a computer screen. Each rectangle is called a **cell**.

(a) What number is in cell B3?
(b) What number is in cell D5?
(c) In which cell is the word TOTALS?
(d) Why does the reference D8 appear above the grid?
(e) Above the grid you can see =SUM(D1:D6). Can you explain this?
(f) What is 34 + 25 + 25 + 91 + 10 000?
(g) Write down the references of the cells which contain *even* numbers.

England need 134 runs to win

The England cricket team is poised for a great victory at Headingley.

The last 3 batsmen scored 29, 47 and 63 runs.
Did England win?

$$\begin{array}{r} 29 \\ 47 \\ +63 \\ \hline 139 \\ {\scriptstyle 11} \end{array}$$

Task

In one very strange cricket match all 11 batsmen's scores are consecutive numbers.

1 What is the smallest total they could have scored?

2 What are the scores of the batsmen if the total is

   (a) 121 runs?   **(b)** 374 runs?   **(c)** 616 runs?

3 Could the total be   **(a)** 84 runs?   **(b)** 95 runs?

It is sometimes useful to add numbers set out in a straight line.

The addition sums at the top of the page could be written like this:
$$29 + 47 + 63 =$$
Add the units digit first:
$$29 + 47 + 63 = {}_19$$
and then the tens (hundreds, thousands etc.)
$$29 + 47 + 63 = 139$$

Other examples are:

1 $328 + 637 =$

  $328 + 637 = {}_15$

  $328 + 637 = 65$

  $328 + 637 = 965$

2 $423 + 518 + 169 =$

  $423 + 518 + 169 = {}_20$

  $423 + 518 + 169 = {}_110$

  $423 + 518 + 169 = 1\ 110$

Exercise

1. England need 15 runs to win.
   Which of these are winning totals?
   (a) $5 + 8$ **(b)** $7 + 6$ **(c)** $8 + 8$ **(d)** $9 + 4 + 5$ **(e)** $7 + 6 + 8$

2. The two opening batsmen score the following number of runs. What is their total?
   (a) $24, 35$ **(b)** $14, 33$ **(c)** $70, 28$ **(d)** $53, 28$ **(e)** $65, 27$

3. What is the total distance that the team have to travel between matches?

   (a) $\begin{array}{r} 103 \\ +241 \\ \hline \end{array}$ **(b)** $\begin{array}{r} 718 \\ +225 \\ \hline \end{array}$ **(c)** $\begin{array}{r} 698 \\ +143 \\ \hline \end{array}$ **(d)** $\begin{array}{r} 365 \\ +537 \\ \hline \end{array}$ **(e)** $\begin{array}{r} 412 \\ +339 \\ \hline \end{array}$

4. The table shows distances, in miles, between towns in Britain.

Bristol	Gloucester	Leeds	Manchester	Norwich	Nottingham	York	London
36							
213	178						
172	137	44					
233	211	172	185				
145	110	74	71	119			
220	191	24	71	181	87		
120	102	198	202	116	131	211	

Find the distances travelled on the following journeys.

(a) Bristol to Gloucester then Gloucester to Nottingham.
(b) Leeds to Manchester then Manchester to Nottingham.
(c) Nottingham to Norwich then Norwich to London.
(d) Bristol to Gloucester then Gloucester to Nottingham then Nottingham to York.
(e) York to Leeds then Leeds to Nottingham then Nottingham to London.
(f) London to Norwich then Norwich to Nottingham then Nottingham to Manchester.

Subtraction

Crimson Tide (PG) (1995) ★★★★

Starring: Gene Hackman, Denzel Washington
Don't miss this exciting submarine drama.
Running time: 135 minutes

Tatjana has two video tapes, each of 180 minutes.

On the first she has two episodes of 'Neighbours', each 25 minutes long.
On the second she has recorded 'Champions of Nature', which is
30 minutes long.

 **Can she record 'Crimson Tide' on either tape without wiping
out her earlier recordings?**

She checked by thinking about this in the following way.

$$
\begin{array}{r}
180 \\
-135 \\
\hline
45
\end{array}
\text{ (Crimson Tide)}
$$

Working out:
$$
\begin{array}{r}
1\,8^1 0 \\
-1\ 3_{,}5 \\
\hline
4\ 5
\end{array}
\quad \text{or} \quad
\begin{array}{r}
17\,\cancel{8}^{10}\cancel{0} \\
-1\ 3\ 5 \\
\hline
4\ 5
\end{array}
$$

Only 45 minutes of other programmes can be recorded. Which tape should she use?

Task

Tatjana wants to record all the programmes listed below. What is the smallest
number of video tapes she can use (180 minutes on each) and which programmes
should she put on each tape?

The Flintstones	25 mins	Charlie Brown	30 mins	The Waltons	1 hr
From Earth to Moon	1 hr 35 mins	Storm Forces	25 mins	High School High	45 mins
The Simpsons	30 mins	Tom and Jerry	10 mins	Hercules	55 mins
Finian's Rainbow	2 hrs 15 mins	Dappledown	30 mins		

Sometimes it is necessary to borrow more than once.

EXAMPLE 1   1000 − 747

Either
$$
\begin{array}{r}
1^10^10^10 \\
-_1 7_{,}4_{,}7 \\
\hline
2\,5\,3
\end{array}
$$
or
$$
\begin{array}{r}
\overset{9\ 9}{\cancel{1}0^1\cancel{0}^1\cancel{0}} \\
-7\,4\,7 \\
\hline
2\,5\,3
\end{array}
$$

EXAMPLE 2   1000 − 658

Either
$$
\begin{array}{r}
1^10^10^10 \\
-6_{,}5_{,}8 \\
\hline
3\,4\,2
\end{array}
$$
or
$$
\begin{array}{r}
\overset{9\ 9}{\cancel{1}0^1\cancel{0}^1\cancel{0}} \\
-\ 6\,5\,8 \\
\hline
3\,4\,2
\end{array}
$$

Exercise

1 Robert's mother is on a diet.
She wants to lose 56 pounds (lbs).
How much more has she to lose after she has lost:

(a) 4 lbs   **(b)** 7 lbs   **(c)** 11 lbs

          $56 - 7 =$ $56 - 11 =$

(d) 16 lbs   **(e)** 19 lbs   **(f)** 28 lbs
(g) 39 lbs   **(h)** 43 lbs   **(i)** 48 lbs.

2 How much time would Tatjana have left on her 180 minute tape if she had recorded the following programmes?

(a) Sunset Beach (40 minutes)
(b) Deep Space Nine (45 minutes)
(c) Instant Gardens (25 minutes)
(d) The Mystery of Flight (110 minutes)

3 England need 132 runs to win a cricket match.
How many more must be scored when:

(a) one opening batsman gets 24, and the other has 0
(b) the first two batsmen get 53 altogether
(c) the first three batsmen get 76 altogether
(d) the first six batsmen get 105 altogether
(e) the first nine batsmen get 128 altogether.

4 **(a)** Tatjana's father needs to saw pieces of wood to the following sizes:

(i) 700 mm   **(ii)** 140 mm   **(iii)** 806 mm
(iv) 693 mm   **(v)** 715 mm   **(vi)** 932 mm.

In each case work out how much wood he has left if he takes a new piece of wood 1 m long (1000 mm) each time.

(b) If Tatjana's father starts with 1 m pieces of wood, but also uses up any left-over pieces, what is the smallest number of 1 m pieces he would need to use to cut all the pieces in part (a)?

Short multiplication and division

Leicester City in Transfer Scoop

Leicester City have signed soccer aces Roberto Luigi and Guiseppe Maldini. At 18 million Euros each, this is seen as the buy of the decade.

Numbers are grouped in threes from the units digit.

1 thousand = 1 000   (3 noughts)
4 thousand = 4 000
65 thousand = 65 000

1 million = 1 000 000   (6 noughts)
3 million = 3 000 000
17 million = 17 000 000

Task

Match these numbers and words correctly.

C forty thousand

12 000 000

D seventy-six million

A two thousand

2 000

5 000

40 000

E twelve million

B five thousand

76 000 000

 What do the transfer fees for these two players cost Leicester City in pounds (£s)?

Cost of players = 2 × 18 000 000 Euros
= 36 000 000 Euros.

> 2 × 18 = 36
> 2 × 18 000 000 = 36 000 000

The exchange rate, at present, is 1 Euro = £0.66 (⅔ of a £).
So to change Euros to £s multiply by 2, then divide the answer by 3.

36 000 000 × 2 =
36 000 000 × 2 = 72 000 000

> 36 × 2 = 72
> 36 000 000 × 2 = 72 000 000

72 000 000 ÷ 3 =
36 000 000 ÷ 3 = 24 000 000

> 72 ÷ 3 = 24
> 72 000 000 ÷ 3 = 24 000 000

Total cost of transfer fees = £24 000 000.

 Each player is paid £40 000 a week. How much is this per year?

Each player = £40 000 × 52 per year
= £2 080 000 per year.
Total wages for Luigi and Maldini = 2 × £2 080 000 per year
= £4 160 000 per year.

> There are 52 weeks in a year.
> 4 × 52 = 208
> 40 000 × 52 = 2 080 000

Exercise

1 Programmes cost £2 each.
Find the total cost of
(a) 3 programmes   **(b)** 30 programmes   **(c)** 300 programmes.

2 Tickets in the main stand cost £20 each. Find the total cost of
(a) 3 tickets bought by three friends   **(b)** 30 tickets bought by a school
(c) 300 tickets bought by away fans.   party

3 Tickets for the section behind the goal cost £12 each.
Find the total cost of
(a) 5 tickets bought by five friends   **(b)** 50 tickets bought by a coach
(c) 5 000 tickets bought by home fans.   party

4 The local theatre is showing
Swan Lake.
Here are the ticket prices.

The Touring Ballet Company present
——— SWAN LAKE ———
27 December - 20 January

Ticket Prices:

Section	A	(Balcony)	£8 each
Section	B	(Upper Circle)	£11 each
Section	C	(Dress Circle)	£14 each
Section	D	(Stalls)	£17 each

Avonford Theatre A_T

What is the total cost of tickets for:
(a) a couple if they sit   **(b)** a family of five if they sit
    (i) in section A   **(i)** in section B
    (ii) in section B   **(ii)** in section C

(c) a small coach party of   **(d)** a large coach party of fifty people
    twenty people if they sit   if they sit
    (i) in section A   **(i)** in section C
    (ii) in section C   **(ii)** in section D.

5 Change the following to £s using the method shown on the opposite page.
(a) 15 Euros   **(b)** 18 Euros   **(c)** 270 Euros
(d) 4 800 Euros   **(e)** 540 Euros   **(f)** 324 000 Euros

6 Four friends go on several outings together.
How much did each outing cost per person, if these are the total costs:
(a) A theatre trip £80   **(b)** A visit to the cinema £52
(c) A weekend break £720   **(d)** A week in Prague £2 400.

7 A coach party of forty people visit the following places in London.
How much is the cost per person for each outing if the total cost is:
(a) Madame Tussaud's   £480
(b) Buckingham Palace   £1 400
(c) West End Show   £960
(d) Chelsea versus Arsenal football match   £600.

Long multiplication and more division

The Patel family are taking a 16-day holiday costing £128 per day. How much is this altogether?

Fly to the Rockies

Canada Travel

Cruise to Alaska

Spectacular mountains, ice-scapes, glaciers, SNOW, SNOW, SNOW...

You need to calculate: £128 × 16

Look at the calculation. Explain in simple words how you do it.

$$128 \times 10 = 1\,280$$
$$128 \times 6 = 768$$

```
  128
×  16
-----
 1280
  768
-----
 2048
```

Total cost of holiday: £2 048

They look at another holiday. It is £910 for 14 days.
Rita works out how much this is per day.

Explain, step by step, what Rita has done.

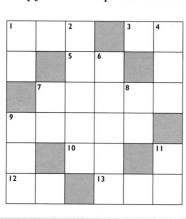

```
        65
    14 |910
        84
        70
        70
        ...

    £65 a day
```

Rough Work

```
 14      14
 ×5      ×7
 ---     ---
 70      98

 14
 ×6
 ---
 84
```

Task

Copy and complete this cross-number.

1		2		3	4
		5	6		
	7			8	
9					
		10			11
12			13		

Across
- 1   12 × 12
- 3   225 ÷ 5
- 5   330 ÷ 15
- 7   672 × 60 add 3
- 9   479 × 21
- 10 361 ÷ 19
- 12 512 ÷ 8
- 13 49 × 9

Down
- 1   391 ÷ 23
- 2   One more than 60 × 700
- 4   19 × 27
- 6   11797 × 2
- 7   800 ÷ 20
- 8   319 ÷ 11
- 9   14 × 14
- 11 612 ÷ 12

Their next holiday is to Nassau and will cost £3 545 altogether.
There are four people in the family, so how much is this each?

You need to calculate: £3545 ÷ 4

Explain, step by step, how you would do this without a calculator.

Exercise

1 How much is the total cost of a flight for 8 people if the cost:
(a) to Amsterdam is £79 each   **(b)** to Montego Bay is £290 each
(c) to Bermuda is £369 each   **(d)** to Rio is 312 Euros.

2 How much is the total cost of a holiday for a group of 6 friends if the price per person for:
(a) a weekend break in New York is £269
(b) 12 days in the Rockies is £1 145
(c) a 7-day Mediterranean cruise is £699?

3 How much would it cost in the currency given to stay for 17 days at the following places:
(a) £65 per day
(b) 187 Euros per day
(c) 97 dollars per day
(d) 238 Euros per day.

4 How much would a newspaper girl earn in a year if she was paid:
(a) £7 per week   **(b)** £16 per week
(c) £23 per week   **(d)** £14 per week?

5 How much do each of the following holidays cost per day?
(a) 7 days based in Vancouver for £560
(b) 8 days in Florida for £1 024
(c) 5 days on a River Nile cruise for £1 845
(d) 9 days at a Eurocamp for £144

6 The cost of a ferry journey from Hull to Amsterdam is £26 for one person. What is the total cost for:
(a) 35 people   **(b)** 48 people   **(c)** 53 people?

7 How much is the cost per day of each of the following holidays?
(a) an 11-day Ski holiday in the Alps for £1 375
(b) a 16-day holiday in Canada for £2 048
(c) a 14-day Greek Island cruise for £1 386
(d) a 28-day Andes trek for £1 484.

Multiples and divisibility tests

Mr. X Becomes Lottery Millionaire for a Second Time

Mr. X, who does not wish to be named for security reasons, became a multi-millionaire for the second time last night. He says the secret is to select at least one multiple of three in every line.

? **What is a multiple?**
How can you easily identify one?

> *Sometimes you only need to look at the end of the number.*

All even numbers are divisible by 2.
714 is an even number as it ends with a 4.
865 is not an even number because it does not end with 0, or 2, or 4, or 6, or 8.

> *Even numbers all end in 0, or 2, or 4, or 6, or 8.*

All numbers ending with a 5 or 0 are divisible by 5.

> *So 4635 can be divided exactly by 5, but 4636 cannot.*

Task

How does Mr X decide which numbers to select?

1　Divide these numbers into two groups;　**(a)** those divisible by 3
(b) those not divisible by 3.

11　　36　　1 042　　2 139　　4 096
507　　2 087　　4 086　　7 125

2　Add the single digits of each number in the first group (a).

> 36
> $3 + 6 = 9$

3　What do you notice about all the answers? Is this also true if you add the single digits of each number in the second group (b)?

? **Which of the first group of numbers do you think are divisible by 9?**
How did you decide?

A number can be divided by 4 *exactly*, if 4 goes exactly into the **last two digits**. e.g. 1732 is a multiple of 4 because 4 goes exactly into 32.

> *4 will go into any number of hundreds, so we only need to know if 4 will go into the tens and units.*

There is a similar test for divisibility by 8, but the **last three digits** must be looked at in this case. Unfortunately, there is no test for divisibility by 7.

Exercise

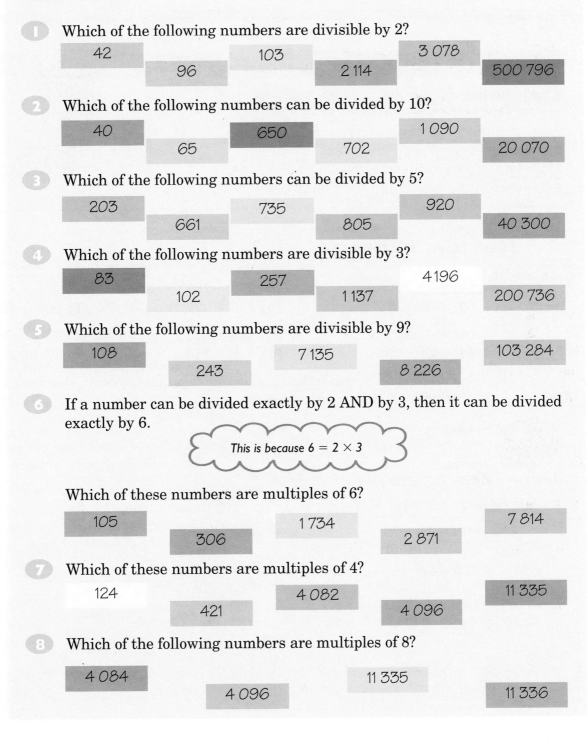

1 Which of the following numbers are divisible by 2?

42   103   3 078
96   2 114   500 796

2 Which of the following numbers can be divided by 10?

40   650   1 090
65   702   20 070

3 Which of the following numbers can be divided by 5?

203   735   920
661   805   40 300

4 Which of the following numbers are divisible by 3?

83   257   4 196
102   1 137   200 736

5 Which of the following numbers are divisible by 9?

108   7 135   103 284
243   8 226

6 If a number can be divided exactly by 2 AND by 3, then it can be divided exactly by 6.

This is because 6 = 2 × 3

Which of these numbers are multiples of 6?

105   1 734   7 814
306   2 871

7 Which of these numbers are multiples of 4?

124   4 082   11 335
421   4 096

8 Which of the following numbers are multiples of 8?

4 084   11 335
4 096   11 336

Finishing off

Now that you have finished this chapter you should be able to:

- add numbers up to 1000
- subtract numbers less than 1000
- write numbers in words and figures
- do long and short multiplication
- do short division (or successive short divisions)
- know about multiples and tests for divisibility

Review exercise

1   **(a)** 63 + 22   **(b)** 145 + 251   **(c)** 205 + 473
    (d) 149 + 38   **(e)** 576 + 47   **(f)** 603 + 98

2   **(a)** 68 − 21   **(b)** 140 − 50   **(c)** 186 − 78
    (d) 245 − 168   **(e)** 503 − 279   **(f)** 1 000 − 364

3   Add two adjacent (neighbouring) bricks together to obtain the number which goes into the brick on top.

EXAMPLE I

EXAMPLE 2

(a)

(b)

(c)

(d)

(e)

(f)

(g)

(h)

4   **(a)** 17×4 **(b)** 17×400 **(c)** 239×8
     (d) $239 \times 8\,000$ **(e)** 69×7 **(f)** 69×70

5   **(a)** 43×35 **(b)** 621×78 **(c)** 507×93
     (d) 477×23 **(e)** 517×88 **(f)** $4\,091 \times 238$

6   **(a)** $820 \div 4$ **(b)** $717 \div 3$ **(c)** $625 \div 5$
     (d) $32\,400 \div 9$ **(e)** $572\,000 \div 5$ **(f)** $41\,200 \div 20$

7   Which of the numbers

        73   405   612   804

   (a) is divisible by 2?
   (b) is divisible by 3?
   (c) is divisible by 9?

8   Use the fact that $2\,664 \div 72 = 37$ to find the answers to the
    following questions:
    (a) $2\,664 \div 37 =$ **(b)** $2\,664 \div 74 =$
    (c) $2\,664 \div 36 =$ **(d)** $2\,664 \div 9 =$
    (e) $37 \times 72 =$ **(f)** $37 \times 36 =$
    (g) $370 \times 36 =$ **(h)** $37\,000 \times 18 =$

9   Use the fact that $2\,080 \div 32 = 65$ to find the answers to the
    following questions:
    (a) $2\,080 \div 65 =$ **(b)** $2\,080 \div 16 =$
    (c) $32 \times 65 =$ **(d)** $64 \times 65 =$
    (e) $20\,800 \div 64 =$ **(f)** $2\,080\,000 \div 64 =$

Activity   Speed test!
            See how quickly you can answer these.

1	$25 + 60 + 18 =$	**11**	$327 \times 63 =$
2	$41 + 173 + 68 =$	**12**	$516 \times 88 =$
3	$514 + 307 + 266 =$	**13**	$210 \div 6 =$
4	$399 + 28 + 514 =$	**14**	$2\,891 \div 7 =$
5	$19 - 8 =$	**15**	$832 \div 8 =$
6	$65 - 32 =$	**16**	$832 \div 16 =$
7	$236 - 197 =$	**17**	$27 \times 8 =$
8	$1\,050 - 688 =$	**18**	$27 \times 16 =$
9	$403 \times 6 =$	**19**	$1\,764 \div 9 =$
10	$589 \times 7 =$	**20**	$1\,764 \div 36 =$

THE AVONFORD STAR

Giant Clock for Avonford

The Mayor of Avonford, Rubena Ali, yesterday unveiled plans for a huge clock for the civic park.

With a diameter of 10 m it will be erected near the park entrance.

As part of the celebrations the Avonford Star will issue a wristwatch to every person who attends the jubilee party in the park.

Artist's impression

? **Which of the two clock faces has the larger angle between the hands?**

Task

1 Place your hand on a desk. Spread your little finger and thumb out as far as you can.

   (a) Which fingers have the largest angle between them?

   (b) Which fingers have the smallest angle between them?

   (c) Don't move your little finger or thumb. Can you change answers (a) and (b).

   (d) Are the answers the same for other people in your class?

2 Look around in your classroom for angles where lines meet. Choose three different angles you can see and write them down in order of size, smallest to largest.

Types of angle

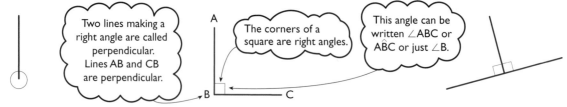

Two lines making a right angle are called **perpendicular**. Lines AB and CB are perpendicular.

The corners of a square are right angles.

This angle can be written ∠ABC or AB̂C or just ∠B.

A **whole turn**.

A **quarter of a turn**.

A **straight line**.

Angles which are smaller than a right angle are called **acute** angles. Acute means sharp.

Angles larger than a right angle but smaller than a straight line are called **obtuse**. Obtuse means blunt or not pointed.

Angles which are larger than a straight line are called **reflex** angles. These are so large that they go back on themselves.

Exercise

1 Write down the order of size of these angles, smallest first.

2 Write down which of these angles are acute, which are obtuse and which are reflex.

3 **(a)** How many right angles make angle *K* in Question 2?
(b) How many right angles make a whole turn?

4 Draw and label
(a) an obtuse angle   **(b)** a reflex angle   **(c)** an acute angle.

5 A whole turn can be made up of an acute angle and a reflex angle. Copy these sums and fill in the boxes.

Acute angle

Reflex angles

whole turn = reflex + acute

whole turn = obtuse +

whole turn = straight line + acute +

whole turn = right angle + right angle +

whole turn = right angle + straight line + acute +

whole turn = straight line +

Now make up three different whole turn sums of your own.

Activity   Where can you see right angles in your classroom?
Write down five different places where right angles occur, for example the corner of a window.
How many right angles are there altogether in your classroom?
Can you count them all?
Think of ways to **estimate** the number of right angles in the room.
Compare your estimate with other people in your class.

Measuring angles

Task

Look carefully at these acute angles.

? **Which angle is the smallest?**
Which angle is the largest?

Write down the angles in order of size,
smallest to largest.

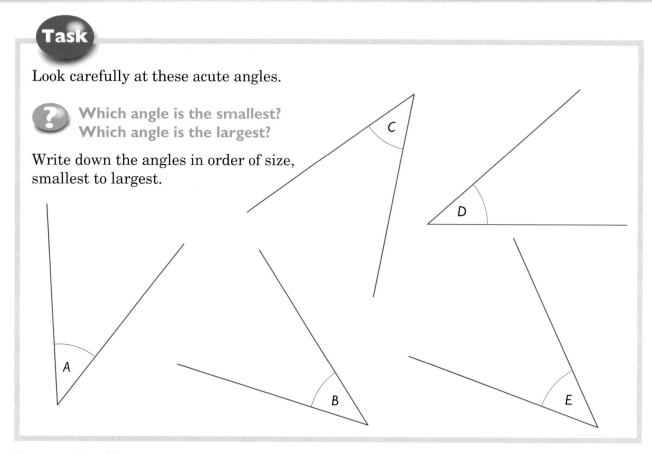

You *may* be able to arrange the angles in the correct order just by looking at them.
To be sure you need to *measure* them using a protractor.

" Do the right thing!

The protractor is placed over the angle
and the size of the angle is shown on the
scale on the outside edge.
Angles are measured in **degrees**.
This angle is 42°.

42 degrees

MADE IN ENGLAND

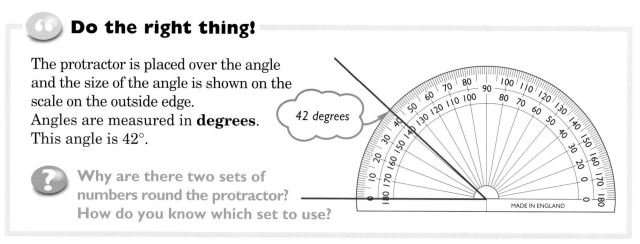

? **Why are there two sets of**
numbers round the protractor?
How do you know which set to use?

? **How many degrees are there**
(a) in a right angle? (b) on a straight line? (c) in a whole turn?

? **How would you use a protractor**
to measure this angle?

Exercise

Before you start this Exercise, bring your vocabulary up to date.

- A flat surface is called a **plane**. This page is part of a plane.
- A line goes on for ever across a plane, in both directions.
- A small part of a line, like AB, is called a **line segment**.
- Two lines **intersect** at a **point** and angles are formed.

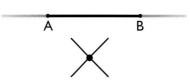

It is important to be accurate when measuring angles.
The centre of the protractor must be on the centre of the angle.
The start line must be lined up *exactly* over one of the angle lines.
Your eyes must be directly over the protractor when reading the scale.

1 Measure angles *A* to *E* on the opposite page and write them down in order of size.

2 Write down the size of these angles.

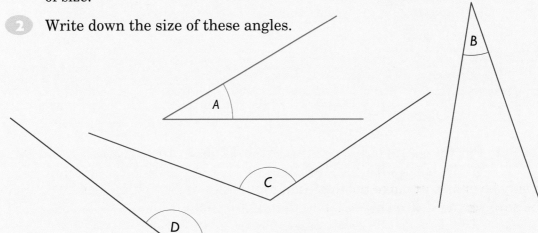

3 Write down the size of these angles.

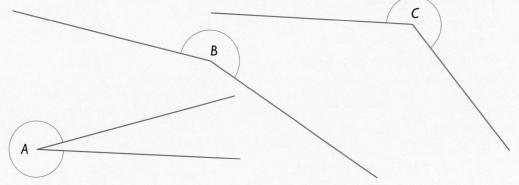

Investigation Draw a large triangle.
Measure the angles inside it and write them down. Add up the three angles.

Repeat this for two other triangles.
What do you notice?

Drawing angles

Protractors can be used to draw angles very accurately.

Following these steps to draw an angle of *exactly* 57°.
Use a sharp pencil.
Keep your eyes over your drawing.

STEP 1 Draw a line across a clean sheet of paper, about half way down the page. Put a mark near one end of the line. This is where the angle will be.

STEP 2 Put the centre of the protractor on the mark with the start line of the protractor over the line you have drawn.

STEP 3 Draw a mark on the paper next to 57°.

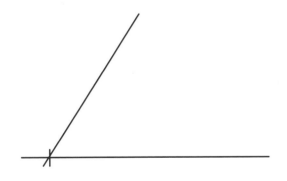

STEP 4 Take away the protractor and use your ruler to draw a straight line through the two marks.

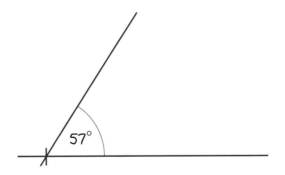

STEP 5 Draw the arc and label the angle.

? How do you use a protractor to draw a reflex angle?

Exercise

1 Follow the 5 steps given opposite to draw each of these angles.
Be as neat and as accurate as possible.

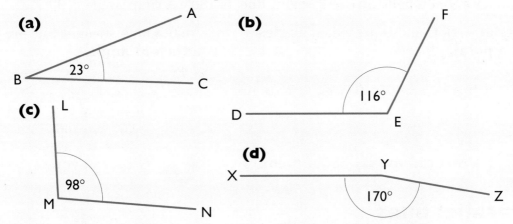

(a)

A

B 23° C

(b)

F

D 116° E

(c)

L

M 98° N

(d)

X Y Z

170°

(e) An angle of 86°   **(f)** An angle of 163°
(g) An angle of 117°   **(h)** An angle of 92°

2 Make an accurate drawing of this
reflex angle of 207°.
You have to do a calculation to
draw the correct smaller angle with
your protrator.

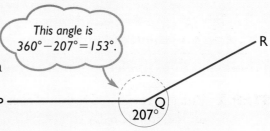

This angle is
360° − 207° = 153°.

R

P 207° Q

3 Use the method in Question 2 to draw and label these reflex angles.
Write down the calculation next to each one.
(a) 200°   **(b)** 243°   **(c)** 300°
(d) 270°   **(e)** 181°   **(f)** 315°

4 Draw and label these angles.
Remember to be as neat and as accurate as possible.
(a) 263°   **(b)** 132°   **(c)** 283°   **(d)** 310°
(e) 8°   **(f)** 72°   **(g)** 357°   **(h)** 360°

Investigation

How many different angles can you
find at A?
Name each one and give its size.
For example ∠CAE = 120°.

C D

50°

B 60° 70° E

A

Angle calculations

From your work on page 30 you know that **there are 360 degrees in a whole turn.**
It follows that a half-turn, or straight line, is 180°. A right angle is 90°.

Angles *A*, *B*, *C* and *D* are called **angles at a point**.

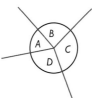

Angles on a straight line are called **adjacent angles**.

 What can you say about them?

 What can you say about X and Y?

Parallel lines

When two lines are always the same distance apart (equidistant) they are **parallel**.
Railway lines are parallel.

Parallel lines

 **Can you see five examples of parallel lines in your classroom?
Can you think of five other examples outside the classroom?**

In these diagrams angles are made where lines **intersect**.

Corresponding angles

Alternate angles

Vertically opposite angles

 Can you explain the names?
What does the word perpendicular mean?

 Task

I Use a ruler and **set square** to draw a pair of parallel lines.

 How does this work?

2 Draw another straight line which intersects both parallel lines.

3 Measure a pair of corresponding angles and write them down.

4 Measure a pair of alternate angles and write them down

5 Measure a pair of opposite angles and write them down.

6 Write down what you notice each time.

Repeat this for another pair of parallel lines with a different intersecting line.

Exercise

The angle facts on the opposite page enable you to solve angle *problems*.

EXAMPLE   What is angle *X*?

The angles round a point add up to 360°.
118° + 87° = 205°
So *X* = 360° − 205°
X = **155°**.

1 Find the value of each lettered angle in these diagrams:
For each one write down the angle fact(s) that you use.

2 Make a *sketch* copy of each of these diagrams.
For each one calculate the lettered angle and write down your reason.

3 Calculate angles *W*, *X*, *Y* and *Z*.

What is *W* + *X* + *Y* + *Z*?

4 What is the angle between the spokes of this wheel?

Investigation

Copy this diagram.
Use it to calculate the value of *A* + *B* + *C*.
Write down your reasoning.

Angles in a triangle

The angles inside a shape are called **interior angles**.
The investigations on pages 31 and 35 shows you that
the interior angles of a triangle add up to 180°.

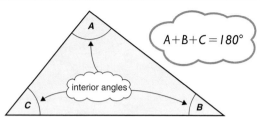

Task

1 Draw any large triangle on a piece of paper.
   Mark each angle and shade each one with a
   different colour.

2 Tear each angle out from the triangle.
   Glue the angles next to each other on to another
   piece of paper so that the 'points' are at the same
   place.

3 Repeat this with two different triangles. Write down what you notice.

? **How does this task show you that the sum of the interior angles of a triangle is 180°?**

Task

Any shape with **four straight sides**
is called a **quadrilateral**.

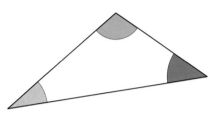

1 On a clean sheet of paper draw a large quadrilateral.
   Label the angles in it A, B, C and D.

2 Draw a diagonal line across it between two opposite corners.

3 Looking at your diagram, what do you think
   the angles A, B, C and D add up to?

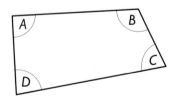

   Write down a reason for your answer.

4 Now use a protractor to measure angles A, B, C and D.
   Work out A+B+C+D to see if you were correct in part 3 of the task.

5 Draw a different quadrilateral and check the sum of its angles.

Exercise

1 Find the value of each unknown angle in these diagrams:

2 What do angles *A, B, C, D,*
and *E* inside this **pentagon**
add up to?

3 Each slope of the roof of this
house makes an angle of 37°
with the horizontal.
What is the angle inside the apex?

4 For safety, the angle this ladder makes with the
horizontal ground must be between 65 and 75 degrees.
(a) Between what values must the acute angle
   between the vertical wall and the ladder be?
(b) What do the words horizontal and vertical mean?

*The ladder
is vertical*

*The ground
is horizontal*

Investigation

In this diagram angle *X* is called an
exterior angle.

A and *B* are the two *opposite* interior angles.

1 Copy this diagram:

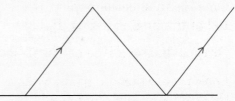

2 Use it to show how an exterior angle
of a triangle is related to the two
opposite interior angles.
Explain your reasoning.
Find the angle in Question 1 above
which shows this.

Finishing off

Now that you have finished this chapter you should:

- know that an angle is a measure of turning
- know that a whole turn is 360°, the angle on a straight line is 180° and a right angle is 90°
- be able to recognise angles which are acute, obtuse and reflex
- be able to measure and draw angles accurately using a protractor
- know that the angles at a point add up to 360° and adjacent angles add up to 180°
- know the meanings of the words perpendicular and parallel
- be able to recognise corresponding angles and know that they are equal
- be able to recognise alternate angles and know that they are equal
- know that the angles inside a triangle add up to 180°, and those in a quadrilateral to 360°.

Review exercise

1 **(a)** Write down these angles in order of size, with the largest first.

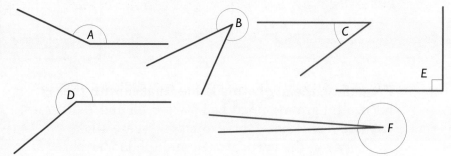

(b) Write down which of the above angles are
   (i)   obtuse   **(ii)** reflex   **(iii)** acute.

2 Write down the size of these angles.
Measure them as accurately as you can.

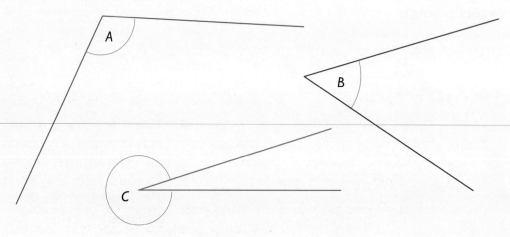

3 Make accurate drawings of these angles and label them.

(a) 30°

(b) 28°

(c) 146°

(d) 323°

(e) 90°
(g) 300°

(f) 168°
(h) 265°

4 **(a)** How many right angles are there on a straight line?
(b) How many degrees are there in a right angle?
(c) How many degrees are there in a whole turn?
(d) How many right angles are there in 270°?
(e) How many right angles are there in a whole turn?

5 Write down the following angles in order of size, with the smallest first.

53°   An obtuse angle   A straight line   240°   A right angle   3°   300°

6 Find the value of the lettered angles in these diagrams:

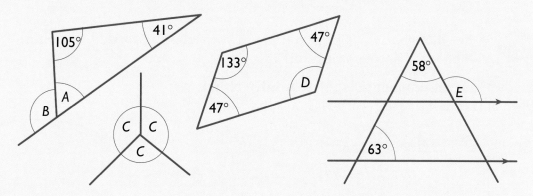

What can you say about the sides of the quadrilateral?

Activity Draw four different angles on one sheet of paper and label them with letters. Measure each angle and write down their sizes on a separate sheet of paper.

Swap your set of drawings with a friend and measure each other's angles. Compare your answers.

Do you agree, to *exactly* the same number of degrees?
If you can't agree, ask someone else to decide who is right.

5 Displaying data

Hannah is organising an end-of-year event for her year group.

She decides to ask everyone in her class what they would like to do.

She writes down each person's suggestion.

disco	ice skating
theme park	disco
disco	zoo
cinema	theme park
zoo	disco
theme park	ice skating
disco	theme park
zoo	cinema
theme park	ice skating
disco	disco

? Which is the most popular suggestion?
Was it easy to tell?

Hannah has collected some information, or **data**. Her data are not written down in an organised way, so it is difficult to make much sense of it.

Task

Collect data from everyone in your class to find out what they would like to do for an end-of-year event.

Try to record your data in a way which makes it easy to see which are the most popular suggestions.

? What different ways have people in your class recorded this data?
Which ways are most useful?

One way of collecting data is to use a **tally chart**.
Here is Hannah's data recorded in a tally chart.

ACTIVITY	TALLY	FREQUENCY
Disco	ℍ ‖	7
Theme park	ℍ	5
Cinema	‖	2
Zoo	‖‖	3
Ice skating	‖‖	3
	TOTAL	20

> Frequency means the number of people.

> This is sometimes called *a **frequency table***.

? What does each line in the tally column mean?
What does ℍ mean?
How many people has Hannah asked in her survey?
Which activity is the most popular?

Exercise

1 Jason is doing a survey about the traffic passing his house during the morning rush-hour.
He notes down each type of vehicle that he sees.
Here are Jason's results:

car	car	car	lorry	car	bicycle	bicycle
van	car	car	car	car	bus	car
lorry	car	car	motorbike	bus	car	car
car	car	lorry	van	car	car	
car	car	bus	bicycle	car	car	
car	car	motorbike	lorry	lorry	lorry	
bicycle	car	car	car	lorry	lorry	

(a) Make a tally chart to show Jason's results.
(b) How many vehicles did Jason see altogether?
(c) What was the most common vehicle?

2 Maddy is making a patchwork quilt.
She is copying this design.
Make a tally chart to show how many squares of each colour Maddy needs.

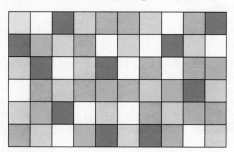

3 Mark throws a die 30 times.
Here are the scores he gets:

2 3 1 5 5 2 6 4 1
2 1 3 6 5 3 3 3 2
4 5 6 1 6 2 4 3 2
5 2 4

(a) Make a tally chart to show Mark's results.
(b) Which number came up most often?
(c) Do you think the same number would come up most often if Mark threw the die another 30 times?

Investigation
1 Find a book and count the number of letters in each word for 50 words. Record your data in a tally chart.
2 Repeat part 1 using a different type of book.
3 Which book do you think has longer words on the whole? Why do you think this is?

Pictograms and bar charts

Here are the results of Hannah's survey again.
They are shown in a **frequency table**.

Activity	Disco	Theme park	Cinema	Zoo	Ice-skating
Frequency	7	5	2	3	3

Hannah wants to show her data in
a graph or chart.
She draws this **bar chart**.

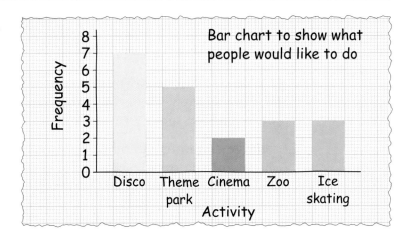

> Make sure you always label the axes
> and give the chart a title.

 Do you think the bar chart is more useful than the tally chart?

Another way that Hannah could
show her data is by using a
pictogram like this:

Disco
THEME PARK
CINEMA
Zoo
ICE-SKATING

☆ = 1 PERSON

> You can use any symbol you like
> for the picture.

 Task

Look back to the data you collected for the last lesson.

Draw a bar chart and a pictogram to illustrate your data.

Make a poster to show your work.

 Which do you think shows the data better, the pictogram or the bar chart?
Which is easier to draw?

Exercise

1 Joe works at the village shop. He wants to know how many pints of each type of milk he should order.

This pictogram shows the number of pints of each type of milk that Joe sells one morning.

(a) What does the symbol ⎰ mean?

(b) How many pints of each type of milk did Joe sell?

(c) How many pints of milk did Joe sell altogether?

(d) Draw a bar chart to show this data.

2 Lisa has drawn a bar chart to show how the people in her class travel to school.

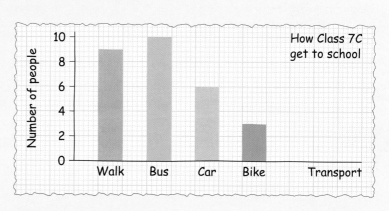

(a) What is the most popular way to get to school in Lisa's class?

(b) How many people walk to school?

(c) How many people come to school by bus or car?

(d) How many people are there in Lisa's class?

(e) Draw a pictogram to show this data.

3 Jack is doing a survey to find out the most popular terrestrial TV channel.

This frequency table shows his results.

Channel	BBC1	BBC2	ITV	C4	C5
Frequency	8	5	7	4	1

(a) Draw a pictogram to illustrate this data.

(b) Draw a bar chart to illustrate this data.

(c) Which way of displaying the data do you think is better? Why?

Pie charts

AVONFORD STAR

Football Team Improve Performance This Year

After last year's disappointing season, Avonford Town have had a much better run this year, winning $\frac{2}{3}$ of the matches played.

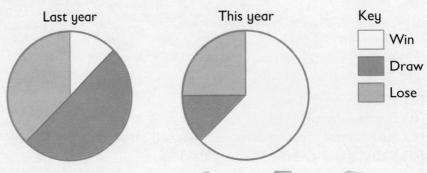

Last year   This year   Key
☐ Win
▨ Draw
▨ Lose

The diagrams used in the *Avonford Star* report shown above are called pie charts.

The yellow section in each chart shows the number of wins. In the chart for last year, the yellow section is $45°$ or $\frac{1}{8}$ of the circle. This means that the team won $\frac{1}{8}$ of their matches.

 What fraction of the matches do you think the team lost this year?

 Task

Copy the table opposite.

Decide what fraction of the matches Avonford Town won, lost and drew in each year and fill in the 'Fraction' column of the table.
The team played 32 matches last year and 40 matches this year. Use this to fill in the 'Number of matches' column.

Draw two bar charts to illustrate these data.

		Fraction	No. of Matches
Last Year	Won	$\frac{1}{8}$	
	Lost		
	Drew		
This Year	Won		
	Lost		
	Drew		

 Does a pie chart have any advantages over a bar chart or a pictogram?

 What fractions correspond to pie chart angles of
   (a) 90°   (b) 180°   (c) 60°   (d) 120°   (e) 30°?

Exercise

1 This pie chart shows the favourite sports of a group of children.

(a) What is the most popular sport?
(b) Which two sports are equally popular?
(c) Which is the least popular sport?
(d) Which sport is preferred by about $\frac{3}{8}$ of the children?
(e) Write the sports in order of popularity, starting with the most popular one.

Key

Football
Swimming
Hockey
Tennis
Athletics

2 Ellie kept a record of the weather for several weeks in the summer. On half of the days it was sunny, on $\frac{1}{8}$ of the days it rained, and the rest of the time it was cloudy.

Ellie also kept a record of the weather for the same amount of weeks in the autumn. On $\frac{1}{3}$ of the days it rained, $\frac{1}{4}$ of the days it was sunny, and the rest of the time it was cloudy.

Draw two pie charts to show this information.

3 Stuart has carried out a survey to find out how people get to school.
He has surveyed three classes: 7P, 7Q and 7R.
Here are his results.

CLASS	7P	7Q	7R
WALK	14	10	9
BUS	10	8	12
CAR	4	3	6
BIKE	2	7	4
TOTAL	30	28	31

Here are the three pie charts that Stuart has drawn.
He has forgotten to write a key for the pie charts.
The pie charts have become mixed up.
Decide which pie chart is for each class, and make a key.

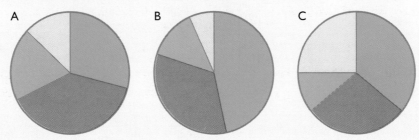

A   B   C

Investigation Find out how to use ICT to draw a pie chart.

Grouping data

Mr Harris has given his class a test. He has given each student a mark out of 50.

Here are the results for his class.

32	38	43	21	30	46	29	35
37	42	27	25	33	32	16	48
39	37	26	19	40	23	35	34
8	24	35	39	41	36		

Mr Harris is going to give each student a grade.
He wants to make a tally chart to show his results.

 What problem will there be with making a tally chart of these data?

Mr Harris can solve the problem by using **grouped data**.
This means that he will collect the data in groups.
Each group will be given a different grade.
Here is Mr Harris' tally chart.

Grade	Mark	Tally	Frequency
E	1–10	I	1
D	11–20	II	2
C	21–30	HHT III	8
B	31–40	HHT HHT IIII	14
A	41–50	HHT	5
		Total	30

 What other ways could Mr Harris have grouped the data?

Task

Ask everyone in your class to measure his or her handspan in millimetres.
Collect the results using a grouped tally chart.
Compare your results with the rest of the class.

 **Has everyone grouped the data in the same way?
Which way do you think is best?**

You can draw bar charts, pictograms and pie charts using grouped data.

Here is a bar chart to show Mr Harris' data.

Exercise

1 Zoe has measured the heights of everyone in her class.
She has measured to the nearest centimetre. Here are her results.

132 121 146 134 114 125 137 129
127 130 124 136 141 118 129 136
123 128 135 132 129 117 140 135
139 131 127

(a) Copy and complete this tally chart.

Height (cm)	Tally	Frequency
110–119		
120–129		

(b) Draw a bar chart for Zoe's data.

2 Matt works at a swimming pool. He is doing a survey to find out what age groups use the swimming pool most.
He writes down the ages of all the people who visit the pool one morning.
Here are his results.

32 55 41 12 13 13 62 45 23
6 4 3 29 27 56 19 17 34
47 8 7 11 15 70 33 26 14
37 13 14 22 30 46 52 15 14
31 53

(a) Make a tally chart using groups 0–9, 10–19, and so on.
(b) Draw a bar chart.
(c) How many people visited the pool that morning?
(d) Which age group used it the most?

3 Sarah keeps a record of her scores when she plays her new computer game. Here are her scores for the first few weeks.

17 55 82 134 168 143 182 174
240 113 194 98 257 322 286 301
126 264 228 319 160 200 258 320
247 281 177 346

(a) Make a tally chart using groups 0–49, 50–99, 100–149, and so on.
(b) Draw a bar chart.
(c) What do you think the bar chart will look like after another few weeks?

Finishing off

When you have finished this chapter you should be able to:

- collect and organise data using a tally chart
- draw bar charts and pictograms
- understand pie charts
- group data using a tally chart.

Review exercise

1 This pictogram shows the results of a football team for its matches one season.

Win

Lose

Draw   = 4 matches

(a) How many matches did the team win?
(b) How many did they lose?   **(c)** How many did they draw?
(d) Draw a bar chart to illustrate this data.

2 Mrs Williams teaches History to two Year 7 classes. One day she gives both classes the same test. She gives each student a grade A, B, C, D or E. Mrs Williams draws this bar chart to show the results.

(a) Copy and complete this table.

Grade	A	B	C	D	E
Frequency for 7T	4				
Frequency for 7X	3				

(b) How many students are there in Class 7T?
(c) How many students are there in Class 7X?
(d) Which class do you think did better in the test?

3 Sonia helps in the school tuck shop.
One day she keeps a record of what
drinks she has sold.
Here is her list.

(a) Make a tally chart.
(b) How many drinks did Sonia sell
altogether?
(c) Draw a pictogram to illustrate
the data.

Cola Lemon Coffee Cola Orange
Tea Tea Cola Lemon Coffee
Cola Cola Cola Lemon Orange
Tea Cola Tea Orange Coffee
Tea Cola Lemon Cola Lemon
Orange Tea Cola

4 This pie chart shows the different types of pets
owned by a group of children.

(a) What fraction of the children own cats?
(b) What pet is owned by about $\frac{1}{3}$ of the
children?
(c) Write the pets in order of popularity,
starting with the most popular.

5 A skating rink keeps a record of the number of visitors it has every day
during the month of July.
The numbers are written on this calendar.

JULY						
Mon	Tues	Weds	Thurs	Fri	Sat	Sun
		1 73	2 52	3 121	4 324	5 286
6 35	7 67	8 112	9 89	10 95	11 274	12 239
13 93	14 104	15 78	16 115	17 127	18 310	19 262
20 48	21 83	22 306	23 283	24 259	25 261	26 249
27 250	28 315	29 352	30 296	31 245		

(a) Why are there more visitors on Saturdays and Sundays?
(b) What day do you think the school summer holidays began?
(c) Make a grouped tally chart using groups 0–49, 50–99, and so on.
(d) Draw a bar chart to illustrate the data.

6 Symmetry

THE AVONFORD STAR

Elegant Design for New Town Hall

The design for Avonford's new Town Hall was revealed today.

Here is an architect's drawing of the front view.

Task

Look at the Town Hall and write down the answers to these questions.

1 How many ground floor windows are there?
2 There is just one entrance – where is it?
3 How many 1st floor windows are there?
4 How many 2nd floor windows are there?
5 How many flagpoles are there?
6 How many chimneys are there?
7 How many small windows are there on each side of the entrance?
8 How many large windows are there on each side of the entrance?

? Sometimes there is an odd number of features, sometimes even. Why is this?

? What do you think is the main design feature of the Town Hall?

The Town Hall is **symmetrical**.
Many buildings are designed like this.

If you stand a mirror on the centre of the drawing, in line with the flagpole, the Town Hall will look exactly the same in the mirror as it does behind the mirror.
This kind of symmetry is called **reflection symmetry**.

The Town Hall has one line on which you can stand a mirror and see reflection symmetry.
This is called a **line of symmetry**.

This green cross, seen on first aid kits, has *four* lines of symmetry.
Two of them are diagonal, one is horizontal and one is vertical.
Try them out with a mirror.

? How many lines of symmetry does a rectangle have?

Exercise

1 Which of these road signs have reflection symmetry?

(a) (b) (c) (d) (e) (f)

2 Copy or trace each of these shapes and draw their lines of symmetry.
Write down how many lines of symmetry each shape has.

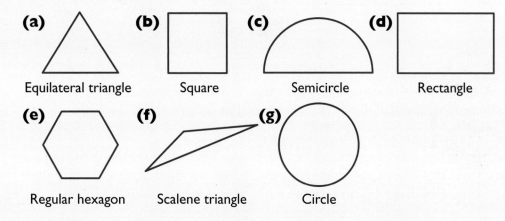

(a) Equilateral triangle (b) Square (c) Semicircle (d) Rectangle

(e) Regular hexagon (f) Scalene triangle (g) Circle

3 Copy or trace these capital letters carefully and draw their lines
of symmetry.

A B C D E F G H

4 **(a)** Look around the room you are in and see if you can find ten items
which have a symmetrical pattern.
Write them down saying how many lines of symmetry each one has.

(b) Now see if you can write down a list of ten items in the same room
which are **asymmetrical**. (This means *not* symmetrical, with no
lines of symmetry.)
For each one describe the features which make it asymmetrical.

Activity Design a logo which has *reflection symmetry*.
You can use squared paper if you wish.
The logo can be for a sports club, music band, your school or anything
you like.
When you have finished, write down how many lines of symmetry it has.

Completing symmetrical shapes

Here is the drawing of the
Town Hall with the line of
symmetry drawn on it.

 Task

Measure and write down the shortest distance of the following:

- from the flagpole to each chimney.
- from the line of symmetry to each small window on the ground floor.
- from the line of symmetry to each large window on the ground floor.
- from the line of symmetry to each first floor window.
- from the flagpole to each outer second floor window.

? **What do you notice about these measurements?**

Trace the drawing and add more windows on the ground and first floors, *making sure that the design remains symmetrical*.

We can use squared paper or
dotted paper to complete
symmetrical shapes.

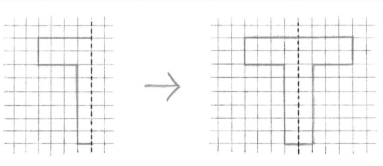

Here is one with two lines of symmetry.

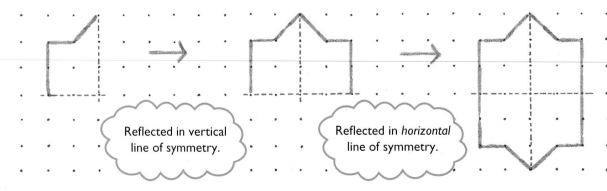

Reflected in vertical
line of symmetry.

Reflected in *horizontal*
line of symmetry.

Exercise

1 Copy these shapes on to squared paper. For each one, copy the line of symmetry and use it to draw the rest of each symmetrical shape.

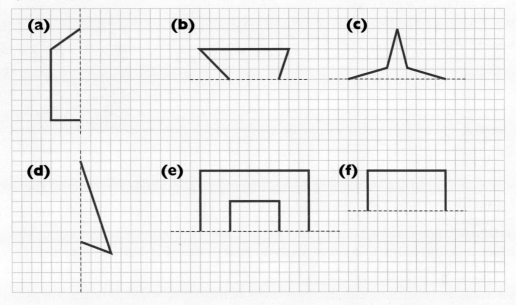

2 Here are parts of shapes which have two lines of symmetry.

Copy them and draw in the rest of the shape.

3 Copy and complete these shapes. The dashed lines are lines of symmetry.

Activity   Work in pairs.
Using squared paper draw half of a shape up to its line of symmetry.
Your drawing should be like those in Question 1.
Now swap with your partner and complete each others' shapes.

Repeat this using shapes that have two or more lines of symmetry like those in Question 2.

Rotation symmetry

Here is a drawing of Avonford Town Council's flag.

Task

Make an exact copy of the flag using tracing paper. Turn the tracing through 180° (half a turn). The tracing should still fit over the flag.

With the tracing exactly over the flag, decide where to stick a pin to rotate the tracing paper around. Mark this point with a cross and test it with a drawing pin.

There are two positions the flag can be in where it looks exactly the same.
We say that the flag has **rotational symmetry of order two**.
The point about which the flag rotates is the **centre** of rotation symmetry.

There are four positions where this square flag looks the same.
Check by tracing the flag.

This flag has **rotational symmetry of order four**.

?   Where is this flag's centre of rotational symmetry?
How could you find it and mark the centre?
Why *is* this point the centre?

Task

Design a flag which has rotational symmetry. Decide the order of rotational symmetry *before* you start.

Use squared paper if you wish. Check the symmetry with tracing paper.

Show the centre of rotational symmetry.

Some shapes have rotation symmetry *and* reflection symmetry.

?   How many lines of reflection symmetry does this
pattern have?
What is the order of its rotation symmetry?

Exercise

1. Which of these dominoes has rotation symmetry?

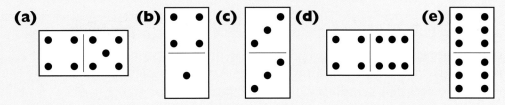

(a)　(b)　(c)　(d)　(e)

2. Write down the order of rotational symmetry of these patterns.
Use tracing paper to help if you wish.

(a)　(b)　(c)　(d)

3. Trace each of these shapes. For each one

   (i) write down how many lines of symmetry it has and draw them
   (ii) write down the order of rotation symmetry and mark the centre
   with a cross.
   Explain how you decided the position of the centre.

(a) Square
(b) Rectangle
(c) Regular octagon
(d)
(e) Scalene triangle
(f)

4. Complete these shapes so that they have both reflection and rotation
symmetry. Mark the centre of rotation symmetry with a cross.

   For each one write down
   how many lines of
   reflection symmetry it has,
   and the order of rotational
   symmetry.

   (a)　(b)

Activity　Design a car wheel which has rotation symmetry.
Before you start decide what the order of rotation symmetry will be.
Use a pair of compasses and a protractor to help you.
When you have finished use tracing paper to check the symmetry.

Finishing off

Review exercise

1 For each of these shapes write down whether they have reflection symmetry or not. Copy each one that does and add to it the lines of symmetry.

(a) I (b) L (c) X (d) Y (e) Z

(f) (g) (h) Quaver (i) Semibreve

2 Which of these national flags have
   (a) reflection symmetry (say how many lines)
   (b) rotation symmetry (say what order)?

Denmark   Jamaica   Japan   Norway

Bangladesh   Trinidad and Tobago   Botswana

3   Copy each of these part-shapes on to squared paper.
    Complete them by reflecting in the lines of symmetry.
    Mark the centre of those which also have rotation symmetry.

(a)

(b)

(c)

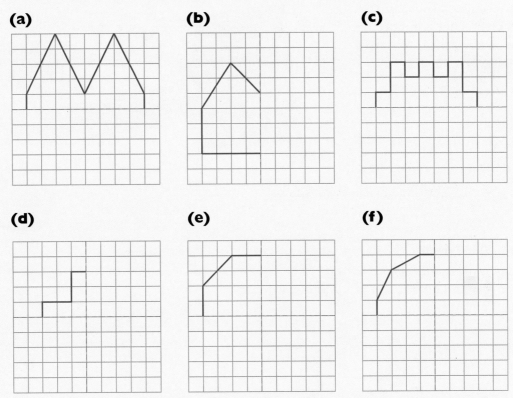

(d)

(e)

(f)

4   Here is a photograph of Vaux-le-Vicomte, a chateaux outside Paris in
    France. Can you spot three things about it which are *not* symmetrical?
    Write them down.

Hannah sees these adverts in her mother's magazine and asks what the figures mean.

Spring bargains

$\frac{1}{4}$ **OFF**

1/3 OFF SPECIAL LINES

1/2 PRICE SALE

Her father is preparing tea.

He cuts a tomato into two equal pieces.

Each of these is a half

Hannah's father takes a pizza out of the oven and cuts it into 3 equal pieces.

Each of these is a third

Then he cuts each piece again.

Now there are 6 pieces, so each piece is a sixth

Task

Here is a picture of a chocolate bar. Copy it enough times to show the fractions $\frac{1}{12}$, $\frac{2}{12}$, $\frac{3}{12}$, etc. up to $\frac{11}{12}$.
Some of these fractions can be written in a simpler way.
Which are they?

Hannah counts the money from her money box.

What fraction of a pound (£) is 10p?

How many pennies make £1? What fraction of a £1 is a penny?

The decimal system can be used for tenths, hundredths, thousandths, etc.

? **Where does the decimal point go?**

Fraction	H hundreds	T tens	U units	$\frac{1}{10}$ tenths	$\frac{1}{100}$ hundredths	$\frac{1}{1000}$ thousandths	Decimal
$\frac{3}{10}$				3			0.3
$\frac{7}{100}$					7		0.07
$6 + \frac{5}{10} + \frac{1}{100}$			6	5	1		6.51
$7\frac{13}{100}$			7	1	3		7.13

Exercise

1 Copy these diagrams and shade these fractions:

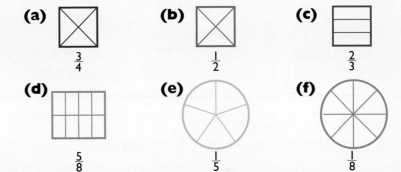

(a) $\frac{3}{4}$ (b) $\frac{1}{2}$ (c) $\frac{2}{3}$

(d) $\frac{5}{8}$ (e) $\frac{1}{5}$ (f) $\frac{1}{8}$

2 Copy the table and write these numbers in the columns.

H	T	U	$\frac{1}{10}$	$\frac{1}{100}$	$\frac{1}{1000}$

(a) $\frac{7}{10}$

(b) $\frac{3}{100}$

(c) $\frac{11}{100}$

(d) $\frac{9}{1000}$

(e) $\frac{21}{1000}$

(f) $6 + \frac{3}{10}$

(g) $7 + \frac{19}{100}$

3 What is the value of the red circled digit?

EXAMPLE 61④3·71   Answer: 4 tens or 40
8·3⑨4   Answer: $\frac{9}{100}$

(a) 1⑥·32   (b) 4·⑦8   (c) 19·7④   (d) 0·⑤
(e) 11·30⑧   (f) 3·⑥1   (g) 0·0③   (h) 3·00⑦
(i) 62·0⑨4   (j) ⑧·63   (k) 49·21⑥   (l) 5·001⑨

4 Write these numbers as decimals:
(a) $\frac{2}{10}$ (b) $\frac{5}{100}$ (c) $\frac{43}{100}$ (d) $\frac{17}{1000}$

(e) $\frac{2}{100}$ (f) $\frac{9}{10}$ (g) $\frac{156}{1000}$ (h) $\frac{29}{100}$

(i) $\frac{11}{1000}$ (j) $\frac{7}{100}$ (k) $\frac{403}{1000}$ (l) $\frac{37}{10000}$

(m) $6 + \frac{5}{10}$ (n) $7 + \frac{3}{10} + \frac{2}{100}$ (o) $5\frac{23}{100}$ (p) $8\frac{17}{1000}$

(q) $6\frac{7}{100}$ (r) $9\frac{3}{10}$ (s) $11\frac{46}{100}$ (t) $2\frac{13}{10000}$

5 Write these in order, smallest first.
(a) 8.9, 9.1, 8.79, 8.901

(b) 0.1 hours, 5 minutes, $\frac{1}{4}$ of an hour, 5.9 minutes

(c) 10 cm, 0.11 metres, $\frac{1}{20}$ metre, 9.98 millimetres

Scales and dials

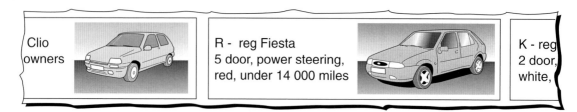

Dan's father sees this advert in the newspaper.
He goes to look at the car and Dan checks the car's mileage.

The gauge says

   The white numbers are the whole number of miles and the red digit
gives the tenths of a mile.

It could be written as **13785·6** miles.

Task

Ask your teacher for a sheet giving mileages covered by cars of different ages.
Take the cars with the same registration number or letter (for older cars), and work
out the average mileage. (Do this by adding to find the total mileage and dividing the
answer by the number of cars.)

EXAMPLE 1   Dan's father takes the car for a test drive.
Dan looks at the speedometer.

> 40 − 30 = 10
> This is divided into 5 intervals
> 10 ÷ 5 = 2
> so each section is worth 2.

Dan's father is travelling at 34 mph.

EXAMPLE 2   Dan's mother wants a new unit to be fitted into their caravan.
She measures the space it is to go in.

> 70 − 69 = 1
> This is divided into 10 intervals
> 1 ÷ 10 = 0·1
> so each section is worth 0·1.

The tape measure reads 69·3 cm.

Exercise

1 Write the numbers shown on these mileage gauges as decimals:
(a) 7619   **(b)** 41293   **(c)** 63217   **(d)** 11193
(e) 362148   **(f)** 712350   **(g)** 42895   **(h)** 732152

2 The dials show speeds in m.p.h. Read the speeds below:

(a)

(b)

(c)

(d)

3 The tapes below are given in cms. What measurements are shown?

(a)

(b)

(c)
(d)

4 These thermometers show temperature in °Fahrenheit.
What temperature do they show?

(a)

(b)

(c)

(d)

(e) Normal body temperature is 98·4°.
Which of the thermometers shows normal body temperature?

5 Read the following scales:

(a)

(b)

(c)

(d)

(e)

(f)

Addition of decimals

BACK TO SCHOOL

Geometry set	£3.70
Fountain pen	£6.50
Calculator	£5.25

Special Offer

Joseph decides he needs all of these
items before he goes back to school.
How much does it cost altogether?

Joseph pays with two £10 notes.
How much change does he receive?

$$£^1 2^1 \cancel{0}^9 \cdot \cancel{0}^9 0$$
$$-£\ 15 \cdot 45$$
$$\overline{£\quad 4 \cdot 55}$$

```
   3.70
   6.50
+  5.25
 ──────
  15.45
   1 1
```

Task

Instead of paying with £10 notes, Joseph pays with money from his money-box.
The coins he has are shown in the table.

Value of coin	1p	2p	5p	10p	20p	50p	£1
Number of coins	6	8	3	9	16	6	10

What is the smallest number of coins that Joseph can use to pay £15·45?
What is the largest number of coins that Joseph can use to pay £15·45?

Joseph's father buys him some new sportswear for the new term.

SOCCER WORLD
HIGH ST. AVONFORD

SOCCER BOOTS	£39.99
SHORTS	£14.99
TRACKSUIT	£59.99
TOTAL	**£114.97**

THANK YOU FOR
YOUR CUSTOM

The assistant rings the items into the till.
Joseph's father checks the bill.

Soccer boots	£40
Shorts	£15
Tracksuit	£60

£40 + £15 = £55
£55 + £60 = £115

Joseph's father has added an extra 3p for the
boots, shorts and tracksuit.
So   £115 − 3p = £114·97. ✔

If a mixture of pence and pounds are to be added, write the pence as a decimal of a pound.

EXAMPLE   Spare protractor   25p
                 Cartridges   £1·45

Write this item as £0·25

£0·25
£1·45
‾‾‾‾‾
£1·70

He pays with a £5 note.

$$£5 \cdot {}^1 00$$
$$-£1_1 \cdot 70$$
$$\overline{£3 \cdot 30}$$

or

$$£\cancel{5}^4 \cdot {}^1 00$$
$$-£1 \cdot 70$$
$$\overline{£3 \cdot 30}$$

Put zeros in to help you

Change = £3·30.

Exercise

1   Work out
   (a) 2.3 + 3.7   **(b)** 2.04 + 4 + 2.2   **(c)** 62.3 + 6.23 + 0.62
   (d) 0.19 + 0.01 + 0.8   **(e)** 0.90495 + 0.00205 + 0.093
   (f) 10.92 − 6.31   **(g)** 2 − 0.05   **(h)** 0.602 − 0.257

2   Work out the cost of the items for each of these people.

   (a) Emily needs a pen, cartridges, crayons and a protractor.
   (b) Simon needs a geometry set, a plain file and a pen.
   (c) Anna wants cartridges, a protractor, a ruler and crayons.

3   What is the change from £1 if you buy:
   (a) a chocolate bar at 28p   **(b)** a Crunchie bar at 35p
   (c) gum at 22p a packet   **(d)** a Nutty bar at 43p.

4   **(a)** Amanda buys some emery boards,
        cotton wool, nail scissors, and nail
        polish.
        (i) How much is this altogether?
        (ii) How much change will she get
            from a ten-pound note?

   (b) Lionel buys some hair gel,
        deodorant and soap.
        (i) How much is this altogether?
        (ii) How much change will he get
            from a ten-pound note?

   emery boards   99p
   cotton wool   £1.45
   nail scissors   £2.49
   nail polish   £4.50
   hair gel   £2.19
   deodorant   £2.29
   soap bar   £2.35

5   Find the total cost of these items:

   (a)
Tee-shirt	£17·99
Shorts	£19·99
Sunglasses	£27·99

   (b)
Trainers	£54·99
Sportsbag	£35·99
Sweatshirt	£39·99

6   **(a)** Find the total cost of decorating
        this teenager's bedroom.

   (b) Check your answer in the same way
        that Joseph's father did on the opposite
        page.

Paint	£15·99
Pillowcases	£10·99
Curtains	£29·99
Duvet cover	£23·99
Sheet	£24·99
Table lamp	£14·99

Finishing off

Now that you have completed this chapter you should be able to:

- understand what a fraction is
- understand what a decimal fraction is
- read scales and dials
- add decimals and decimal money
- subtract decimals and decimal money

Review exercise

1 Write down the shaded parts as fractions.

(a)   (b)   (c)   (d)   (e)

2 What are the shaded parts as fractions?

(a)   (b)   (c)   (d)   (e)

(f) Write the fractions above as decimals.

3 Write the numbers in the
table as decimal numbers:

H	T	U	$\frac{1}{10}$	$\frac{1}{100}$	$\frac{1}{1000}$
		4	6		
	1	5		3	
					9
3		1	2		7
				5	9

4 Remember each penny is $\frac{1}{100}$th of a £1.
So 7p = $\frac{7}{100}$th of a £1 = £0·07 and 30p = $\frac{30}{100}$th of a £1 = £0·30.
Write these amounts as £s:
(a) 11p   **(b)** 23p   **(c)** 8p   **(d)** 2p   **(e)** 195p   **(f)** 263p.

5 Read the letters from the following scales.

(a)

10 11 12 13 14

A   B   C D

(b)

50   60   70

W   X   Y   Z

(c)

16   17   18

L   M   N

(d)

```
— 100
      ← F
—  80
      ← G
—  60
      ← H
```

6 Carlo's mother buys these groceries:
(a) What is the total cost?
(b) How much change does she get from £5?

bread	53p
milk	57p
bacon	£1·43
eggs	£1·39

7 **(a)** Find the total cost of all of these items:

Winnie the Pooh book	£9.99	Slimline diary	£1.99
Return to Fantasia video	£12.99	Card	£1.40
Wrapping paper	95p		

(b) How much change would you get from £30?

8 David has £23·98 in his money box.
Find the amount he has left after each shopping trip.
(a) Flowers for Granny's birthday – £6·95
(b) Ticket and programme for Goliaths v Spartans – £8·50
(c) Easter eggs and card – £3·98

9 Carlo's father goes shopping with £200 of vouchers which he has been
given for his birthday. He goes to the fishing
shop and buys the following:

Carbon fishing rod	£84.99
Thigh waders	£59.99
Fixed spool reel	£34.99

(a) **(i)** How much is this altogether?
  (ii) How much money has he still to spend?

He decides to buy a bite alarm for £36·99.

(b) How much money will he need to pay in addition to the vouchers?

Phil draws a map of his town on a grid showing the important places.

KEY

A	Library
B	Shop
C	Phil's house
D	Sports centre
E	Swimming pool
F	Windmill
G	School
H	Cinema
I	Church
J	Post Office

Each building is marked at a point.
You can use the gridlines to help you write down the exact position of a building.

The library is at position (4, 2).

Go up 2 squares.

Go along 4 from Phil's house.

We say that the library has **co-ordinates (4, 2)**.

The first number, **4**, gives the distance along.

The second number, **2**, gives the distance up.

? **What are the co-ordinates of the windmill?**
What are the co-ordinates of the school?

Task

1 Look at Phil's map:

    (a) What has co-ordinates (7, 1)?
    (b) What has co-ordinates (9, 4)?

2 Write down the co-ordinates of all the other buildings on Phil's map.

 Phil says that the Post office is at (3, 7).
What has he done wrong? Why does Phil's mistake matter?

Exercise

Jane draws a map of her local boating lake.

1. What is at the co-ordinates (9, 3)?

2. What is at the co-ordinates (10, 2)?

3. What is at the co-ordinates
   (a) (8, 2) **(b)** (2, 8)?

4. What is at the co-ordinates
   (a) (6, 2) **(b)** (2, 6)?

5. Write down the co-ordinates of all the trees.

6. Write down the co-ordinates of all the ducklings.

7. Write down the co-ordinates of:
   (a) the red boat **(b)** the rock **(c)** the duck **(d)** the swans.

8. Write down all the co-ordinates of the stepping stones.

9. John says that there is a boat at (4, 2).
   Explain why he is wrong.

Using co-ordinates in mathematics

In mathematics co-ordinates are plotted on a pair of axes like this:

The vertical axis is called the y axis.

The horizontal axis is called the x axis.

The *x* co-ordinate is always given first.

The distance along from (0,0)

The point A is written (4, 3).
We say A has co-ordinates (4, 3).

Go along 4 *Then up 3*

? **What are the co-ordinates of points B and C?**
Would the point (3, 2) lie inside the shaded shape?
What about the point (2, 3)?

Any point can be plotted using co-ordinates.
The point (0, 0) has a special name. It is called the **origin**.

Task

I Write down the co-ordinates of the points D, E and F.

2 (a) Draw a grid like the one above.
  (b) Plot the points (2, 5), (5, 5), (5, 2) and (2, 2) and join them.
  (c) What shape have you drawn?

3 (a) Draw another grid and make up your own shape.
  (b) Give the co-ordinates of the corners to a friend so that they can draw your shape.

? **Why is it important that the x co-ordinate is always given first?**

Exercise

1 Write down the co-ordinates of each point plotted below:

(a)

(b)

(c)

(d)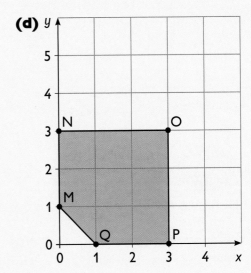

2 Follow these instructions.

> Draw an x axis from 0 to 10 and a y axis from 0 to 6.
> Plot the following points and join them up.
>
> (0, 3),   (4, 4),   (5, 5),   (5, 4),   (8, 3),   (9, 4),
> (9, 1),   (8, 2),   (5, 1),   (5, 0),   (4, 1),   (1, 2).
>
> Now put a dot at (2, 3).
> Draw a jagged line from (1, 2) to (2, 2).
> Draw straight lines from (3, 3) to (3, 2), from (4, 3) to (4, 2) and
> from (5, 3) to (5, 2).

What have you drawn?

Activity Draw your own picture and write a set of instructions giving the
co-ordinates. Follow Question 2 as a guide.
Give your instructions to a friend to draw your picture from.

Using negative numbers, fractions and decimals

Look at this star.
Now look at the axes. You will notice two things.

- There are negative (minus) co-ordinates, to the left for x and down for y.
  The point D is $(-3, -4)$.
- Some of the co-ordinates are not whole numbers.
  B is $(4\frac{3}{4}, 1\frac{1}{2})$ or $(4.75, 1.5)$.

 What are the co-ordinates of the other points, A, C and E?

Task

Here is a sketch of a star with 8 points. A is $(0, 5)$.

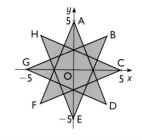

? What is the length of OB?
How many degrees is angle AOB?

Draw this star accurately on graph paper.
What are the co-ordinates of the other points?

⚠ Always look carefully at your graph paper to see how many small squares fit along each big one.

? What are the co-ordinates of the points on these two graphs?

(a)

(b)

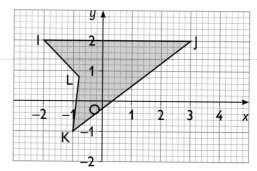

Exercise

1 Write down the co-ordinates of the points which make this bow-tie.

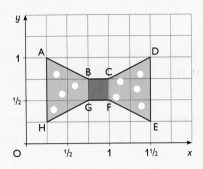

2 Draw axes, using the values of 0 to 5 for both x and y.
Plot these points and join them in order:

$(2, 4\frac{1}{2})$, $(4\frac{1}{2}, 4\frac{1}{2})$, $(2\frac{1}{2}, 1\frac{1}{2})$, $(0, 1\frac{1}{2})$ and back to $(2, 4\frac{1}{2})$.

Describe the shape you have drawn.

3 Draw axes, using the values of -1 to 6 for x and -4 to 4 for y.
Plot these points and join them in order:

$(-1, -1)$, $(2, 3)$, $(6, 0)$.

What fourth point would be needed to make a square?

4 Draw axes, using the values of -6 to 6 for both x and y.
(a) Plot these points and join them in order:

$(4, 6)$, $(6, 0)$, $(4, -6)$, $(-4, -6)$, $(-6, 0)$, $(-4, 6)$ and back to $(4, 6)$.

(b) Describe the shape you have drawn.
(c) Are all the sides the same length?
(d) Are all the angles exactly equal?

5 Write down the co-ordinates of the points on the following graphs.

(a)

(b)

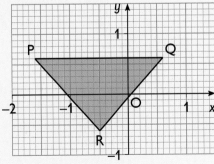

Investigation   Find out how to draw a star with 9 points. Draw one for yourself.
Now complete the instructions for a friend.
'Plot the following points and join them up in order:
....*'*

Finishing off

Now that you have finished this chapter you should be able to:

- use positive and negative co-ordinates
- use co-ordinates that are not whole numbers
- use different sorts of graph paper.

Review exercise

1 Here is a map showing seven towns and the roads between them. The distances along the axes are in kilometres.

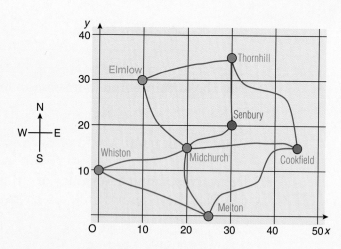

Elmlow is at the point (10, 30).
Melton is at (25, 0).

(a) What are the co-ordinates of **(i)** Whiston **(ii)** Midchurch?

(b) How far is it from **(i)** Thornhill to Senbury **(ii)** Midchurch to Cookfield?

(c) A new town is to be built at (45, 35).
    (i)   How far will the new town be from Thornhill?
    (ii) How far will the new town be from Cookfield?

2 Draw axes, using the values of 0 to 14 for x and 0 to 6 for y.

(a) Plot these points and join them in order:
    (0, 3), (4, 6), (9, 6), (13, 3), (9, 0), (4, 0) and back to (0, 3).
(b) Describe the shape you have drawn.
(c) Are all the sides the same length?
(d) Are all the angles the same size?

3 Draw axes, using the values of −6 to 6 for x and −4 to 4 for y.
Plot these points and join them in order:
$(-4\frac{3}{4}, 0)$, $(-3\frac{1}{2}, 3\frac{1}{2})$, $(0, 0)$, $(3\frac{1}{2}, 3\frac{1}{2})$, $(4\frac{3}{4}, 0)$, $(3\frac{1}{2}, -3\frac{1}{2})$, $(0, 0)$.
What additional point is needed to make the shape you have drawn symmetrical?

4 Write down the co-ordinates of the points on these graphs.

(a)

(b)

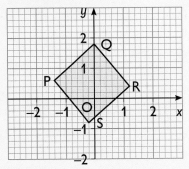

5 Greg and Debbie are playing a game called Treasure Hunt.
Their game is shown below.

Debbie 'buries' the
treasure at the
point (5, 7).
Greg has to guess
where Debbie has
hidden the treasure.
He guesses the
point (4, 4).
Debbie says that he is
a distance of 4 away.

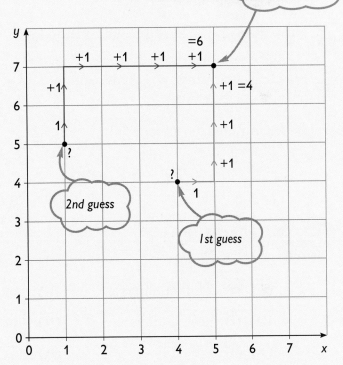

The distance is the shortest distance away from the treasure travelling
only along the grid lines.

Greg then guesses (1, 5).
Why is this a sensible next guess?
He is now a distance of 6 away.
Greg will win when he works out where the treasure is.

Play the game with a partner.

Investigation   Investigate what tactics you should use when playing
Treasure Hunt.
What is the least number of guesses which guarantees you find
the treasure?

Charlie's start time

Charlie's end time

Charlie is skating in a competition.

? **How many minutes does his routine last?**

? **How can you see it is $\frac{1}{12}$ of an hour from the clock face?**

That is $\frac{1}{12}$ of an hour

There are 60 minutes in an hour.

$$\frac{1}{12} \text{ of } 60 = \frac{1}{\cancel{12}_1} \times \cancel{60}^{5}$$

$$= 5$$

You can also write this as $\frac{60}{12}$ and then cancel

Task

1 Find **(a)** **(i)** $\frac{1}{3}$ of 60 minutes **(ii)** $\frac{2}{3}$ of 60 minutes

(b) **(i)** $\frac{1}{4}$ of 28 days **(ii)** $\frac{3}{4}$ of 28 days

(c) **(i)** $\frac{1}{7}$ of £56 **(ii)** $\frac{2}{7}$ of £56

2 How many degrees does the minute hand of a clock turn through in
(a) 60 minutes **(b)** 5 minutes **(c)** 1 minute **(d)** 23 minutes **(e)** $2\frac{1}{2}$ hours?

As soon as Charlie finishes another skater starts. They all take exactly 5 minutes.

Two skaters take $\frac{1}{12} + \frac{1}{12} = \frac{2}{12}$ of an hour.

Three take $\frac{1}{12} + \frac{1}{12} + \frac{1}{12} = \frac{3}{12}$ of an hour.

? **How can you say $\frac{2}{12}$ and $\frac{3}{12}$ more simply?**

? **What fraction of an hour do 5 skaters take?**

? **The competition lasts $1\frac{1}{2}$ hours. How many skaters take part?**

Exercise

1 Work out. Simplify your answers when possible.

(a) $\frac{1}{3} + \frac{1}{3}$ **(b)** $\frac{1}{8} + \frac{3}{8}$ **(c)** $\frac{1}{4} + \frac{1}{4} + \frac{1}{4} + \frac{1}{4}$ **(d)** $\frac{1}{3} + \frac{2}{3}$ **(e)** $\frac{3}{5} - \frac{1}{5}$

(f) $\frac{7}{10} - \frac{3}{10}$ **(g)** $\frac{1}{4} + \frac{1}{2}$ **(h)** $\frac{3}{4} + \frac{1}{4}$ **(i)** $1\frac{1}{2} - \frac{1}{4}$ **(j)** $\frac{3}{4} + \frac{3}{4}$

2 Use this diagram to write these fractions in order, smallest first.

$\frac{2}{5}, \ \frac{1}{2}, \ \frac{1}{8}, \ \frac{3}{7}, \ \frac{5}{6}, \ \frac{2}{3}, \ \frac{3}{4}$

3 Find
(a) $\frac{1}{4}$ of an hour (1 hour = 60 minutes)
(b) $\frac{1}{4}$ of a mile (1 mile = 1 760 yards)
(c) $\frac{1}{4}$ of a pound (1 pound = 16 ounces)

4 By how much are these items reduced?

5 1 pound = 16 ounces. Work out

(a) $\frac{1}{2}$ of a pound   **(b)** $\frac{1}{8}$ of a pound   **(c)** $\frac{1}{16}$ of a pound

6 A dartboard is a circle divided into 20 sectors. Work out one-twentieth of 360°.

7 Find

(a) $\frac{2}{5}$ of 60 minutes   **(b)** $\frac{3}{4}$ of 64 kg   **(c)** $\frac{1}{4}$ of 100 cm   **(d)** $\frac{1}{3}$ of 45 minutes

(e) $\frac{2}{3}$ of 18 kg   **(f)** $\frac{5}{16}$ of 32 ounces   **(g)** $\frac{3}{7}$ of 28 days   **(h)** $\frac{4}{9}$ of 360°

(i) $\frac{4}{7}$ of \$42   **(j)** $\frac{6}{11}$ of £33   **(k)** $\frac{3}{10}$ of 1000 m   **(l)** $\frac{4}{9}$ of 63 km

(m) $\frac{11}{25}$ of 100 kg   **(n)** $\frac{3}{20}$ of £40   **(o)** $\frac{7}{12}$ of 132 g

Cancelling down

Half-past five.
$\frac{1}{2}$ of an hour = 30 minutes out of 60.

Half-past five. Tea-time!
You can have some tea and some cake.

$$\frac{1}{2} = \frac{30}{60}$$

These fractions are the same.

Philip eats two pieces of cake at tea-time.

This means he has eaten a quarter of the cake.

So $\frac{2}{8} = \frac{1}{4}$.

? **Why are these fractions the same or equivalent?**

Dividing top and bottom by 2.

$$\frac{2}{8} = \frac{\cancel{2}^1}{\cancel{8}_4} = \frac{1}{4}$$

$$\frac{30}{60} = \frac{\cancel{30}^1}{\cancel{60}_2} = \frac{1}{2}$$

Dividing top and bottom by 30.

These fractions are in their simplest terms, or their **lowest terms**.

Task

Which of these fractions below is the same as two thirds $\left(\frac{2}{3}\right)$?

Write down the letter of each fraction in the order that you find them.

1 A $\frac{4}{6}$	**2** C $\frac{15}{25}$	**3** B $\frac{12}{18}$	**4** F $\frac{14}{20}$	**5** D $\frac{8}{10}$	**6** S $\frac{16}{24}$
7 O $\frac{20}{30}$	**8** V $\frac{10}{12}$	**9** X $\frac{12}{16}$	**10** P $\frac{16}{20}$	**11** L $\frac{14}{21}$	**12** N $\frac{24}{30}$
13 U $\frac{34}{51}$	**14** Z $\frac{24}{28}$	**15** T $\frac{32}{48}$	**16** Q $\frac{30}{40}$	**17** U $\frac{30}{35}$	**18** F $\frac{7}{28}$
19 E $\frac{30}{45}$	**20** J $\frac{30}{42}$	**21** L $\frac{22}{33}$	**22** Y $\frac{28}{42}$	**23** R $\frac{6}{9}$	**24** C $\frac{7}{35}$
25 I $\frac{18}{27}$	**26** D $\frac{42}{48}$	**27** G $\frac{8}{12}$	**28** W $\frac{14}{28}$	**29** H $\frac{24}{36}$	**30** T $\frac{26}{39}$

You can cancel as often as you like.

Cancelling by 2 and by 3

$$\frac{12}{54} = \frac{\cancel{12}^6}{\cancel{54}_{27}} = \frac{\cancel{6}^2}{\cancel{27}_9} = \frac{2}{9}$$

OR

$$\frac{12}{54} = \frac{\cancel{12}^2}{\cancel{54}_9} = \frac{2}{9}$$

Cancelling by 6

Exercise

1 Cancel to simplest terms.

(a) $\dfrac{5}{10}$ **(b)** $\dfrac{3}{12}$ **(c)** $\dfrac{2}{16}$ **(d)** $\dfrac{4}{20}$ **(e)** $\dfrac{6}{12}$

(f) $\dfrac{11}{44}$ **(g)** $\dfrac{9}{24}$ **(h)** $\dfrac{25}{30}$ **(i)** $\dfrac{24}{56}$ **(j)** $\dfrac{18}{66}$

(k) $\dfrac{27}{72}$ **(l)** $\dfrac{21}{49}$ **(m)** $\dfrac{21}{28}$ **(n)** $\dfrac{8}{48}$ **(o)** $\dfrac{18}{81}$

(p) $\dfrac{45}{60}$ **(q)** $\dfrac{24}{36}$ **(r)** $\dfrac{28}{35}$ **(s)** $\dfrac{54}{63}$ **(t)** $\dfrac{88}{96}$

2 **(a)** Which of these fractions are the same as four-fifths $\left(\dfrac{4}{5}\right)$?

Write down the letters of those you find.

(i) O $\dfrac{12}{18}$ **(ii)** Y $\dfrac{8}{10}$ **(iii)** D $\dfrac{3}{9}$ **(iv)** O $\dfrac{20}{25}$ **(v)** U $\dfrac{24}{30}$

(vi) A $\dfrac{16}{20}$ **(vii)** G $\dfrac{12}{16}$ **(viii)** R $\dfrac{28}{35}$ **(ix)** E $\dfrac{12}{15}$ **(x)** L $\dfrac{3}{12}$

(b) Which of these fractions are the same as four-ninths $\left(\dfrac{4}{9}\right)$?

Again, write down the letters of those you find.

(i) K $\dfrac{20}{44}$ **(ii)** I $\dfrac{10}{20}$ **(iii)** G $\dfrac{8}{18}$ **(iv)** N $\dfrac{21}{28}$ **(v)** O $\dfrac{24}{54}$

(vi) O $\dfrac{32}{72}$ **(vii)** G $\dfrac{14}{35}$ **(viii)** A $\dfrac{16}{30}$ **(ix)** L $\dfrac{16}{48}$ **(x)** D $\dfrac{20}{45}$

(c) Which of these fractions are the same as five-sixths $\left(\dfrac{5}{6}\right)$?

Again, write down the letters of those you find.

(i) K $\dfrac{6}{16}$ **(ii)** J $\dfrac{18}{20}$ **(iii)** A $\dfrac{15}{18}$ **(iv)** T $\dfrac{25}{30}$ **(v)** T $\dfrac{40}{48}$

(vi) H $\dfrac{45}{54}$ **(vii)** W $\dfrac{25}{35}$ **(viii)** W $\dfrac{48}{64}$ **(ix)** I $\dfrac{10}{12}$ **(x)** S $\dfrac{30}{36}$

Activity   Ask your teacher for the worksheet that goes with this activity. Shade in every part of the worksheet which contains a fraction equivalent to $\dfrac{7}{9}$.

Multiplying fractions

Sally's mother cuts a pizza into 2 halves.
She then cuts each half piece into 3 slices.

She has cut the whole pizza into 6 pieces,
so each slice is one-sixth, or $\frac{1}{6}$.

In fact she did $\frac{1}{3}$ of $\frac{1}{2} = \frac{1}{3} \times \frac{1}{2}$

> Multiplying $1 \times 1 = 1$
> at the top and $3 \times 2 = 6$
> at the bottom.

$= \frac{1}{6}$.

The next day Sally's mother cuts a quiche
into 3 equal pieces. She puts 2 of these
pieces into Sally's lunch-box.

At school, Kevin has forgotten his lunch.
Sally gives him one of her pieces of quiche.
Kevin and Sally now each have one-third,
or $\frac{1}{3}$, of quiche.

$$\frac{1}{2} \text{ of } \frac{2}{3} = \frac{1}{\cancel{2}^1} \times \frac{\cancel{2}^1}{3}$$

$$= \frac{1}{3}.$$

> Multiplying $1 \times 1 = 1$ at the top
> and $1 \times 3 = 3$ at the bottom.

Task

Draw your own fraction diagrams to find the following.

1 **(a)** $\frac{1}{2}$ of $\frac{1}{4}$ **(b)** $\frac{1}{2}$ of $\frac{1}{5}$ **(c)** $\frac{1}{3}$ of $\frac{1}{4}$ **(d)** $\frac{1}{4}$ of $\frac{1}{4}$ **(e)** $\frac{1}{4}$ of $\frac{1}{5}$

Now try these:

2 **(a)** $\frac{1}{2}$ of $\frac{4}{5}$ **(b)** $\frac{1}{3}$ of $\frac{3}{8}$ **(c)** $\frac{1}{3}$ of $\frac{6}{8}$ **(d)** $\frac{1}{4}$ of $\frac{6}{8}$ **(e)** $\frac{2}{5}$ of $\frac{5}{8}$

Check the results of your drawings by using the cancelling and multiplying method
shown above.

Cancelling can be done with any number of fractions:

$$\frac{6}{7} \times \frac{14}{27} \times \frac{3}{4} = \frac{6}{\cancel{7}^1} \times \frac{\cancel{14}^2}{27} \times \frac{3}{4}$$

> Cancel by 7 ...

$$= \frac{\cancel{6}^3}{\cancel{7}_1} \times \frac{\cancel{14}^{2}}{27_9} \times \frac{\cancel{3}^1}{\cancel{4}_1}$$

> ... and lastly by 3.

$$= \frac{6}{\cancel{7}_1} \times \frac{\cancel{14}^2}{27_9} \times \frac{\cancel{3}^1}{4}$$

> ... and now by 3.

$$= \frac{\cancel{6}^{3_1}}{\cancel{7}_1} \times \frac{\cancel{14}^{2^1}}{27_{9_3}} \times \frac{\cancel{3}^1}{\cancel{4}_1}$$

$$= \frac{\cancel{6}^3}{\cancel{7}_1} \times \frac{\cancel{14}^{2_1}}{27_9} \times \frac{\cancel{3}^1}{\cancel{4}_{2_1}}$$

> Cancel by 2 and then
> by 2 again ...

$$= \frac{1}{3}.$$

Exercise

1 (a) $\frac{1}{2} \times \frac{1}{5}$ (b) $\frac{1}{3} \times \frac{1}{7}$ (c) $\frac{1}{6} \times \frac{1}{4}$

(d) $\frac{1}{3} \times \frac{2}{5}$ (e) $\frac{1}{4} \times \frac{3}{5}$ (f) $\frac{3}{7} \times \frac{5}{8}$

2 (a) $\frac{2}{5} \times \frac{1}{4}$ (b) $\frac{3}{8} \times \frac{4}{9}$ (c) $\frac{3}{10} \times \frac{5}{12}$

(d) $\frac{7}{9} \times \frac{3}{14}$ (e) $\frac{5}{18} \times \frac{6}{25}$ (f) $\frac{8}{27} \times \frac{9}{32}$

3 (a) $\frac{5}{8} \times \frac{2}{3}$ (b) $\frac{3}{16} \times \frac{4}{5}$ (c) $\frac{7}{9} \times \frac{6}{14}$

(d) $\frac{11}{12} \times \frac{2}{9}$ (e) $\frac{5}{14} \times \frac{7}{8}$ (f) $\frac{2}{39} \times \frac{13}{14}$

4 (a) $\frac{15}{8} \times \frac{8}{5}$ (b) $\frac{3}{2} \times \frac{4}{3}$ (c) $\frac{5}{2} \times \frac{2}{5}$

(d) $\frac{13}{4} \times \frac{8}{13}$ (e) $\frac{14}{11} \times \frac{11}{7}$ (f) $\frac{15}{4} \times \frac{8}{3}$

5 (a) $\frac{2}{15} \times \frac{5}{12} \times \frac{8}{9}$ (b) $\frac{3}{8} \times \frac{5}{9} \times \frac{16}{25}$ (c) $\frac{7}{8} \times \frac{12}{21} \times \frac{16}{20}$

(d) $\frac{15}{33} \times \frac{14}{25} \times \frac{11}{21}$ (e) $\frac{12}{45} \times \frac{15}{81} \times \frac{27}{2}$ (f) $\frac{54}{33} \times \frac{49}{56} \times \frac{11}{63}$

6 (a) $\frac{2}{5} \times 15$ (b) $\frac{5}{8} \times 40$ (c) $\frac{3}{7} \times 21$

(d) $\frac{6}{7} \times 42$ (e) $\frac{5}{9} \times 45$ (f) $\frac{2}{13} \times 52$

Activity   Find this palindrome.

❖ ☆ ❖ ▲, ❖ ● ☨ ❖ ▲, ❖ ❑ ❖ ▲ ❖ ☨, ● ❖ ▲ ❖ ☆ ❖

1 First work out the answer to this question:

▲ $\frac{6}{11} \times \frac{33}{42}$ Now find the answer below and write the corresponding letter in place of every ▲ in the palindrome above.

2 Now try this one:

☆ $\frac{3}{10} \times \frac{5}{21}$ Find this answer and replace every ☆ with the corresponding letter from the answers below.

3 Continue with these:

● $\frac{1}{12} \times \frac{3}{4} \times 2$ ❖ $\frac{2}{5} \times \frac{10}{7} \times \frac{3}{9} \times \frac{14}{6}$

☨ $\frac{5}{9} \times \frac{42}{48} \times \frac{45}{35}$ ❑ $\frac{5}{17} \times \frac{51}{42} \times \frac{28}{35}$

A $\frac{4}{9}$	C $\frac{2}{7}$	L $\frac{5}{8}$	M $\frac{1}{14}$	N $\frac{3}{7}$	P $\frac{1}{8}$

Introduction to percentages

Percentage means *out of 100* and is written as %.   20% means $\frac{20}{100}$.

Task

Which percentage do you think belongs to each label?

C DEPOSIT   **A** VAT   **G** SALES REDUCTION

D OXYGEN CONTENT OF AIR   **H** French: John could do better!

F Half-Price Sale   **B** Three quarters   **E** Full marks

10%   100%   75%   21% $17\frac{1}{2}\%$ 20%   40%   50%

Percentages can be written as fractions . . .

$$30\% = \frac{30}{100}$$

$$= \frac{30^3}{100_{10}} = \frac{3}{10}$$

$$65\% = \frac{65}{100}$$

$$= \frac{65^{13}}{100_{20}} = \frac{13}{20}$$

. . . and cancelled in the same way.

You can find a percentage of a quantity:

$$10\% \text{ of } £600 = \frac{10}{100} \times £600$$

$$= \frac{10}{100_1} \times £600^6$$

$$= £60$$

10% OFF See inside for details   25% EXTRA FREE   SAVE 50%   40% OFF

30% OFF next purchase   20 per cent discount

Special rate 6.25% until May

The whole amount is called **100%**.

Example   82% of apples in a box are good, ripe apples.
What percentage of the apples are not fit to eat?

(100 − 82)% = 18% of the apples are not fit to eat.

Exercise

1 Write these percentages as fractions.
   (a) 37%   **(b)** 53%   **(c)** 7%   **(d)** 11%
   (e) 9%   **(f)** 29%   **(g)** 17%   **(h)** 6%

2 Write these percentages as fractions and cancel to their lowest terms.
   (a) 20%   **(b)** 25%   **(c)** 40%   **(d)** 75%
   (e) 24%   **(f)** 5%   **(g)** 64%   **(h)** 88%

3 Find 10% of each of these amounts.
   (a) £30   **(b)** £500   **(c)** $450   **(d)** $70
   (e) 240 m   **(f)** 60 litres **(g)** 70 kg   **(h)** 500 g

4 There is 30% off goods in a sale.
   Find the reduction for these items.
   (a) A computer game priced at £50
   (b) A computer priced at £1 000
   (c) A holiday priced at $800
   (d) A tent priced at £750

   You may find it quicker to find 10% first and then multiply by 3.

5 Find these percentages.
   (a) 25% of 840 m   **(b)** 75% of 20 km
   (c) 60% of 20 kg   **(d)** 30% of 80 kg
   (e) 5% of £300   **(f)** 2% of $450

6 **(a) (i)** A jumper is made from a mixture of wool and viscose.
       It is 80% wool.
       What is the percentage of viscose?
   (ii) Another jumper is made from a mixture of polyester and cotton.
       It is 70% polyester.
       What is the percentage of cotton?

   (b) 83% of the pupils in a school are present.
       What percentage are absent?

   (c) 94% of a class of music pupils pass their examination.
       What percentage fail?

   (d) 98% of the oranges in a crate are of good quality.
       What percentage are bad?

7 Write 50%, 25%, and 75% as fractions in their lowest terms.
   These results are useful to know off by heart.

Ratio and proportion

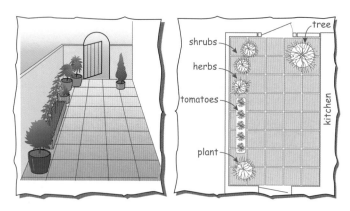

Andy and his father are making a patio.

They lay the slabs using mortar.

To mix the mortar they need 1 part cement to 4 parts sand.

This can be written as *the ratio* 1 : 4 (read as 1 to 4).

 They have a 50 kg bag of cement.
How much sand should be mixed with it?

Task

Air Wales has different sorts of aeroplanes. On all of them the ratio of 1st class to 2nd class seats is 1 : 9.

I One aeroplane has 20 1st class seats.
  (a) How many 2nd class seats does it have?
  (b) How many seats does it have overall?
  (c) What fraction of the seats are 1st class? 2nd class?

 I + 9 = 10. What has this got to do with the aeroplane?

2 Another aeroplane has 400 seats.
How many are 1st class? 2nd class?

3 Another airline has 3 classes of seats, in the ratio

First : Standard : Backpacker = 1 : 8 : 3

How many of each are there on a 240-seater aeroplane?

Order matters with ratios.
Sand : cement = 4 : 1.

But cement : sand = 1 : 4.

We will probably need 1 250 kg of mortar altogether.

5 parts altogether (1 part + 4 parts) will be 1250 kg.
So 1 part is $\frac{1250}{5} = 250$ kg.
So 250 kg of cement are needed and $250 \times 4 = 1\,000$ kg of sand.

Ratios can be cancelled down like fractions:

Example I $2 : 8 = 1 : 4$

Cancelling by 2.

Example 2 $3 : 12 : 15 = 1 : 4 : 5$

Cancelling by 3.

Exercise

1. The ratio of cement : sand is 1 : 4.
   How much sand is needed if:
   (a) 200 kg of cement is used?
   (b) 70 kg of cement is used?

2. The ratio of cement : sand is 1 : 4.
   How much cement is needed if:
   (a) 320 kg of sand is used?
   (b) 240 kg of sand is used?

3. Andy's father makes a different mixture to use as a
   base for a shed. It is 1 part cement, 2 parts sand,
   and 3 parts coarse aggregates (tiny stones).
   (a) Write down the ratio cement : sand : coarse aggregrates.
   (b) 250 kg of cement is used.
      (i) How much sand is needed?
      (ii) How many kilograms of coarse aggregates are needed?

4. To fill the flower pots, Andy mixes a compost of 7 parts loam, 3 parts peat,
   and 2 parts sand.
   (a) Write down the ratio of loam : peat : sand.
   (b) How much peat and how much sand is needed if 14 kg of loam is used?
   (c) How much loam and how much sand is needed if $1\frac{1}{2}$ kg of peat is used?

5. Andy wants to make 60 kg of compost altogether.
   (a) How many parts altogether?
   (b) How many kilograms in one part?
   (c) How much loam, peat and sand is needed?

   > Compost mix is 7 parts loam, 3 parts peat and 2 parts sand.

6. Andy's mother makes 12 jars of strawberry jam and
   8 jars of raspberry jam.
   (a) (i) Write down the ratio of
       strawberry jam : raspberry jam.
      (ii) Simplify your ratio.
   (b) What is the ratio of raspberry jam : strawberry jam?
   (c) (i) What is the ratio of jars of raspberry jam : total number of jars
       of jam?
      (ii) Simplify your ratio.

7. Simplify these ratios:
   (a) 6 : 8   **(b)** 8 : 6   **(c)** 8 : 4   **(d)** 40 : 45
   (e) 16 : 24   **(f)** 6 : 3   **(g)** 7 : 28   **(h)** 11 : 33
   (i) 12 : 15 : 21   **(j)** 25 : 20 : 40   **(k)** 9 : 12 : 15   **(l)** 63 : 28 : 56

Finishing off

Now that you have finished this chapter you should be able to:

- cancel a fraction
- find a fraction of a quantity
- change percentages to fractions
- find a percentage of a quantity
- multiply fractions
- understand ratios and proportion.

Review exercise

1 Write down the fraction shaded.

(a) (b) (c)

(d) (e) (f)

2 Cancel these fractions to their lowest terms.

(a) $\frac{6}{8}$ (b) $\frac{12}{15}$ (c) $\frac{25}{30}$ (d) $\frac{12}{16}$ (e) $\frac{21}{35}$

(f) $\frac{24}{32}$ (g) $\frac{12}{20}$ (h) $\frac{240}{360}$ (i) $\frac{72}{81}$ (j) $\frac{19}{38}$

3 Write these percentages as fractions.
(a) 11% (b) 3% (c) 79% (d) 91%

4 Write these percentages as fractions, and cancel them to their lowest terms.
(a) 12% (b) 4% (c) 80% (d) 92%
(e) 45% (f) 18% (g) 32% (h) 75%

5 Work out the following.

(a) $\frac{1}{3}$ of £24 (b) $\frac{1}{4}$ of 1 760 yards

(c) $\frac{5}{8}$ of 16 ounces (d) $\frac{3}{4}$ of £16

6 A sale has 20% off the marked prices.
Work out how much each of these cost in the sale.

7 Find
(a) 30% of £650
(b) 25% of $8
(c) 60% of 45 Euros
(d) 75% of 48 kg
(e) 5% of 40 metres
(f) 55% of 80 km

8 Work out (evaluate)
(a) $\frac{1}{4} \times \frac{1}{3}$
(b) $\frac{2}{7} \times \frac{1}{3}$
(c) $\frac{1}{2} \times \frac{8}{13}$
(d) $\frac{3}{4} \times \frac{1}{3}$
(e) $\frac{2}{5} \times \frac{4}{11}$
(f) $\frac{1}{7} \times \frac{14}{33}$

9 Simplify these
(a) $\frac{2}{3} \times \frac{9}{14} \times \frac{7}{8}$
(b) $\frac{2}{3} \times \frac{15}{16} \times \frac{4}{5}$
(c) $\frac{7}{8} \times \frac{3}{4} \times \frac{16}{49}$
(d) $\frac{12}{17} \times \frac{1}{5} \times \frac{5}{11}$
(e) $\frac{1}{4} \times \frac{2}{7} \times \frac{2}{9}$
(f) $\frac{2}{3} \times \frac{7}{10} \times \frac{5}{6}$

10 Simplify the following ratios:
(a) $16:20$
(b) $15:3$
(c) $48:36$
(d) $36:18:27$
(e) $33:55:66$
(f) $72:45:54$

11 A fertiliser is made of 2 parts hoof and horn meal, 2 parts lime and 1 part potash.
(a) How much lime and how much potash is needed if 3 kg hoof and horn meal is used?
(b) How much of each should be used if 20 kg of fertiliser is wanted altogether?

12 Look at this graph. The line goes through the whole number point (12, 4).
(a) What other whole number points does the line go through?
(b) Use your answers to part (a) to write down some equivalent fractions to $\frac{4}{12}$.

Activity Make 2 copies of this grid on squared paper.

(a) (i) Shade one square. What fraction of the grid is this?
(ii) Shade 5 more squares. What fraction of the grid are your 5 squares?
(iii) What fraction of the grid is now shaded?
(iv) Complete this statement $\frac{1}{36} + \frac{5}{36} = \frac{?}{36} = \frac{?}{6}$

(b) (i) Shade in squares to represent $\frac{1}{2} + \frac{1}{6}$
(ii) Complete this statement $\frac{1}{2} + \frac{1}{6} = \frac{?}{6} = \frac{?}{3}$

(c) What is $\frac{1}{2} - \frac{1}{6}$?

10 Number patterns

Factors

Terry is preparing for a party by putting glasses onto a shelf.
He arranges 18 glasses in a rectangle.

3 by 6

 Are there any other ways that Terry could arrange the glasses into rectangles? Is a 3 by 6 rectangle different from a 6 by 3 rectangle?

We say that 3 and 6 are **factors** of 18 because they divide exactly into 18.

 What are the other factors of 18?

Task

1 There are 24 children in a class. How many different ways can their desks be arranged in a rectangular shape?

2 How can 144 chairs be arranged for an assembly? Find all the possible rectangular arrangements. Which ones are the most practical?

Multiples

Terry has some trays which hold 6 glasses each.
He starts to stack the trays of glasses.

 How many glasses are in each of the piles that Terry has made?

The numbers 6, 12, 18, 24, . . . are called **multiples** of 6.
They are the answers to the 6 times table:

$$1 \times 6 = 6$$
$$2 \times 6 = 12$$
$$3 \times 6 = 18$$
$$4 \times 6 = 24 \quad \text{and so on.}$$

 What are the first 12 multiples of 2?

The multiples of 2 are called **even numbers**.
Numbers which are not multiples of 2 are called **odd numbers**.

 How can you decide that a number is odd?

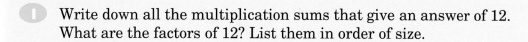

Exercise

1 Write down all the multiplication sums that give an answer of 12.
What are the factors of 12? List them in order of size.

2 Write down in order of size all of the factors of the following.
(a) 8   **(b)** 6   **(c)** 7   **(d)** 16   **(e)** 20   **(f)** 15

3 Write down the numbers that are factors of both 24 and 36.
The largest of these is called the highest common factor (HCF).
What is the HCF of 24 and 36?

4 Write down your four times table up to 12×4.
What are the first 12 multiples of 4?

5 Write down the first three multiples of the following.
(a) 3   **(b)** 7   **(c)** 13   **(d)** 10   **(e)** 5   **(f)** 11

6 Write down the first three multiples of both 24 and 36.
The smallest of these is called the lowest common multiple (LCM).
What is the LCM of 24 and 36?

7 Sean buys 36 plants.
(a) Show all the different ways he can arrange them into rectangular trays.
(b) Another day Sean buys 3 trays of 36 plants.
How many plants does he buy altogether?

8 Sally has bought 10 raffle tickets for the tombola.

(a) Which of her tickets are odd numbers?
How do you know? Explain your answer.
(b) All numbers which are multiples of both 3 *and* 5 win prizes.
Which of Sally's tickets win a prize?

9 James is stacking trays of 8 glasses. Sarah is stacking trays of 12 glasses.
When they have finished they find that they both have the same number of
glasses in their piles. How many glasses do they each have?

10 Chris is organising a barbecue.
The local shop sells rolls in packets of 6, and sausages in packets of 10.
Chris buys three packets of rolls and two packets of sausages.

(a) How much does he spend?
(b) How many hot dogs can he make?
(c) Chris does not want to have any rolls
or sausages left over.
How many packets of each does he buy?

Squares

Jamie has several square patio slabs and he wants to arrange them to make a square patio. He has 16 slabs and he arranges them into a 4 by 4 square.

 Is there any other way of arranging 16 slabs into a square?

One of the slabs is cracked. Jamie now tries to arrange the remaining 15 slabs into a square.

 Can you arrange 15 patio slabs into a square?

Jamie now uses some of the patio slabs to make smaller squares.

1 by 1

2 by 2

3 by 3

Task

1 How many slabs are used for each square above?
2 How many slabs would be used in the next 7 squares in Jamie's pattern?
3 What patterns can you spot in these numbers?

The numbers 1, 4, 9, and 16 are called **square numbers**.

Square numbers are the answers when a number is multiplied by itself.
We write

$$1^2 = 1 \times 1 = 1$$
$$2^2 = 2 \times 2 = 4$$
$$3^2 = 3 \times 3 = 9$$
$$4^2 = 4 \times 4 = 16.$$

We read this as 3 squared.

1 is the first square number.

 How can you find 97^2 using your calculator?

Square roots

A square which uses 25 patio slabs must have 5 slabs along each side.
5 is called the **square root** of 25.

$$5 \times 5 = 25$$

A quick way to write this is using the square root sign $\sqrt{\ }$.

$$\sqrt{25} = 5$$

 What size square should you use to arrange 49 patio slabs into a square?

 What is $\sqrt{49}$? What is $\sqrt{15}$?

Exercise

1 Write down the first ten square numbers.

2 Jenny wants to arrange oranges into different sizes of trays.
Which of the following numbers of oranges can she arrange into square trays?

(a) 9 **(b)** 27 **(c)** 16 **(d)** 64 **(e)** 58 **(f)** 100

Explain how you know in each case.

3 How many oranges are there in each of the following square boxes?

(a) **(b)** **(c)**

4 Imad wants to break off squares of chocolate from a larger bar of 25 pieces.
How many different sizes of square can he break off?

5 **(a)** How many small pieces of chocolate would there be in a square bar with 6 pieces along each side?

(b) How many small pieces of chocolate would there be in a square with 12 pieces along each side?

(c) Katy has a square bar with 64 pieces of chocolate. How many small pieces are there along each side of the square bar?

(d) What is the square root of 64?

6 Find

(a) $\sqrt{81}$ **(b)** $\sqrt{169}$ **(c)** $\sqrt{1}$ **(d)** $\sqrt{100}$ **(e)** $\sqrt{121}$

7 **(a)** Find

(i) $\sqrt{900}$ **(ii)** $\sqrt{1600}$ **(iii)** $\sqrt{2500}$ **(iv)** $\sqrt{3600}$

(b) What pattern do you notice?

(c) Now write down the value of

(i) 80^2 **(ii)** 90^2 **(iii)** 100^2 **(iv)** 700^2

8 Find

(a) **(i)** 0.1^2 **(ii)** 0.2^2 **(iii)** 0.3^2 **(iv)** 0.4^2

(b) What pattern do you notice? Continue this pattern up to 0.9^2.

Investigation How many squares are there on a chess board?
There are more than 64 squares!

Primes

Ben wants to arrange seven video tapes into as many different rectangular boxes as possible.

 How many different ways can he do this?

Ben finds that there are only two ways of packing the tapes.

1 by 7

7 by 1

1 and 7 are the factors of seven.

Seven is called a **prime number**.

 7 is a prime number since it has exactly two factors, 1 and itself.

Prime numbers always have exactly two different factors.

 How many different ways could you pack eleven tapes into rectangular boxes? Is eleven a prime number? How do you know?

How can you find other prime numbers?
Start by looking at the ways of packing 2 tapes.

There are only two ways.
So 2 is a prime number.

1 by 2   2 by 1

Task

1   Write down the first ten prime numbers?
     What do you notice about these numbers?

2   How can you check whether a number is prime?

3   What is the biggest prime number you can find?

 Are there any other even prime numbers? Why?

 Is one a prime number?

Exercise

1 How many different ways can you pack the following numbers of tapes into rectangular boxes.

(a) (b) (c)

Which numbers are prime?
How do you know?

2 Which of the following numbers are prime?

(a) 9   **(b)** 23   **(c)** 51   **(d)** 61   **(e)** 29

Explain your reasons for each one.

3 Draw a 2 – 61 grid like the one shown.

2	3	4	5	6	7
8	9	10	11	12	13
14	15	16	17	18	19
20	21	22	23	24	25
26	27	28	29	30	31
32	33	34	35	36	37
38	39	40	41	42	43
44	45	46	47	48	49
50	51	52	53	54	55
56	57	58	59	60	61

(a) On your grid put a ring around every number that is prime.

(b) How can you be sure that each number you have ringed is a prime?

(c) How do you know that you have not missed any out?

(d) Shade in all the multiples of 6.
What do you notice about where all the prime numbers are?
Why do you think this happens?

4 John and Maria are having an argument.
John says that the numbers 12 898 and 3 021 735 are both prime.
Maria says that they are not.

Who is right?
How can you prove your answer?

Cubes

A **centicube** is a 1 cm by 1 cm
by 1 cm cube.
You can fit centicubes together
to make cuboids.

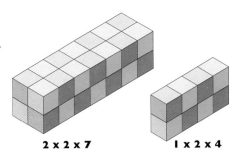

2 x 2 x 7   **1 x 2 x 4**   **1 x 3 x 9**

Task

How many centicubes are in each cuboid shown above?

? The first cuboid is pulled apart into 28 centicubes.

Can you use all these centicubes to make a cube?

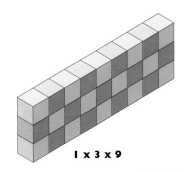

$2 \times 2 \times 7 = 28$

You can use 28 centicubes to
make a 3 by 3 by 3 cube
with 1 centicube left over.

A solid with all sides the same length.

? Is there a different way that you could make a cube without any centicubes left over?

Task

1 (a) Can the $1 \times 2 \times 4$ or $1 \times 3 \times 9$
cuboids be turned into cubes?

(b) What size cube will they make?

2 How many centicubes are in the
cubes opposite?

Numbers like 1, 8, 27, 64 . . . are called **cube numbers**.

? Why do you think they are called cube numbers?

$1^3 = 1 \times 1 \times 1 = 1$
$2^3 = 2 \times 2 \times 2 = 8$
$3^3 = 3 \times 3 \times 3 = 27$
$4^3 = 4 \times 4 \times 4 = 64$

Example What size cube could you make from 27 centicubes?

You can make a cube of side 3 from 27 centicubes.
3 is called the **cube root** of 27.

$3 \times 3 \times 3 = 27$

Exercise

1 How many centicubes are in the following cubes?

2 Which of these cuboids can be turned into cubes?

What is the biggest size of cube that can be made from each?

How many centicubes are left over?

3 What size cube can be made from 8 centicubes?
What is the cube root of 8?

4 What size of cube can be made from 64 centicubes?
What is the cube root of 64?

5 Find
(a) 9^3 **(b)** 10^3 **(c)** 12^3 **(d)** 0.1^3 **(e)** 0.2^3

Investigation   **1**   Steven has a box of 100 centicubes.
He realises that he can't make one big cube but he can make several smaller cubes using all the centicubes.

How many ways can *you* find of doing this?

2   Sarah has a box of 216 centicubes and she makes a large cube using all of these.
What is the length of one of its sides?

She can also use all of these to make three smaller cubes.
How?

Powers of 2

A certain type of bacteria grows by splitting into 2 every hour.

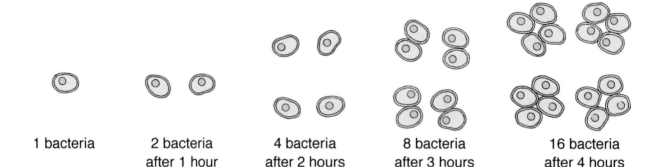

| 1 bacteria | 2 bacteria after 1 hour | 4 bacteria after 2 hours | 8 bacteria after 3 hours | 16 bacteria after 4 hours |

These are the numbers of bacteria present each hour:

$2, 4, 8, 16, 32, \ldots$

This sequence of numbers has been obtained by doubling to get from one number to the next.

 Write down the next 3 numbers in the pattern.
What is the 10th number in the pattern?

The numbers are all **powers of 2**.

Task

David earns £5 a day for his newspaper round.

His employer wants to change the amount that he pays David.
He will pay 1p for the first day, 2p for the second, 4p for the third and will double his pay every day after that.

David thinks that he will be better off. His employer thinks that he will save money.

Who is right?

The mathematical way of writing the *powers of 2* is:

$$2^1 = 2$$
$$2^2 = 2 \times 2 = 4$$
$$2^3 = 2 \times 2 \times 2 = 8$$
$$2^4 = 2 \times 2 \times 2 \times 2 = 16$$

 Work out 2^6 and 2^{10}.

 How many times would you have to double to get a number bigger than one million?
What power of 2 is this?

Exercise

1 Write the correct power for each of these numbers.
(a) $8 = 2^?$ **(b)** $32 = 2^?$ **(c)** $128 = 2^?$

2 The diagram below shows how a knockout tournament is arranged to produce one winner when 8 people play.

(a) How many games are played?

(b) Draw a diagram to show how to organise a tournament for 16 players. How many rounds are needed?

(c) How many rounds are needed if the number of players is
(i) 64 **(ii)** 256 **(iii)** 512
(iv) 20?

3 BINARY numbers can be written using just the digits 0 and 1 if the column headings are powers of 2.

(a) Continue the pattern 1, 2, 4, 8, 16, 32, . . . to find the next three column headings.

You add up all the columns with '1' in.

?	?	?	32	16	8	4	2	1	
			1	0	0	1	0	1	= 32 + 4 + 1 = 37
				1	1	0	1	0	= 16 + 8 + 2 = 26
				1	0	0	1	= 8 + 1 = 9

So 37 is represented by the binary number 100101.

(b) Change the following *binary* numbers to numbers from our usual counting system.
(i) 110 **(ii)** 1011 **(iii)** 110101 **(iv)** 11011101

(c) Write the following as *binary* numbers
(i) 5 **(ii)** 7 **(iii)** 12 **(iv)** 31

(d) Why are *binary* numbers used for computers?

Finishing off

Now that you have finished this chapter you should know the meanings of the following terms:

- odd number
- even number
- factor
- multiple
- prime number
- square number
- square root
- cube number
- cube root
- powers of two.

Review exercise

1 Write down the first five multiples of the following.
   (a) 3   **(b)** 7   **(c)** 12   **(d)** 11   **(e)** 9   **(f)** 30

2 Write down all the factors of the following.
   (a) 15   **(b)** 24   **(c)** 19   **(d)** 27   **(e)** 16   **(f)** 13
   Which of the above numbers are prime?

3 Avonford Town's nursery has bricks in the shape of cubes.
   They are to be packed into rectangular trays.
   Draw all the possible arrangements for each set.

(a) 8 bricks

(b) 16 bricks

(c) 12 bricks

(d) 9 bricks

(e) 27 bricks

(f) 64 bricks

   Which bricks can be packed into square trays?
   Which bricks could be packed into cube shaped boxes?

4

| 7 | 9 | 21 | 27 | 13 | 63 | 16 |
| 29 | 42 | 25 | 100 | 8 | 17 | 64 |

Which of these numbers are
(a) multiples of both 3 and 7   **(b)** odd   **(c)** squares
(d) cubes   **(e)** prime numbers   **(f)** powers of 2?

5 Terry's younger sister is having a party. Terry is helping her organise it. She wants to give each of her friends a party bag, containing a balloon, a hat and a chocolate.

The local shop sells packets of the following amounts:

(a) Terry's sister invites 12 friends.

  (i)   How many packets of each should they buy?
  (ii) How many balloons are left over?
  (iii) How many party hats are left over?

(b) For his party, Terry doesn't have any balloons, party hats or chocolates left over when he buys his packets from the local shop.
How many friends does *he* invite?

6 Jane buys some oranges for 90p.
Peter buys some oranges from the same shop for 72p.

(a) List all the possible amounts that one orange can cost.

(b) The actual cost is the highest of the answers to part (a).
How much does one orange cost?

Investigation   Joe is investigating triangular numbers.

   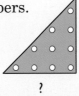

  1   3   6   ?

(a) Why do you think these are called triangular numbers?

(b) What are the next three triangular numbers?
Draw their triangles.

(c) Joe puts two of the triangles together to make a square.
Which other triangular numbers can be used to make a square number?

6 + 10 = 16

11 Everyday measures

Length

How tall are you?

What is the distance from York to London?

There are two types of units used when measuring length.

The **IMPERIAL SYSTEM** uses inches (in), feet (ft), yards (yd) and miles.

The **METRIC SYSTEM** uses millimetres (mm), centimetres (cm), metres (m) and kilometres (km).

Metric Measures		Imperial Measures	
1000 mm = 1 m	1000 m = 1 km	12 in = 1 ft	
100 cm = 1 m *also* 10 mm = 1 cm		3 ft = 1 yd 1760 yd = 1 mile	

Task

What is the approximate length of the following items?

- The width of a thumb nail
- The height of a doorway
- A hand span
- The length of your longest stride

Use these measurements to help you estimate the length of 10 objects around your school.
Measure the lengths of the objects accurately.
How accurate are your estimates?

Measuring – to the nearest cm and the nearest mm

The ruler shows that the length of the line is a bit more than 5 cm.

The length of the line is 5 cm (to the nearest cm)

or   54 mm

or   5.4 cm.

These measurements are accurate to the nearest mm.

? **Is 54 mm the EXACT measurement of the line?**

Exercise

1 Match each of the objects or distances in List A with an appropriate measure of length from List B.

There may be more than one suitable answer.

List A
The distance from London to Edinburgh
The length of a swimming pool
The width of a man's hand
The height of a fully grown woman
The width of a sewing needle
The width of your maths book

List B
4 inches
20 centimetres
1.6 metres
1 millimetre
440 miles
50 metres
8 inches
5 ft 4 in

2 How many centimetres are there in
(a) 3 m   **(b)** 4.2 m   **(c)** 500 m   **(d)** 36 mm?

3 How many metres are there in
(a) 8 km   **(b)** 32 km   **(c)** 1.7 km   **(d)** 320 cm
(e) 25 cm   **(f)** 52 cm   **(g)** 2.6 km   **(h)** 64 mm?

4 How many millimetres are there in
(a) 5 cm   **(b)** 23 cm   **(c)** 2.6 cm   **(d)** 0.35 cm?

5 Measure the following lines
(a) to the nearest cm   **(b)** to the nearest mm.

6 The map shows the position of Jody's house, and Jody's friends' houses.

(a) Which of Jody's friends lives furthest away from her house?
(b) One day Jody decides to visit Jill, Mary, Ben and Oliver, in that order.
   How far must she walk?
(c) After visiting Oliver she returns home.
   Has she walked more or less than 1 mile?

This is my map

Mass (or weight)

The *weight* of the cake is 3 pounds 2 ounces or 1.5 kilograms.
In science and maths this is called the *mass* of the cake.

Imperial
16 ounces (oz) = 1 pound (lb)
14 pounds = 1 stone
160 stone = 1 ton
also 2240 lb = 1 ton

Metric Measures
1000 grams (g) = 1 kilogram (kg)
1000 kg = 1 tonne
1000 milligrams (mg) = 1 g

 What is the mass of (a) a brick
(b) an elephant
(c) a grain of rice?

 Task

Find a selection of objects in your classroom. For example, pencil, ruler, rubber, exercise book, board rubber, wrist watch, ink cartridge, thick pen, computer disc, pencil case.

Without weighing them, compare the weights of these objects.

Make a list of the objects in order of their weight, from lightest up to heaviest.

Compare your list with a friend's. Do you agree?

Volume

This bucket holds 2 gallons.
It has a *volume* of 2 gallons.

2 gallons

We can also say it has a capacity of 2 gallons

Imperial
8 pints = 1 gallon

This carton of orange juice holds 1 litre.
It has a *volume* of 1 litre.

Metric Measures
1000 millilitres (ml) = 1 litre
100 centilitres (cl) = 1 litre

 What volume of liquid can be contained in (a) a can of soft drink
(b) a medicine spoon
(c) a car's petrol tank?

Exercise

1. How many grams are there in **(a)** 2 kg   **(b)** 3.5 kg?

2. How many litres are there in   **(a)** 5000 ml   **(b)** 330 ml?

3. The ingredients needed to make a fruit cake are listed in this recipe.
A beaten egg weighs 25 g or 1 oz.

   Find the total weight of the ingredients
   (a) in metric units
   (b) in imperial units.

Fruit Cake		
Margarine	100 g	(4 oz)
Caster Sugar	100 g	(4 oz)
Self-raising Flour	225 g	(8 oz)
Currants	50 g	(2 oz)
Mixed peel	25 g	(1 oz)
2 eggs, beaten		

4. A bottle contains 250 ml of shampoo. How many times can you wash your hair if you use 25 ml each time?

5. A 2 litre bottle of lemonade is used to fill two 330 ml glasses, a 150 ml cup and 10 ml is spilt.
   How much lemonade is left in the bottle?

6. The luggage allowance on an aircraft is 20 kg.
   Louise wishes to pack the following items in her suitcase.
   The suitcase has a mass of 2 kg.

Item(s)	Mass
Coat	500 g
Shoes	1500 g
Toiletries	400 g
Hairdryer	800 g
Clothes	5 kg
Books	2 kg
Travel documents/money	200 g

   (a) What is total mass of her luggage?

   (b) What is the total mass of souvenirs that she can buy without exceeding the luggage allowance on the return trip?

7. In the USA people usually give their weight in pounds. What is the weight in stones and pounds of someone weighing
   (a) 110 pounds   **(b)** 135 pounds   **(c)** 167 pounds?

Activity

2.5 kg   2 lb   1 tonne

350 g   7 stone   4 oz

Find an item to match each of the weights given above.

Time

The clocks below all show the same time.

This clock uses Roman numerals.

This is a 24-hour clock.

It is five minutes past four in the afternoon.

? **Which of the clocks let you know that it is afternoon?**

Units of time
60 seconds = 1 minute   24 hours = 1 day
60 minutes = 1 hour   365 days = 1 year (except in a leap year)

Task

Work out the following.

1 What is your age in days?   **2** What is your age in minutes?

3 Are you older or younger than 350 000 000 seconds?

Timetables

This is part of the timetable for the Trans-Pennine Express:

This train leaves before midnight

This train does not stop at Manchester Piccadilly

York	2309	0048	0238	0348
Leeds	2338	0117	0307	0417
Huddersfield	2359	0140	0330	0440
Manchester Vic.	0034	0225	0417	0531
Manchester Picc.	–	0243	0433	0548
Manchester Airport	0115	0310	0500	0605

This is exactly 5 o'clock in the morning.

? **How long does the 0348 train from York take to reach Manchester Airport?**

0348 to 0400 is 12 minutes ...   12 min

... then 2 hours to 0600 ...

+   2 hr

+   5 min

_____

2 hr   17 min

... and another 5 minutes to 0605

Total time is 2 hours and 17 minutes.

? **Why do you not get the correct answer if you work out 605 − 348?**

Exercise

1. Write these times using the 24-hour clock.
   (a) 9.25 am
   (b) 12.15 pm
   (c) 12.15 am
   (d) twenty to three in the afternoon.

2. Write these times using am or pm.
   (a) 0728
   (b) 1305
   (c) 2311

3. (a) How many hours in 240 minutes?
   (b) How many seconds in 5 minutes?

4. Use the train timetable printed opposite to answer the following questions.
   (a) Where will the 2309 departure from York be at midnight?
   (b) Humza's flight departs from Manchester Airport at 0515 and he has to check in 30 minutes before that. Which train should he catch from York?
   (c) Humza's friend lives in Huddersfield. What time should he be at Huddersfield station if he is to catch the same train?
   (d) Which is the fastest train?

5. (a) How long do the Sports Highlights last?
   (b) Rosa wishes to record the X-Files and the Late Night Film. What is the start time for these programmes using the 24-hour clock?

TV Guide	
9.00 pm	News and Weather
9.25 pm	The X-Files
10.10 pm	Sports Highlights
11.25 pm	Late Night Film
1.10 am	Close

   (c) Rosa has a 120 (2 hr) tape and a 180 (3 hr) tape. Which should Rosa use to record both the X-Files and the Late Night Film? Will there be any spare tape?

6. The time required to cook a turkey is 20 minutes, plus 20 minutes for each pound weight.
   (a) How long will a 10 pound turkey take to cook?
   Peter wants to have the turkey ready for 1.00 pm.
   (b) When should he start cooking?

Investigation The time for the earth to orbit the sun is not exactly 365 days. Every 4 years we have a leap year.

What does this tell you about the true length of a year?

Every 100 years is not a leap year but every 400 years is.
Was the year 2000 a leap year?

Use all this information to calculate the true length of a year.

Finishing off

Now that you have finished this chapter you should be able to:

- find length, mass, capacity and time
- use metric and imperial units
- estimate lengths
- change units
- use the 24-hour clock and read timetables
- measure to the nearest cm and mm.

Review exercise

1 How many seconds are there in a day?

2 For each of the objects in List A, select a suitable mass from List B.

List A	List B
An elephant	5 lb
A feather	1 ton
A new born baby	8 oz
A sack of potatoes	3 g
A bag of sweets	4.5 kg

3 Borrow a copy of the *Guiness Book of Records* from the library.
How many of these records can you find, and what are they?
(a) The length of the world's longest river.
(b) The height of the tallest woman.
(c) The record for running 100 metres.
(d) The volume of blood in the human body.
(e) The weight of the heaviest man.`

Now list four more interesting records that you have discovered.

4 The timetable shows the times of the late buses to Tom's village each evening.

Railway station	1905	1925	1945	2005	2025
Theatre	1919	1939	1959	2019	2039
High Street	1922	1942	2002	2022	2042
Back Lane	1935	1955	2015	2035	2055
Village green	1945	2005	2025	2045	2105

(a) How much time is there between buses?
(b) How many buses is this each hour?
(c) Tom arrives at the railway station at 7.15 pm.
   (i) Which bus will he catch?
   (ii) How long will he have to wait?
(d) Tom wishes to see a show at the theatre.
   The performance does not finish until 8.30 pm.
   Should he book a taxi to get him home?

5 **(a)** How many ml are there in 2 litres?
(b) How many feet are there in 6 yards?
(c) How many ounces are there in 3 pounds?

6 A rectangular parcel is to be decorated with ribbon as shown. How much ribbon is needed?

7

FRIARS FISH AND CHIPS OPENING TIMES		
	Lunch	*Evenings*
Monday	–	5.00 – 10.30
Tuesday	11.30 – 1.30	6.00 – 11.00
Wednesday	11.30 –1.30	6.00 – 11.00
Thursday	–	4.30 – 6.30 8.00 – 11.00
Friday	11.30 – 1.30	4.30 – 11.00
Saturday	11.30 – 1.30	6.00 – 11.00

(a) On which days is the fish and chip shop closed at lunch time?
(b) Can you buy chips at 7.00 pm on a Thursday?
(c) For how many hours a week is the shop open?
(d) On which evening is the shop open for the longest time?

8 A lift has a weight restriction of 1000 kg.
An average person has a mass of 65 kg.
How many people can safely be carried in the lift?

Activity Find 10 examples of *capacity* (or volume) written on packaging or in catalogues.
Make a table like this and say whether the units are imperial or metric.

Item	Capacity	Units
Shampoo	200 ml	metric

12 Flat shapes

THE AVONFORD STAR

New Boating Pond in the Park

Avonford Council are to create a new boating pond in the civic park.
Here are several possible shapes for the pond, proposed by the
council architects.
All these shapes have the same area of water.

Task

1 Draw a shape *with straight sides* which you think would make a good boating pond.
   Write down a description of the shape.
   Your teacher may ask you to describe the shape to the rest of your class, so be precise!
   Write down why you think it would be a good boating pond.

2 Draw a shape which you think would be unsuitable for a boating pond.
   Write down a description of the shape.
   Write down your reasons for it being unsuitable.

Any shape made with straight sides is called a **polygon**.
There are many different types of polygon. To describe them we give them special names.

Triangle	***Quadrilateral***	***Pentagon***	***Hexagon***
3 straight sides, 3 angles	*4 straight sides*	*5 straight sides*	*6 straight sides*

If all the *sides* of a polygon
are *the same length* and if
all its *angles are the same*
it is called a **regular
polygon**.

Regular triangle   Regular quadrilateral   Regular pentagon   Regular hexagon

Exercise

In this chapter you are asked to describe some polygons. This vocabulary will help you.

A polygon has a number of **sides**.
A point where two sides meet is called a **vertex** (plural **vertices**).

In a quadrilateral a **diagonal** joins two opposite vertices.

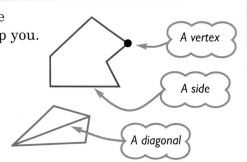

A vertex

A side

A diagonal

1 Write down a description of these shapes.
Say whether they are regular or non-regular.

(a)

(b)

(c)

(d)

(e)

(f)

(g)

(h)

(i)

(l)

(m)

(j)

(k)

2 Which of the following shapes are
(a) regular
(b) quadrilaterals
(c) irregular (this means *not* regular)
(d) hexagons
(e) squares (regular quadrilaterals)
(f) triangles
(g) irregular pentagons
(h) regular hexagons.

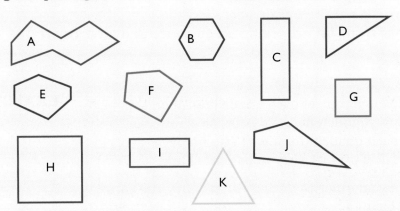

Classifying triangles and quadrilaterals

Task

Copy the three boating pond designs which are triangles on page 106.
Next to each one write down how it is different to the others.

Ten of the designs are quadrilaterals.
Sketch each one and write down how each quadrilateral is different from the others.

Types of triangle

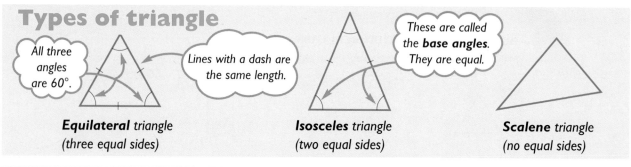

Equilateral triangle
(three equal sides)

Isosceles triangle
(two equal sides)

Scalene triangle
(no equal sides)

Types of quadrilateral

Rectangle
(four right angles)

Square
(rectangle with
four equal sides)

Parallelogram

Rhombus

Trapezium

These lines are
parallel (in the same
direction).

Kite

Arrowhead

? How many rectangles are there in the newspaper article on page 106?
Why is a parallelogram so called?
What is the difference between a kite and an arrowhead?

Task

Make a sketch copy of each quadrilateral on this page.
Make sure you include the dashes or arrows correctly.
Next to each quadrilateral write its name
and the *rules* it must obey to be that shape.

Compare your rules to a friend's. Are they the same?
Do they have to be?

EXAMPLE

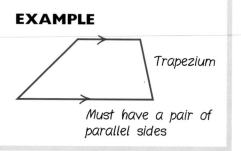

Trapezium

*Must have a pair of
parallel sides*

Exercise

1 Which of these triangles are
(a) equilateral
(b) scalene
(c) isosceles?

2 Which of these quadrilaterals are
(a) squares   (b) irregular   (c) rectangles
(d) regular   (e) kites   (f) parallelograms
(g) rhombuses   (h) trapeziums
(i) arrowheads?

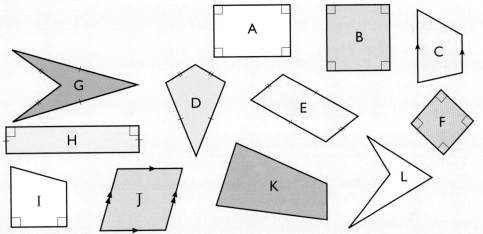

3 Describe each of these shapes as fully and as accurately as you can.

Circles

THE AVONFORD STAR

Boating Pond to be a Circle!

All the polygon designs proposed by the council architects have been rejected by Avonford's Model Boat Club.

'Only a circle is suitable for sailing in all wind directions' said club spokesperson Amy Brown.

Architect's impression

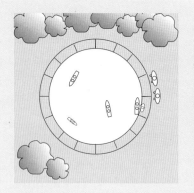

To draw a plan of a circular pond you need a pair of compasses. The distance between the point and the pencil can be adjusted.

Do the right thing!

Follow these steps to draw a perfect circle.

STEP 1 Mark a cross on a clean sheet of paper. Use a sharp pencil.

STEP 2 Place the point of the compasses at the beginning of the centimetre scale on your ruler.
Adjust the distance between the point and the pencil to 6 cm.

STEP 3 Place the point on the cross and move the pencil round to draw a circle.
The cross is at the centre of the circle.

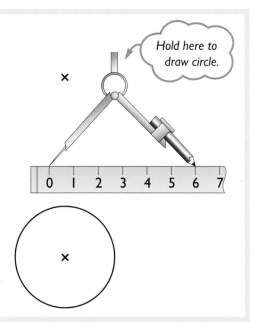

Hold here to draw circle.

 What size is the largest circle you can draw with your compasses?
What size is the smallest circle you can draw with your compasses?

Parts of a circle

The circle you have drawn in the activity has a radius of length 6 cm.

What is the diameter of the circle you have drawn?
What can you say about the radius and diameter of a circle?

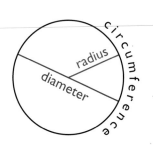

Exercise

1 Use a pair of compasses to make accurate drawings of these circles.

(a) A circle with radius 5 cm.   **(b)** A circle with radius 7 cm.
(c) A circle with radius 4.6 cm.   **(d)** A circle with radius 9.3 cm.
(e) A circle with diameter 8 cm.   **(f)** A circle with diameter 12.4 cm.

2 Measure the radius of each of these circles.
For each one write down the length of the diameter as well as the radius.

(a)   **(b)**   **(c)**

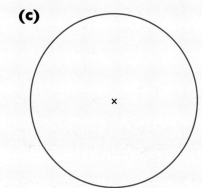

3 Follow these steps to draw a six pointed star.

(a) Open your compasses to about 5 cm and draw a circle.
(b) *Without adjusting the compasses* use them to make marks around the circumference. Draw the first mark on the circumference as a starting point. To make the second mark put the point of the compasses on the first mark, draw a mark, and so on.
(c) Join the marks with straight lines as shown.

4 Use your compasses to draw this flower.

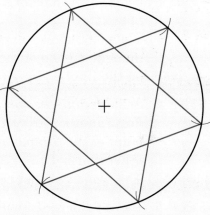

5 Use your compasses to draw a regular hexagon.

6 Use your compasses to draw these patterns. They can be any size.

Constructing triangles

You need to use a pair of compasses to make an accurate drawing of a triangle.

" Do the right thing!

Follow these steps to draw an accurate equilateral triangle.

STEP 1 About half way down a clean sheet of paper draw a line across the page. Make a mark on the line near one end.

STEP 2 Put the point of the compasses on the mark and open them out to make a mark near the other end.

STEP 3 *Without adjusting the gap between the point and the pencil* draw part of a circle above the line.
The point of the compasses must be on one of the marks on the line.

STEP 4 *Still keeping the same gap*, draw another arc with the point of the compasses on the other mark.
The two arcs must cross.

STEP 5 Use a ruler to draw lines from the intersection of the arcs to each mark. Your finished diagram should look like this one.

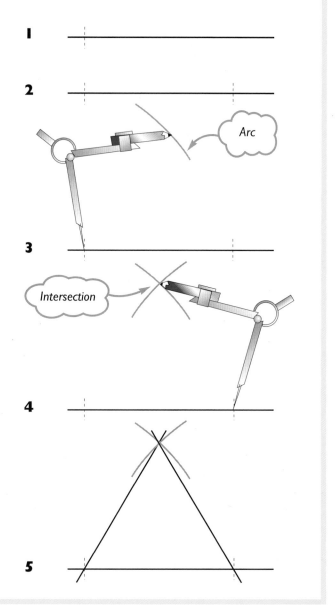

Making an accurate drawing like the one above is called a **construction**.

You have constructed an equilateral triangle.

The arcs and 'extra bits' of line are an important part of a construction.
They must not be rubbed out!

? Without measuring, how do we *know* that all the sides are the same length?

? Measure the angles of your triangle. What do you find?

Exercise

1 Construct equilateral triangles with the following side lengths.
(a) 8 cm   **(b)** 5.2 cm   **(c)** 11 cm   **(d)** 2.6 cm

2 **(a)** Follow these steps to draw a triangle which is **isosceles** but not equilateral.

> **STEP 1**   Draw a line and make two marks on it 7 cm apart.
>
> **STEP 2**   Adjust the compasses to 9 cm to draw two intersecting arcs.
>
> *These are called the **base angles**.*
>
> **STEP 3**   Complete the isosceles triangle. It has one side of 7 cm and two sides of 9 cm.

(b) Measure the base angles. What do you find?

3 Follow the method above to construct isosceles triangles with sides of these lengths:
(a) one side of 6 cm and two sides of 8 cm
(b) one side of 10 cm and two sides of 6 cm.

4 To construct a **scalene** triangle the compasses have to be different for each arc. Construct the triangles which have the following lengths:
(a) 8 cm, 7 cm and 5 cm   **(b)** 9 cm, 5.5 cm and 6 cm

5 Construct triangles with sides of the following lengths, if possible:
(a) 5.2 cm, 5.2 cm and 5.2 cm   **(b)** 10.4 cm, 4.3 cm and 8.7 cm
(c) 3.2 cm, 7.7 cm and 11.2 cm   **(d)** 5 cm, 10 cm and 4 cm
(e) 6.8 cm, 4.1 cm and 6.8 cm   **(f)** 4.6 cm, 5.9 cm and 9.9 cm

Which of these triangles are isosceles?
Which two triangles cannot be drawn?

6 **(a)** Construct a triangle with sides of lengths 2 cm, 4 cm and 2.5 cm.
(b) Construct a triangle with sides of lengths 4 cm, 8 cm and 5 cm.
(c) Measure the angles in each triangle.
What do you notice? Why is this?

Constructions with angles

THE AVONFORD STAR

New 'Safe' Slide in the Park

A new children's slide has been built in the civic park.
   'The old one was too steep for new regulations', said
Leisure Manager John Stubbs.
The steps must be at an angle of 60 degrees to the horizontal
and the slide at 40 degrees.
   'The old one was more fun', said Tom Wilson, aged 4.

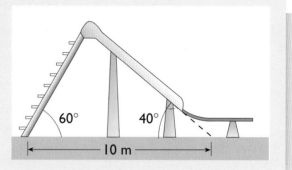

The council's engineers need an accurate drawing of the new slide.
Follow these steps to construct one.

> **Do the right thing!**
> **Constructing triangles with angles**
>
> **STEP 1**   Draw a line across the page.
>   This represents the horizontal ground.
>   Make two marks 10 cm apart.
>
>
>
> **STEP 2**   On one mark use a protractor to   **STEP 3**   On the other mark draw an
>   draw an angle of 60°.   angle of 40°. Label both angles.

?   The triangle you have constructed has been drawn to a scale of 1 cm to 1 m.
       What is the height of the apex of the triangle?

> **Do the right thing!**
> **Constructing rectangles**
>
> Follow these steps to construct a rectangle with sides of 11 cm and 7 cm.
>
>

Exercise

Sometimes you will find it helpful to use
letters, like a, b and c for this triangle, to stand
for the lengths of the sides.

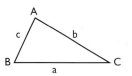

1 Construct each of these triangles as accurately as you can.
The sides can be any length you like.
Do not forget to use a sharp pencil.
Write next to each one what sort of triangle it is.

(a)   50° 40°

(b) 60° 60°

2 Construct triangles with the following angles.
For each triangle measure the third angle and write its size down.
Is it what you expect each time?
(a) 32°, 65°   **(b)** 72°, 34°   **(c)** 12°, 22°   **(d)** 25°, 125°.

3 Make accurate constructions of these triangles.
For each one measure and write down
the lengths of the other two sides.

A B 28° 65° C 8 cm

P Q 32° R 6 cm

L M 70° 70° N 4.3 cm

X Y 15° 145° Z 5.2 cm

4 Construct an accurate drawing of a rectangular postcard with sides of
lengths 14 cm and 7 cm.

5 Here is a sketch
of a triangle.

Make an accurate copy of it
using the measurements shown.
Measure and label the length
of the unlabelled side.

A 7 cm B 48° 8 cm C

6 Construct a triangle with sides of length 5.8 cm and 7.2 cm with an angle
of 63° between them.

7 Construct a rhombus with sides of length 5 cm.

Finishing off

Now that you have finished this chapter you should:
● know what a polygon is, and when it is a regular polygon
● be able to recognise and construct rectangles and squares
● be able to recognise and construct equilateral, isosceles and scalene triangles
● be able to construct triangles with given angles and lengths
● be able to recognise and sketch quadrilaterals which are parallelograms, rhombuses, trapeziums, kites and arrowheads
● be able to recognise and sketch pentagons and hexagons
● be able to construct a circle, and know what a radius and diameter of a circle are.

Review exercise

1   Describe these shapes as fully and accurately as you can.

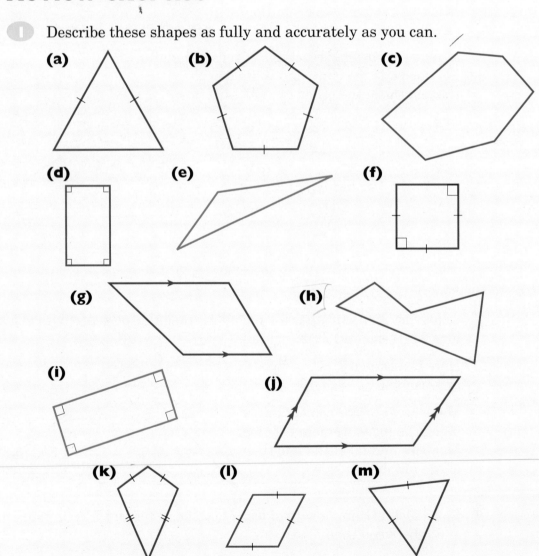

2 Construct two circles, one of radius 4 cm and the other with radius 8 cm *using the same centre for both circles.*
These are called **concentric** circles.

3 Construct an equilateral triangle with sides of length 6.3 cm.

4 **(a)** Construct a triangle with lengths 3 cm, 4 cm and 5 cm.
(b) Construct another triangle with lengths 6 cm, 8 cm and 10 cm.
(c) Write down two things you notice about these triangles.

5 Construct a square with sides of length 5.1 cm.

6 Construct an isosceles triangle with sides of length 5.9 cm and *one* angle of 26°.
What are the other two angles?

7 Julie wishes to measure the height of a tree. Using a **clinometer** she measures angle A to be 25°.
The ground is horizontal.
Construct a scale drawing to find the height of the tree.

8 Construct a parallelogram with sides of length 6.5 cm and 4.3 cm.

Activity

1 Construct a polygon of your choice.
On a separate piece of paper write down a description of it, including angles and lengths.
Swap your *description* with a friend's.
Do not let your friend see your polygon.

2 Construct the shape described by your friend.

Has your friend produced an exact copy of *your* shape?
Use tracing paper to check.

If one shape will fit *exactly* over another shape we say that the two shapes are **congruent**.
Congruent shapes are the *same shape* and the *same size*.
Two shapes are congruent even if one has to be turned over to fit over the other.

13 Multiplying and dividing decimals

My dear friend,
I would so much like you to
come and visit me this summer. It
would be great fun showing you
round my hometown. We could go

Jenny invites her two pen pals, Monique and Anna, to stay with her.

Monique arrives from France, and Anna arrives from the USA.

Monique and Anna both buy a souvenir when they are out shopping.

The exchange rate is   £1 = 9·98 French Francs
                        £1 = 1·57 dollars

> *9·98 francs is about*
> *10 francs*

They calculate the cost of the souvenir in their own currencies.

Monique works out:

> *10 × 8 = 80, so the answer is about 80 francs.*

Anna works out:

$$\begin{array}{r} 998 \\ \times \quad 8 \\ \hline 7984 \\ \hline {\scriptstyle 7\,6} \end{array}$$

> *Remember there are two decimal places.*

$$\begin{array}{r} 157 \\ \times \quad 8 \\ \hline 1256 \\ \hline {\scriptstyle 4\,5} \end{array}$$

The souvenir costs £8, or 79·84 francs, or 12·56 dollars.

Task

Work out the answers in these patterns:

> *Divide the first number by 10 ...*

Pattern A

180	× 300	= 54 000
18	× 300	=
1·8	× 300	=
0·18	× 300	=
0·018	× 300	=

> *and so divide the answer by 10.*

Pattern B

180	× 3	=
180	× 0·3	=
180	× 0·03	=
180	× 0·003	=

> *Divide the second number by 10 and work out the answers.*

? **How can you decide where to place the decimal point?**

EXAMPLE   Work out 12·99 × 1·57

> *There are 2 + 2 decimal places here ...*

$$\begin{array}{r}
12.99 \rightarrow \quad\quad 1299 \\
\times 1.57 \rightarrow \quad\quad \times 157 \\
\hline
129\,900 \\
64\,950 \\
9093 \\
\hline
203\,943 \rightarrow 20{\cdot}3943
\end{array}$$

> *... so put 4 decimal places in your answer.*

Exercise

1 Find the total cost of these items which Monique buys:
   (a) 3 CDs at £14·95 each

   (b) 5 books at £6·95 each

   (c) 2 lipsticks at £7·36 each

2 Change these amounts to Swiss francs by multiplying by 2·35
   (£1 = 2·35 Swiss francs).
   (a) £5   **(b)** £8   **(c)** £19

3 Change these amounts to dollars by multiplying by 1·57 (£1 = $1·57).
   (a) £5   **(b)** £8   **(c)** £19

4 The numbers in these multiplications are correct, but there are no decimal points in the answers. Copy them and put the decimal point in the correct place.

   EXAMPLE   Question 7·6 × 5·31 = 40356
                 Answer   7·6 × 5·31 = 40·356

   (a) 6·1 × 0·9 = 549   **(b)** 15·6 × 0·04 = 624
   (c) 0·79 × 0·03 = 237   **(d)** 1·4 × 2·68 = 3752
   (e) 0·816 × 13·7 = 111792   **(f)** 0·98 × 3·71 = 36358
   (g) 5·8 × 5 = 29   **(h)** 7·92 × 6 = 4752

5 Work out
   (a) 0·3 × 0·2   **(b)** 0·5 × 0·2
   (c) 0·1 × 0·3   **(d)** 0·6 × 0·8
   (e) 0·01 × 0·4   **(f)** 0·06 × 0·3
   (g) 0·07 × 0·07   **(h)** 0·005 × 0·005

6 Work out (evaluate)
   (a) 8·3 × 0·6   **(b)** 0·69 × 7
   (c) 15·3 × 0·8   **(d)** 2·29 × 0·05
   (e) 2·8 × 0·17   **(f)** 0·34 × 5·6
   (g) 18·7 × 0·61   **(h)** 0·12 × 0·12

7 Write as decimals

   (a) (i) 6 × 0.1   **(ii)** $\frac{6}{10}$

   (b) (i) 7 × 0.01   **(ii)** $\frac{7}{100}$

   (c) (i) 3 × 0.001   **(ii)** $\frac{3}{1000}$

Division of decimals by a whole number

On Saturday, Karen and three of her friends go to the cinema.
The tickets total £19.

It is £4·75 each.

$4)\overline{19} \rightarrow 4)\overline{19.00} \rightarrow 4)\overline{19.^30^20}$
4.75

? How can you work this out with ordinary numbers?

> Karen works it out and writes in two noughts for pence, and then divides.

Task

Divide **(a)** 11 by 4 **(b)** 17 by 4 **(c)** 17 by 8.

> You can add as many decimal places as you need.

The girls meet two more friends at the cinema and buy some popcorn for £4·40. Karen works out how much this is each.

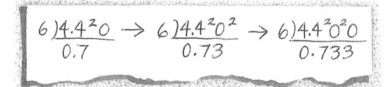

$6)\overline{4.4^20} \rightarrow 6)\overline{4.4^20^2} \rightarrow 6)\overline{4.4^20^20}$
$0.7 0.73 0.733$

Karen decides to call this amount £0·73 each.

Jenny says that 0·73333 is a recurring decimal, and is written as 0·7$\dot{3}$.

Task

Investigate $1 \div 9$, $2 \div 9$, $3 \div 9$, and so on, up to $8 \div 9$.

Now investigate $1 \div 7$, $2 \div 7$, $3 \div 7$, and so on, up to $6 \div 7$.

When a group of digits recur, the dots are placed over the first and last recurring digits.

EXAMPLE $\frac{1}{7} = 0.142857142857142\ldots$
$= 0.\dot{1}4285\dot{7}.$

Exercise

1 Jenny needs a new toothbrush.
How much is this for each toothbrush?
Would it be cheaper to buy a single toothbrush
for 59 pence?

2

(a) How much is each packet of cereal?
(b) How much is each packet of crisps?

3 Monique and Karen love shopping.
They buy several things together and share the cost by dividing by 2.
How much do they pay each if the total cost is:
(a) £1·30   **(b)** £2·50   **(c)** £7·00

4 Divide these numbers by 2.
(a) 1·3   **(b)** 2·5   **(c)** 7
(d) 6·75   **(e)** 0·45   **(f)** 43·6

5 Divide these numbers by 5.
(a) 1·3   **(b)** 2·5   **(c)** 7
(d) 6·75   **(e)** 0·45   **(f)** 43·6

6 Divide these numbers by 4.
(a) 3·4   **(b)** 2·7   **(c)** 5·6
(d) 0·07   **(e)** 1·9   **(f)** 9

7 Divide these numbers by 8.
(a) 5·2   **(b)** 7·3   **(c)** 0·5
(d) 0·17   **(e)** 15·8   **(f)** 11

8 Divide these numbers by 6.
(a) 1·2   **(b)** 2·34   **(c)** 1
(d) 5   **(e)** 3·5   **(f)** 43·6

9 Write these numbers as decimals.
(a) $6 \div 10$ **(b)** $0.6 \div 10$ **(c)** $0.06 \div 10$
(d) $6 \div 100$ **(e)** $6 \div 1000$ **(f)** $0.06 \div 100$
Describe in words the effect of dividing a decimal by 10, 100 and 1000.

10 Divide 1 by 11, 2 by 11, 3 by 11, and so on up to 10 by 11.

Division of decimals (short division)

Stephen has been collecting 5p coins and putting them into a bottle.
He has exactly £7.

 How many coins does Stephen have?

5p = £0·05.
So the question is £7·00 ÷ £0·05.
Stephen changes both amounts to pence.

> £7.00 = 7.00 × 100 pence = 700 pence
> and
> £0.05 = 0.05 × 100 pence = 5 pence

$$5\overline{)700} \qquad 5\overline{)7^{2}00}$$
$$140$$

Now the question is 700 pence ÷ 5 pence. He has 140 coins.

Task

Work out these questions putting your answers into headed columns.

1

	TH	H	T	U	$\frac{1}{10}$	$\frac{1}{100}$	
(a)			2	0 ·	0		×10
(b)			2 ·	0	0		×10
(c)			0 ·	2	0		×10
(d)			0 ·	0	2		×10

2

	TH	H	T	U	$\frac{1}{10}$	$\frac{1}{100}$	
(a)		5	0				×100
(b)			5 ·	0			×100
(c)			0 ·	5			×100
(d)			0 ·	0	5		×100

 What did you notice about these patterns?

3 What would the answers to these be?

(a) 0·4 × 10   **(b)** 0·04 × 100   **(c)** 0·004 × 1000
(d) 0·5 × 10   **(e)** 0·8 × 100   **(f)** 0·09 × 1000

This is used to divide a decimal by a decimal.

EXAMPLE   0·0324 ÷ 0·09

Write this as $\dfrac{0.0324}{0.09}$ then multiply both numbers by 100.

$\dfrac{0.0324 \times 100}{0.09 \times 100} = \dfrac{3.24}{9}$

> You know how to divide
> by a whole number.

$9\overline{)3.24}$ works out as $9\overline{)3.2^{5}4}$ The answer is 0·36.
$\phantom{9\overline{)}}0.36$

Exercise

1 Find how many 2p pieces in
(a) £2 **(b)** £5 **(c)** £7 **(d)** £9?

2 Divide these numbers by 0·02.
(a) 2·00 **(b)** 5·00 **(c)** 7·00 **(d)** 9·00

3 Find how many half-hours in
(a) 3 hours **(b)** 7 hours **(c)** 15 hours **(d)** 18 hours?

4 Divide these numbers by 0·5.
(a) 3 **(b)** 7 **(c)** 15 **(d)** 18

5 How many textbooks 1·2 cm thick will fit onto a shelf 132 cm long?

6 How many magazines 0·6 cm thick will fit into a magazine rack 9·6 cm wide?

7 Work out
(a) 8·4 ÷ 0·4 **(b)** 7·5 ÷ 0·5 **(c)** 6·9 ÷ 0·3
(d) 7·2 ÷ 0·3 **(e)** 3·76 ÷ 0·8 **(f)** 4·626 ÷ 0·9

8 Work out
(a) 0·224 ÷ 0·07 **(b)** 1·542 ÷ 0·06 **(c)** 24·75 ÷ 0·05
(d) 2·912 ÷ 0·08 **(e)** 0·861 ÷ 0·07 **(f)** 32·76 ÷ 0·09

9 Alice wonders what happens to answers when you divide by a number less than 1.
She tried these. Do them yourself and see what she discovered.
(a) 4·2 ÷ 0·1 **(b)** 4·2 ÷ 0·02 **(c)** 4·2 ÷ 0·01
(d) 4·2 ÷ 0·003 **(e)** 4·2 ÷ 0·002 **(f)** 4·2 ÷ 0·0004
(g) 4·2 ÷ 0·0003

10 Copy and complete these statements.
(a) Dividing by 0·1 is the same as multiplying by … .
(b) Multiplying by 1000 is the same as dividing by … .
(c) Dividing by … is the same as multiplying by 0·01.

11 Work out
(a) 1·95 ÷ 0·006 **(b)** 2·24 ÷ 0·004 **(c)** 0·4496 ÷ 0·008
(d) 42 ÷ 0·005 **(e)** 4·1157 ÷ 0·009 **(f)** 3·3152 ÷ 0·007

12 Work out (evaluate)
(a) 22·72 ÷ 0·4 **(b)** 51·6 ÷ 0·06 **(c)** 0·65 ÷ 0·001
(d) 11·2 ÷ 0·2 **(e)** 2 ÷ 0·005 **(f)** 7·2 ÷ 0·4

Equivalent percentages, fractions and decimals

80% of the audience think there are 1 000 grams in a kilogram.

$$80\% = \frac{80}{100}$$

Remember % means 'out of 100'.

$$= \frac{4}{5}$$

Cancelling by 20

10% thought there were only 100 g.
$$10\% = \frac{10}{100} = \frac{1}{10}$$

Four-fifths of the audience were right.

To change from fractions to percentages, multiply by 100.

$$\frac{4}{5} = \frac{4}{5} \times 100\%$$

$$\frac{3}{20} = \frac{3}{20} \times 100\%$$

Remember 100% is the same as $\frac{100}{100}$ths or one whole one.

$$= \frac{4}{\cancel{5}_1} \times \cancel{100}^{20} \%$$

$$= \frac{3}{\cancel{20}_1} \times \cancel{100}^{5} \%$$

$$= 80\%$$

$$= 15\%$$

Task

Aimée is doing practice tests for her life-saving theory exam on March 10th.

(a) Write Aimée's marks as percentages. Is she getting steadily better?

Jan 14th $\frac{11}{20}$ *Aimée*

Feb 1st $\frac{39}{50}$ *Aimée*

Feb 28th $\frac{18}{25}$ *Aimée*

(b) The pass mark on the real exam is 70%.
How many marks is this out of **(i)** 20 **(ii)** 50 **(iii)** 25?

(c) Do you think Aimée will pass?

To convert a decimal into a percentage, you multiply by 100.

$$0.4 = 0.4 \times 100\% = 40\%$$
$$0.02 = 0.02 \times 100\% = 2\%$$

? **How do you convert a percentage into a decimal?**

Exercise

1 Change these percentages to fractions and cancel to their lowest terms:

(a)

25% of the audience liked Frosties

(b)

50% of the audience went to bed before 11 pm

(c)

75% of the audience thought Henry VIII had six wives

2 Here are performance figures for 3 train companies.

(a) Find the percentage of trains on time for each company.

(b) Place the companies in order, starting with the best.

Company	Trains run	On time
Gt. Southern	200	164
Rural	50	37
Best West	80	60

3 Change these percentages to fractions in their lowest terms.

(a) 10% further sales reduction

(b) 30% of the ballet students passed with grade A

(c) 70% of holiday-makers travel abroad

4 Change these percentages to decimals.

EXAMPLE 1 $26\% = \frac{26}{100} = 0.26$ **EXAMPLE 2** $7\% = \frac{7}{100} = 0.07$

(a) 10%   **(b)** 30%   **(c)** 45%   **(d)** 83%
(e) 6%   **(f)** 9%   **(g)** 11%   **(h)** $12\frac{1}{2}\%$

5 Change these decimals to percentages.

(a) 0.42   **(b)** 0.38   **(c)** 0.95   **(d)** 0.04
(e) 0.17   **(f)** 0.8   **(g)** 0.03   **(h)** 0.2

6 Change these fractions to percentages.

(a) $\frac{1}{5}$ **(b)** $\frac{1}{25}$ **(c)** $\frac{11}{20}$ **(d)** $\frac{3}{20}$ **(e)** $\frac{16}{25}$ **(f)** $\frac{7}{10}$

Write them in order, smallest first.

7 Change the following to decimals by dividing.

Reminder: $\frac{3}{8} \rightarrow 8\overline{)3.000}$ $8\overline{)3.^30^60^40}$
$\phantom{8\overline{)}}0.375$

(a) $\frac{3}{4}$ **(b)** $\frac{7}{8}$ **(c)** $\frac{5}{6}$ **(d)** $\frac{1}{4}$ **(e)** $\frac{1}{6}$ **(f)** $\frac{5}{8}$

Write them in order, smallest first.

8

But what about changing decimals to fractions?

Remember the column headings T, U, $\frac{1}{10}$ ths, $\frac{1}{100}$ ths.

EXAMPLE 1 $0.6 = \frac{6}{10}$
$ = \frac{3}{5}$

EXAMPLE 2 $0.22 = \frac{22}{100}$
$ = \frac{11}{50}$

Change the following decimals to fractions.

(a) 0.7   **(b)** 0.4   **(c)** 0.5   **(d)** 0.24   **(e)** 0.85   **(f)** 0.84
(g) 0.12   **(h)** 0.04   **(i)** 0.05   **(j)** 0.72   **(k)** 0.88   **(l)** 0.02

Finishing off

Now that you have finished this chapter you should be able to:

● multiply a decimal by an integer (whole number)
● multiply a decimal by a decimal
● divide a decimal by a whole number
● divide a decimal by a decimal
● understand the equivalence of percentages, fractions and decimals.

Review exercise

1 Sally buys three hair-slides. How much is this altogether?

2 Monique buys two perfume sprays. How much is this altogether?

3 Robin buys six tickets for Stand A at Old Trafford. How much does he pay altogether?

```
MANCHESTER UNITED          FA Premiership
                           Sat 26th Feb KO:3pm
                                    £18.75
                           STAND A
                           Block    Row      Seat
Old Trafford               E290     10       44
```

4 Multiply
(a) 0.3×0.2
(b) 0.01×0.6
(c) 0.3×0.07
(d) 0.02×0.5
(e) 0.8×0.9
(f) 0.006×0.03

5 Work out
(a) 6.4×1.1
(b) 7.32×0.84
(c) 4.18×0.23
(d) 8.99×0.15
(e) 6.214×0.027
(f) 30.6×4.7

6 Work out
(a) $7 \div 4$
(b) $0.6 \div 5$
(c) $1.7 \div 2$
(d) $3.9 \div 6$
(e) $26.7 \div 3$
(f) $14.7 \div 9$

7 Complete the following table. Learn the results in this table. They are very useful to remember.

Division	Fraction	Decimal
$1 \div 2$	$\frac{1}{2}$	
$1 \div 4$	$\frac{1}{4}$	
$3 \div 4$		
$1 \div 3$		
$2 \div 3$		

8 Calculate
(a) $4.1 \div 0.2$
(b) $0.36 \div 0.6$
(c) $0.61 \div 0.05$
(d) $17.2 \div 0.08$
(e) $7.2 \div 0.01$
(f) $0.54 \div 0.09$

9 A pack of 24 coloured pencils costs £2·88.
   (a) How much is each pencil?

   Another pack of 18 pencils costs £1·98.
   (b) Which set has the cheapest pencils in it?

10 Is it possible to fit 26 magazines each 0·7 cm thick into a magazine rack 18 cm wide? Show how you would work this out.

11 Put the decimal point in the correct place in these answers.
   (a) $6·4 \times 2·7 = 1728$ **(b)** $9·83 \times 0·014 = 13762$
   (c) $5·26 \times 41·7 = 219342$ **(d)** $0·025 \times 0·68 = 1700$
   (e) $21·13 \times 48·7 = 1029031$ **(f)** $0·004 \times 0·28 = 112$
   (g) $0·9 \times 2·6 = 234$ **(h)** $0·01 \times 35·6 = 356$
   (i) $0·2 \times 16 = 32$ **(j)** $0·47 \times 0·03 = 141$

12 Change these fractions to decimals by dividing.

   EXAMPLE $\frac{3}{8} = \frac{3·000}{8} \rightarrow 8\overline{)3·000}$

   (a) $\frac{3}{8}$ **(b)** $\frac{3}{5}$ **(c)** $\frac{2}{5}$ **(d)** $\frac{5}{8}$
   (e) $\frac{7}{8}$ **(f)** $\frac{1}{6}$ **(g)** $\frac{5}{6}$ **(h)** $\frac{7}{12}$

13 Write down the answers only to these questions. Can you work them out in your head?
   (a) $41·8 \times 100$ **(b)** $16·73 \times 10$ **(c)** $0·009 \times 100$
   (d) $0·003 \times 1000$ **(e)** 13×100 **(f)** $1·3 \times 1000$
   (g) $0·04 \times 10$ **(h)** $0·007 \times 1000$ **(i)** $0·4 \times 10\,000$

14 Write down the answers only to these questions. Can you work them out in your head?
   (a) $73·6 \div 10$ **(b)** $0·03 \div 10$ **(c)** $4·16 \div 100$
   (d) $28·9 \div 100$ **(e)** $5 \div 10$ **(f)** $16·31 \div 100$
   (g) $0·02 \div 100$ **(h)** $0·004 \div 1000$ **(i)** $0·000\,7 \div 100$

15 Change these to percentages.
   (a) $\frac{11}{25}$ **(b)** $\frac{2}{5}$ **(c)** $\frac{3}{8}$ **(d)** $\frac{9}{20}$
   (e) $0·11$ **(f)** 0.07 **(g)** 0.6 **(h)** 0.75
   Write them in order, smallest first.

16 Change these to fractions in their lowest terms.
   (a) $0·6$ **(b)** 0.15 **(c)** 0.28 **(d)** 0.02

17 Change these to decimals.
   (a) $\frac{9}{10}$ **(b)** $\frac{3}{25}$ **(c)** $\frac{17}{20}$ **(d)** $\frac{5}{9}$

18 Change these to fractions in their lowest terms.
   (a) 17% **(b)** 6% **(c)** 30% **(d)** $12\frac{1}{2}\%$

Huyen is making a call from a phone box.
Phone calls cost 8p per minute plus a 6p connection charge.
The cost of her call is calculated using a number machine like this:

no. of
minutes → [×8] → [+6] → cost of call
in pence

input   output

Huyen is on the phone for 5 minutes.

The number of minutes that Huyen is on the phone for is called the **input**.

 What is the cost of Huyen's call?

The cost of the call is called the **output**.

Task

What would the *outputs* be for these inputs using the number machine above?

(a) 10 minutes   **(b)** 7 minutes   **(c)** 2.5 minutes

Think of some other examples of when you pay for what you use.

Huyen makes another phone call.
The output is 78 pence.

 For how long was Huyen on the phone?
How can you check that you are right?

Huyen reverses the number machine to find out what the input was.

To undo ×8 she divides by 8.   ? ← [÷8] ← [−6] ← 78   *To undo +6 she subtracts 6*

She finds out that the input was 9 minutes.

Task

Huyen's machine is used in reverse. What inputs give these outputs?

(a) 22 minutes   **(b)** 38 minutes   **(c)** 1 hour 26 minutes

 Why does this work?

Exercise

1 Different phone companies charge different amounts.
Work out the cost of the following telephone calls:

(a)

8 mins ⟶ ×3 ⟶ +5 ⟶ cost of call in pence

(b)

5 mins ⟶ ×4 ⟶ −6 ⟶ cost of call in pence

(c)

12 mins ⟶ ×6 ⟶ +9 ⟶ cost of call in pence

2 A mobile phone company charges 5p per minute plus a connection charge of 10p for off-peak calls.

(a) Copy and complete the number machine to show this information.

time in mins ⟶ ☐ ⟶ ☐ ⟶ cost of call in pence

The same company charges 8p per minute plus a connection charge of 10p for peak time calls.

(b) Draw a number machine to show this information.

(c) How much would a 12 minute call cost
   (i) off-peak   **(ii)** at peak rate?

(d) Jason makes three phone calls costing the following:
   (a) 55p off peak   **(b)** 82p peak rate   **(c)** £1.30 peak rate.

   How long was each call?

3 Find how long each of the following calls are by reversing the number machine. Check all of your answers.

(a)
time in minutes ⟶ ×5 ⟶ 20p

(b)
time in minutes ⟶ ×5 ⟶ 25p

(c)
time in minutes ⟶ ×2 ⟶ 17p

(d)
time in minutes ⟶ +8 ⟶ 17p

(e)
time in minutes ⟶ ×4 ⟶ −3 ⟶ 45p

(f)
time in minutes ⟶ ×6 ⟶ −8 ⟶ £1.12

Finding the rule

Brian feeds the number 7 into this number machine.

The output is 19.

Task

Write down as many different rules as you can that the number machine could
be using.

Have you got enough information to decide which rule is correct?

Brian thinks that the number machine is adding 12 to his input.
He checks this by using the number 4 as his input.

? **What answer is Brian expecting?**

The number machine gives an output of 10.

Brian checks other inputs to find out what output he will get.
He makes a table of his results:

> Brian chooses his inputs
> logically, so that he can spot
> the rule more easily.

? **What will the output be when the input is 5?**
What will the output be when the input is 10?
What rule do you think the number machine is using?

Brian now draws the number machine
with it's rule:

? **What is the input when the output is 34?**
Check that you are right.

Exercise

1 Work out the rules for the following *adding and subtracting* number machines.

(a) 7 ⟶ ▮ ⟶ 10   **(b)** 12 ⟶ ▮ ⟶ 8

(c) 8 ⟶ ▮ ⟶ 1   **(d)** 3 ⟶ ▮ ⟶ 13

Write down your rule in words.

2 Work out the rules for the following *multiplying and dividing* number machines.

(a) 24 ⟶ ▮ ⟶ 6   **(b)** 7 ⟶ ▮ ⟶ 21

(c) 16 ⟶ ▮ ⟶ 2   **(d)** 3 ⟶ ▮ ⟶ 1

3 Tom has two number machines.

(1) 3 ⟶ ▮ ⟶ ▮ ⟶ 4

(2) 6 ⟶ ▮ ⟶ ▮ ⟶ 17

(a) Write down three possible rules for each number machine.

Tom collects some inputs and outputs for each number machine. Here are his results:

1.

Input	Output
1	0
2	2
3	4
4	6
5	8

2.

Input	Output
1	2
2	5
3	8
4	11
5	14

(b) What would the outputs be for each number machine if the input was
   (i) 12   **(ii)** 20   **(iii)** 100?

(c) What is the rule for each number machine?

Investigation

Find 5 different rules. Compare your rules with a friend's.
Find 10 different rules between you.

4 ⇢ ⟶ 7

Writing down the rule

Nesrene wants to hire a boat at her local boating lake.

She wants to find the cost of hiring a rowing boat for one hour.

The boating company uses the following number machine to work out the cost of hiring rowing boats.

input
number of hours →   → output
cost in £
2   7

 What rules could this machine be using?

She tries several different inputs and writes down her results:

Number of hours	Cost in £
1	4
2	7
3	10
4	?
5	?

 What rule is the number machine using?

Nesrene draws the number machine.

input → [× 3] → [+ 1] → output

She writes down a rule in words:

Cost = 3 × number of hours + 1

Nesrene realises that it would be easier to write:

$C = 3 \times h + 1$

 What do C and h mean?

Task

Make up your own rule for a number machine and write it down. Get a friend to work out your rule by trying several different inputs.

How many inputs and outputs does your friend need to try before working out your rule?

 Why does Nesrene think it is better to write the rule using letters?
How can you check that the rule is correct?

Exercise

1 A boating company has the following charges for hiring canoes and motor boats.

Canoes		Motor Boats	
Number of Hours	Cost in £	Number of Hours	Cost in £
1	3	1	5
2	4	2	10
3	5	3	15
4		4	
5		5	
20		20	
	25		30
	50		50
	100		75

(a) Complete each of the two tables.

(b) Draw a number machine for finding the cost of hiring
   (i) a canoe   (ii) a motorboat.

(c) Write down a rule using letters for each number machine.
   Use h to represent the number of hours the boat is hired for and C to represent the cost.

2 John wants to work out how his electricity bill is calculated.
He has used 6 units of electricity and is charged 13p.

(a) Write down four rules that the Electricity Board could be using.

John collects some more data to help him find the rule:

Number of units	Cost in pence
1	3
2	5
3	7
6	13

(b) What is the cost when the number of units used is
   (i) 4   (ii) 5   (iii) 10   (iv) 2.5?

(c) How many units are used when the cost is
   (i) 15   (ii) 23   (iii) 19   (iv) 29?

(d) Write down the rule that the Electricity Board is using.
   Use U to represent the number of units and C to represent the cost.

Finishing off

Now that you have finished this chapter you should be able to:

- know what number machines are
- find the output of a number machine
- find the input of number machine
- work out the rule for a number machine
- write down the rule using letters.

Review exercise

1 Work out the outputs for these number machines:

(a) $3 \rightarrow \boxed{\times 3} \rightarrow \boxed{-7} \rightarrow \boxed{?}$ **(b)** $8 \rightarrow \boxed{\div 2} \rightarrow \boxed{-1} \rightarrow \boxed{?}$

(c) $2 \rightarrow \boxed{\times 10} \rightarrow \boxed{+30} \rightarrow \boxed{?}$ **(d)** $12 \rightarrow \boxed{\div 3} \rightarrow \boxed{-4} \rightarrow \boxed{?}$

2 Two mobile phone companies are advertising their phones:

MICRO MOBILES
calls only
4p per minute
plus
20p connection

LO-CALLS
calls only
6p per minute
plus
10p connection

(a) Draw a number machine to show how to work out the cost of a call for each company.
(b) Omar wants to use his mobile phone for calls of more than ten minutes.
Which company should he use? Why?
(c) Tim wants to use his mobile phone for calls of no longer than 5 minutes.
Which company should he use? Why?
(d) Serina spends 64p on a call. Work out how long her call would be with each company.

3 Work out the inputs for the following number machines:

(a) $\boxed{?} \rightarrow \boxed{\times 4} \rightarrow 16$ **(b)** $\boxed{?} \rightarrow \boxed{+5} \rightarrow 11$

(c) $\boxed{?} \rightarrow \boxed{-6} \rightarrow 5$ **(d)** $\boxed{?} \rightarrow \boxed{-8} \rightarrow 9$

4 Work out the inputs for the following number machines:

(a) ? → × 2 → + 1 → 5   **(b)** ? → + 4 → − 6 → 10

(c) ? → × 3 → − 2 → 13   **(d)** ? → − 5 → × 3 → 15

5 Michelle wants to find out what the rule is for this number machine. She tries using 4 as her input and gets an output of 21.

4 → ▢ → ▢ → 21

(a) Write down four different rules that the number machine could be using.

Michelle now tries some different inputs.
She makes a table of her results:

input	output
2	11
3	16
4	21
5	

(b) What would the output be if the input was:
   (i) 1   **(ii)** 5   **(iii)** 7   **(iv)** 20?

(c) What rule do you think the number machine is using?
   Draw the number machine.

(d) What would the inputs be if the number machine gave the following outputs?
   (i) 41   **(ii)** 51   **(iii)** 76   **(iv)** 126

6 A leisure company uses the following table for hiring roller blades:

Number of hours	Cost (in £)
1	1
2	3
3	5
4	?

(a) What is the cost for hiring roller blades for
   (i) 4 hours   **(ii)** 6 hours
   (iii) 10 hours
(b) Write down the rule that the leisure company is using.
   Use h to represent the number of hours and c to represent the cost.

Activity Invent your own number machines.
Write down a set of rules for them.

Get a friend to try and work out the rules.

This photograph is taken from a catalogue.
The real height of the toy is 30 cm.
Measure the height in the photograph.

The size of the photograph is $\frac{1}{10}$th of the size in real life.
The real toy is 10 times as big as the photograph.
This is a *scale of $\frac{1}{10}$th* when written as a *fraction*.
As a *ratio*, this is a scale of **1 : 10**.
Measure the width of Tigger's nose in the photograph.

 How wide is Tigger's nose in real life?

Task

The drawings below give the true sizes of 5 dinosaurs.
Choose a suitable scale so that each of the dinosaurs can be displayed on a poster for your classroom wall.
Make a scale drawing of one of the dinosaurs.
Collect together all the drawings from your class to make a poster.

Pachycephalosaurus
8 metres long, about 6 metres high

Diplodocus
25 metres long, about 8 metres high

Deinonychus
3 metres long, about 1.5 metres high

Iguanodon
10 metres long, about 5 metres high

Coelophysis
3 metres long, about 2 metres high

Using a scale

A toy car is made on a scale of $\frac{1}{50}$th.

It is 6 cm long.

The real car will be 6×50 cm = 300 cm or 3 m long.

The real car is 1.7 m wide.

That is 170 cm wide.

The model car will be $170 \div 50 = 3.4$ cm wide.

Exercise

1 The two photographs have been taken from catalogues.
Below each photograph a real measurement is given.
Find the scale of each photograph.

800 mm length

3400 mm length

2 A doll's house is to be built on a $\frac{1}{100}$th scale. Complete the following table, which lists the lengths of various items in the house.

Item	True length	Length on model
Settee (length)	2 m	
Bookcase (height)		1.8 cm
Hall (length)	13.5 m	
Plate		2 mm
Living room (width)	5.8 m	
Toothbrush	20 cm	
Bottle (height)		3 mm

3 As a promotion, a firm wishes to place small toys in their packets of breakfast cereal. The toys are to be a series of 'mini beasts' and will include the following:

- ant (real length 4 mm)
- a ladybird (real length 6 mm)
- a centipede (real length 12 mm)
- a spider (real length 9 mm)
- a bee (real length 15 mm)

The toys must all be smaller than 100 mm but for safety reasons they must be larger than 20 mm.

(a) Choose a suitable scale for the toys.
(b) Work out the length of each toy.
(c) The toys can all be displayed by hanging them from the cut out of a flower printed on the back of the cereal packet.
This flower has a diameter of 10 cm.
What size is the real flower using the same scale?

Drawing plans

Sarah wishes to draw a plan of her bedroom. Her bedroom is 4 metres long.

The space available for her plan is only 10 cm long. She chooses a scale of *2 cm to 1 m*.

 How wide is the plan of her bedroom? How much extra space is there? Why has Sarah chosen a scale that does not use all the available space?

Here is Sarah's plan:

 How wide is the bedroom?

Sarah's bed is 1.8 metres long. On the plan this is 2×1.8 cm = 3.6 cm.

 Sarah has a rug that measures 1.5 m by 0.5 m. Is there enough room for this to go beside her bed?

 Task

Draw an outline plan of your classroom on graph paper. You will need to choose a suitable scale.

Use the same scale to make cut out shapes of the items of furniture in the room. Use the plan and furniture to find a sensible way to rearrange your classroom.

Writing the scale as a ratio

The scale of Sarah's bedroom is 2 cm to 1 metre.

This can be written as   1 cm : $\frac{1}{2}$ metre

> *Change everything to the same unit of measurement.*

1 cm : 50 cm

1 : 50

> *The scale can now be written without the units of measurement. This is called a **ratio**.*

The ratio tells us that the real measurements are 50 times as big as the measurements on the plan.

Exercise

1 The plan is of a bungalow. Find the real measurements of
(a) bedroom 1
(b) the kitchen
(c) the living room.

Scale:
1cm to 2m

2 Complete this table for a scale of 2 cm to 1 metre.

True length	Length on plan
10 m	
	3 cm
	1.6 cm
15 m	
25 cm	
	4 mm
165 cm	
328 cm	

3 The diagram shows a plan of a tennis court. It is not drawn to scale.
Use the measurements on the diagram to draw a scale drawing of a tennis court.

(a) What is the total length of the lines on the court?
(b) What is the total length of the lines on your plan?

4 Use the plan of Sarah's bedroom on the opposite page to answer the following questions.

(a) How wide is the window?
(b) Give the dimensions of the desk.
(c) Sarah has bought 2 sets of drawers. They are each 1 m wide. Can she fit the drawers, her desk and her wardrobe along one wall of her bedroom?

5 Write a scale of 2 cm to 1 m as a ratio.

Activity Draw an outline plan of your bedroom.
Make cut outs for all the items of furniture in your room.
Use these to re-design the layout of your room.

Map scales

1 inch to the mile

1: 25 000

km
0 1 2 3 4 5 6 7

These are all examples of the way that a scale might be given on a map or in an atlas.

The Ordnance Survey map has a scale of 1:50 000.

This means that any length on the map is 50 000 times as big in real life.

> 1 cm on the map is 50 000 cm in real life
> 50 000 cm = 500 m
> 500 m = 0.5 km

A scale of *1:50 000* is the same as *1 cm to 0.5 km.*

© *Crown copyright*

Task

Find Gouthwaite reservoir on the map and measure its length.
The length is about 6.5 cm.
That is a real length of
> 6.5 × 50 000 cm = 325 000 cm
> 325 000 cm = 3250 m
> 3250 m = 3.25 km
The length of the reservoir is 3.25 km.

You are going to walk round the reservoir starting from the village of Bouthwaite. Write a description of the route giving distances between points of interest.

 What is the total length of the walk?

Real distances to map distances

The hotel at Wath advertises that it is 'less than 1 km from the lake'.
> 1 km = 1000 m
> 1000 m = 100 000 cm
> 100 000 cm on the ground = 100 000 ÷ 50 000 cm = 2 cm on the map
The hotel should be less than 2 cm away from the lake.

 Is the advertising correct?

Exercise

1 Use the map on the opposite page to answer the following questions.

(a) How wide is the reservoir at its widest point?

(b) How far is it from Coville House Farm to Lamb Close?

(c) You set off from Longside House (written Ho) and walk along the lakeside path.
After walking 5 km you stop for lunch. Where will you be?

2 The map below shows some of the main features of Lambton Village. Use it to answer the following questions.

(a) Jo walks from Home Farm to school everyday.
How far is this?

(b) How far is it from the school to the playing field?

(c) There is a large oak tree in the middle of the village green.
It has a spread of 10 m. How wide is this when it is put on the map?

(d) Draw a line with measurements on it to show the scale of the map.

3 The scale on a map is 1:20 000.

(a) What are the real distances shown by distances of 2 cm, 12 cm and 3.8 cm and on the map?

(b) What measurements on the map are needed to show real distances of 2 km, 25 km and 6.4 km?

4 From the scales shown below pick out any that are the same.

1 cm to 100 m

0	100	200	300	400	500 m

km
0 1 2 3

1 cm to 1 km

1: 100 000

miles
4
0 1 2 3

1 in to 1 mile

5 A map has a scale of 1 cm to 10 km.

(a) Change 10 km to cm and write the scale as 1 cm to _____ cm.

(b) Now write your scale in the form 1:_____.

(c) Write the following scales in the form 1:_____.

(i) 1 cm to 5 km **(ii)** 1 cm to 20 km **(iii)** 2 cm to 1 km

Finishing off

Now that you have finished this chapter you should be able to:

● understand a scale when it is written as a fraction or as a ratio
● interpret scales on maps and plans
● convert lengths for a given scale
● use a plan to re-design a room.

Review exercise

1 A model railway is built using a scale of 1 : 200.
Copy and complete this table for the lengths of the objects shown.

Object	Real length	Model length
Engine	20 m	
Level crossing (width)		10 cm
Signals (height)		4 cm
Station (length)	100 m	
Tree (height)	5 m	
Suitcase (width)		5 mm
Station cat (length)	40 cm	

2 Write the following scales in the form 1:_____.
(a) 1 cm to 3 m   (b) 5 cm to 1 m   (c) 1 cm to 1 km   (d) 2 cm to 1 km
(e) 1 cm to 5 km   (f) $\frac{1}{20}$th   (g) $\frac{1}{50}$th   (h) $\frac{2}{5}$th

3 Write the following scales in the form 1 cm to _____ km.
(a) 1 : 25 000   (b) 1 : 50 000   (c) 1 : 100 000

4 Write these scales in the form of 1 cm to _____ m or _____ to 1 m.
(a) 1 : 500   (b) 1 : 25   (c) 1 : 50

5 A map has a scale of '1 mile to the inch'. What is the true distance
represented by measurements on the map of
(a) 2 inches   (b) 3.5 inches   (c) $4\frac{3}{4}$ inches?

6 A length of 2.75 m is represented on a scale drawing by a length of 11 cm.
What is the scale of the drawing?

7 The diagram shows the plan of a maze.

Using instructions like 'go forward 6 paces, turn left through 90 . . .', write a set of instructions to enable someone to get to the centre of the maze.

Ask a friend to test your instructions.

Scale $\frac{1}{2}$ *cm to 1 pace*

8 The map shows part of the centre of York.
The Patel family arrive at York station.
They decide to start their visit by walking round the city walls from North St. Postern Tower to Baile Hill.

How far is it from the front of the station to the start of their walk?
How far do they walk round the city walls?

Scale *1 cm to 100 metres*

16 Averages

The mean

 What does 'average contents' mean?
Are there 20 mints in every bag?

Sam and Adam each buy a bag of Choco-mints.
They each count the number of mints in their bag.

Sam has 17 and Adam has 21.

Adam says he will give Sam some of his mints so that they have the same number.

 How many mints does Adam give Sam?
How many do they have each now?

Sam and Adam decide to find out if the average number of mints in each bag really is 20.
They count the number of mints in 16 bags.

| 20 | 21 | 16 | 17 | 19 | 20 | 20 | 21 |
| 20 | 17 | 20 | 21 | 18 | 22 | 20 | 20 |

There are several different ways of finding an average. One of them is the **mean**.

You find the mean by adding up all the mints and dividing it by the number of bags.

Total number of mints = 312
Number of bags = 16
Mean number of mints = 312 ÷ 16 = 19.5.

 Task

James asks his friends how many penalty points they have on their driving licences.

Points	0	1	2	3	4	5	6	7	8	9	10	11
People	9	0	0	4	0	0	3	0	1	0	1	2

If you get 12 or more points within three years, you are disqualified.

(a) How many friends does James ask?
(b) Work out the total number of penalty points for all his friends.
(c) Find the mean number of penalty points per person.

 Can you get $3\frac{1}{2}$ penalty points?

 Could Sam and Adam put all their mints back in the bags so that there are the same number of mints in each bag?

 Do you think the label on the bag is accurate?

Exercise

1 Find the mean of each of these sets of numbers.
   (a) 4, 9, 11, 5, 6   **(b)** 1, 1, 2, 2, 2, 3, 3, 4
   (c) 5, 0, 3, 10, 12, 6, 5, 1, 13, 8

2 Sarah goes ten-pin bowling. Here are the number of pins she knocks down in each turn.

Work out Sarah's mean score.

0	2	5	8	6	7	3	9
6	0	5	7	6	7	5	0
2	3	6	8	7	7	4	9
5	6	8	6				

3 Alex and Paul are training for a 100 m race. They both keep a record of their times, in seconds, that they take to run 100 m.

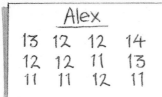

Alex

13	12	12	14
12	12	11	13
11	11	12	11

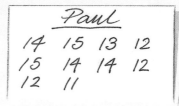

Paul

14	15	13	12
15	14	14	12
12	11		

   (a) Work out Alex's mean time.   **(b)** Work out Paul's mean time.
   (c) Who do you think is the faster runner?

4 Matthew wants to compare the heights of boys and girls in his class. He measures the heights in centimetres. Here are his results.

Boys:	120	131	126	139	137	126	141
	132	129	135	136	128	131	137
Girls:	124	131	139	115	123	136	133
	131	140	113	118	135	123	134
	123	134					

   (a) Find the mean height of the boys.
   (b) Find the mean height of the girls.
   (c) Find the mean height of the whole class.

5 Matthew's friend Jo has worked out the mean height of the boys and girls in *her* class. There are 13 boys and 11 girls in the class.
   The mean height of the boys is 132.5 cm.
   The mean height of the girls is 128.3 cm.
   (a) What is the total height of the boys in Jo's class?
   (b) What is the total height of the girls in Jo's class?
   (c) What is the total height of the whole class?
   (d) Work out the mean height of the whole class.

   A new girl joins Jo's class. She is 129.5 cm tall.

   (e) What is the mean height of the girls now?
   (f) What is the mean height of the whole class now?

The median

Michelle is taking part in a skating competition.
There are 7 judges. Here are the scores each judge gives Michelle.

4.5 **5.1** **4.6** **5.0** **4.5** **4.7** **4.9**

Michelle wants to find her middle score.

First she writes her scores in order.

4.5 4.5 4.6 (4.7) 4.9 5.0 5.1

Then she circles her middle score.

Michelle's middle score is 4.7.
There are 3 scores below 4.7 and 3 scores above 4.7.

Finding the middle value is another way of finding an average.
It is called the **median**.

? **Find the mean of Michelle's scores.**
Which average, *mean* or *median*, do you think Michelle will use when she tells her friends her average score?

To find the median, first write the data in order.
Then find the middle value.

Here are Sam and Adam's data about Choco-mints from the last page, written in order.

There are two middle values.

16, 17, 17, 18, 19, 20, 20, (20, 20) 20, 20, 20, 21, 21, 21, 22

The middle values are both 20, so the median number of sweets in a bag is 20.

? **What would you use for the median if the two middle values had been 20 and 21?**
What about if the two middle values were 20 and 22?
How can you tell whether there will be one middle value or two?

Task

1 Do you think boys' names or girls' names are generally longer?
   Use the *mean* method to find out.

2 Use your data collected in part 1. Compare the name lengths using the *median*.
   Does this give you the same results?

Exercise

1 Write each list of data in order and find the median.
(a) 5, 10, 6, 8, 11, 5, 9, 1, 3, 4, 8
(b) 1, 7, 5, 4, 7, 6, 2, 4, 3, 0, 5, 6, 5, 3, 2, 8
(c) 17, 42, 11, 37, 84, 29, 56, 82, 36, 68, 49

2 This data shows the number of hours of television a group of children watched in a week.

7	10	4	9	15	12	8	6
13	12	8	10	18	9	11	7
12	11	3	6	13	12	10	

Find the median number of hours of television watched.

3 Amy does a survey to find out the shoe sizes of everybody in her class. Here are the results.

4	3	$4\frac{1}{2}$	6	2	2	$2\frac{1}{2}$	3
5	$4\frac{1}{2}$	4	3	$3\frac{1}{2}$	5	$2\frac{1}{2}$	3
4	4	$3\frac{1}{2}$	$2\frac{1}{2}$	3	$4\frac{1}{2}$	$3\frac{1}{2}$	$5\frac{1}{2}$
$1\frac{1}{2}$	$3\frac{1}{2}$	3	2				

(a) Find the median shoe size.
(b) Find the mean shoe size.

4 These are the ages of all the people going on a school skiing trip, including the teachers.

14	16	13	13
29	15	13	14
16	52	14	16
15	13	16	16
44	15	13	14
14	14	15	16
12	13		

(a) Find the mean age.
(b) Find the median age.
(c) Which average do you think describes the data better? Why?

5 Sanjay and Mark are comparing their scores on a computer game which they both have.

SANJAY'S SCORES
234 410 320 94 258 521 345 487
160 339 478 317

Mark's scores
156 32 79 289 541 443 689 220
374 498 168 753 226 413 114

(a) Find the median score for each boy.
(b) Find the mean score for each boy.
(c) Who do you think is better at the game?

The mode

7B are going to watch a video on the last day of
the school year.
Their teacher gives them a choice of four films.

He makes a tally chart to show the votes.

The most popular film is *Star Wars*.
This is called the **mode** of the data.

The mode is another kind of average. It is the most
common item in a set of data.

 Why is the mode useful in this example?
Why can't you use the mean or the median?
Think of some more situations when the mode is the best average to use.

When data are grouped, the group or
class with the most items is called
the **modal class**.

In a bar chart or frequency chart,
the modal class
has the highest bar.

The modal class
is 31–40

 Task

Dawn and James go ten-pin bowling.
Here are their scores (the total number
of pins knocked down) in each turn.

Dawn:	4	0	2	5	10	3	4
	5	4	8				
James:	2	4	3	7	4	6	4
	4	5	6				

Find the mean, median and mode of their scores.

 Who do you think is the better bowler?
Describe the differences between the two sets of data.

(You may find it helps to make a frequency table.)

The range

The mean, median and mode are all ways of finding an average, or typical value.

The **range** is the difference between the largest and smallest values of a set of data.

The range for Dawn's scores is 10 − 0 = 10.
The range for James' scores is 7 − 2 = 5.

The range is *not* an average. It tells you how spread out the data are.
Dawn's scores are more spread out than James'.
James is more consistent.

Exercise

1 David does a survey of the colours of cars passing his house.
Here are his results.

red red blue white red green blue black
white yellow blue red red blue black green
red white blue red blue red red

(a) Make a frequency table. (b) What is the mode?
(c) When might these data be useful?

2 These are the temperatures, in degrees Celsius, in two seaside resorts
each day for two weeks in July.

Blackpool	21°	24°	20°	19°	17°	20°	20°
	22°	25°	26°	23°	20°	19°	15°
Brighton	24°	24°	23°	21°	18°	17°	21°
	22°	21°	23°	24°	22°	20°	19°

(a) Find the mode for each resort. (b) Find the range for each resort.
(c) Which resort do you think had better weather? Why?

3 Nicole does a survey to find out how many days off school everyone in
her class has had over the last two weeks. Here are her results.

2 0 0 0 1 0 1 2 3
5 0 0 3 3 2 0 0 0
1 0 4 0 6 2 2 0 0
3 1 0 0 6 2 2 0 1

(a) Make a frequency table and draw a bar chart to illustrate these data.
(b) Find the mode, mean and median for these data.
(c) Which average do you think describes the data best? Why?

4 Mrs Green gives two Year 7 classes the same French vocabulary test. The
test is marked out of 20. Here are the results for the two classes.

CLASS 7P
Paul 15 Humza 12 Suzie 13 David 17 Chi 11 Kate 14 Wasim 8 Becky 10 Cliff 19
Sam 16 Peter 15 Zena 14 Cathy 18 Simon 9 Peter 12 Sam 14 Petra 16 Stefi 15
Chloe 14 Dan 16 Sarah 11 Martin 13 Jess 15 Jack 13 Mandy 11 George 10

CLASS 7Q
Tom 18 Tasmin 12 Liz 16 Kate 14 Justin 20 Denise 11 Alex 13 Val 20 Luke 14
Roy 9 Seb 12 Bella 15 Pippa 14 Philip 10 Robert 4 Laura 13 Fiona 12 Boris 18
Tim 19 James 16 Kath 5 Jake 20 Grace 13 Sophie 14 Chris 16 Zak 15 Penny 15

(a) Find the mean for each class. (b) Find the range for each class.
(c) Which class do you think has done better?
(d) Which classes' results are more spread out?

Finishing off

When you have finished this chapter you should be able to:

- find the mean, median and mode of a set of data and know that these are average values
- find the range of a set of data and know that it shows you how spread out the data are.

Review exercise

1 Samantha is captain of the school hockey team.
She keeps a record of the number of goals the team score in each match.
Here are Samantha's data.

2 0 1 3 2 2 0 1 4 3
2 3 0 1 4 6 2 2 2 4

(a) Find the mode.
(b) Work out the mean number of goals scored.
(c) Work out the median number of goals scored.
(d) Find the range.

2 Mr Wilson wants to compare the attendance rates of boys and girls in his tutor group.
Here are the number of absences for one term.
One of the boys in the class has been in hospital for most of the term.

Boys
5 12 0 2 0 8 6 3 0
41 1 0 9 4

Girls
3 2 5 1 8 2 6 10 9
5 4 3 9 8 6

(a) Find the mean for the boys and the mean for the girls.
(b) Find the median for the boys and the median for the girls.
(c) Which average do you think is the best way to compare these data?
(d) Find the range for the boys and the range for the girls.
(e) What does the range tell you about the data?

3 Paul gets £3.50 pocket money per week.
He wants to persuade his parents to give him a rise, so he asks some of his friends how much pocket money they get.

Here are the results.

£4.00 £2.50 £5.00 £10.00
£2.80 £3.00 £3.50 £3.00

(a) Find the median of the data. **(b)** Find the mean of the data.
(c) Which average should Paul use when he shows his survey to his parents?

The friend who gets £10 per week has to buy his own clothes out of his pocket money.

(d) Find the mean of the data if the £10.00 is not included.
(e) Do you think Paul should get a rise? Explain your answer.

4 Boxes of drawing pins are labelled 'Average contents 50'.

A quality control inspector wants to check that the label is accurate.
She counts the number of drawing pins in 30 boxes.
Here are her results.

46	50	52	50	49	49	51	47
49	50	50	51	48	51	53	49
51	48	49	50	47	50	51	50
50	50	48	52	51	52		

(a) Make a frequency table for this data and draw a bar chart.
(b) What is the mode?
(c) Find the mean number of drawing pins in a box.
(d) Find the median number of drawing pins in a box.
(e) Do you think the labelling is accurate?

5 A company which makes plant food is testing two new products.

Two batches of identical seeds are planted and each batch is treated with one of the new plant foods. After three weeks the height of the seedlings, in centimetres, is measured.

```
Batch A
    1.5   2.3   2.1   1.8   2.8   1.4   1.8   2.0   1.7
    0.8   1.2   1.8   2.3   0.9   1.3   1.2   0.9   1.6
    2.2   1.7   1.2   1.3   1.5   2.3   2.6

Batch B
    1.8   2.4   1.9   1.8   2.9   3.1   1.6   0.2   1.3
    2.5   1.4   0.3   3.5   1.2   1.5   2.3   1.4   2.4
    3.6   1.4   0.6   0.5
```

(a) Find the mean, the median and the range for each batch of seeds.
(b) Which plant food do you think is more effective? Why?

17 Formulae

THE AVONFORD STAR   **Thursday Sport Special**

Avonford Girls Make Top of League

Following a stunning 4-3 victory over arch rivals Shellbury last night, Avonford Ladies Football Club went top of the table.

Here are the positions of the first four clubs today.

Team	P	W	D	L	Points
Avonford	8	6	2	0	20
Shellbury	8	6	1	1	19
Plystar	8	5	1	2	16
Swynton	8	5	0	3	15

Winning goal scorer, star Karen Eccles

? Look at the table in the newspaper article.
What do the letters P, W, D and L stand for?

Task

I Use the information in the newspaper article.
   (a) Work out how many points a team gets for a win.
   (b) How many for a draw?
   (c) What about if they lose?
Bannington scored 12 points in 8 matches. How many wins, losses and draws could they have had?

The next team in the table is Newchurch.
They have won 4 matches, drawn 2 and lost 4.

Kevin works out their points.

He uses a formula:

$$Points = 3 \times Number\ of\ wins + 1 \times Number\ of\ draws$$
$$Points = 3 \times 4 + 1 \times 2$$
$$Points = 12 + 2$$
$$Points = 14$$

An easier way to write the formula is

$$Points = 3 \times W + 1 \times D$$

W stands for the number of wins.

D stands for the number of draws.

Exercise

1 The cost of buying milk in a supermarket is given by the formula

Cost (in pence) = 50 × Number of litres

(a) Find the cost of buying
(i) 1   **(ii)** 2   **(iii)** 3   **(iv)** 4   **(v)** 5
litres of milk.
(b) How many litres of milk can you buy for £5?
(c) The supermarket increases the price of milk to 60 pence per litre.
Write down the new formula for the cost.

2 A railway company works out its fares using this formula:

Divide the length of the journey in kilometres by 10 and then add 5.
The answer is the fare in £.

(a) Find the fares for journeys of
(i) 50 km   **(ii)** 100 km   **(iii)** 200 km   **(iv)** 5 km.
(b) Ashley has £55. How far can she travel?

3 Look back to the newspaper article on the opposite page.
Here are the bottom four teams in the league.

Team	P	W	D	L	Points
Six Stars	*	2	1	5	*
Torness	9	*	0	7	*
Parkby	8	1	2	*	*
Lower Pass	7	*	*	*	0

(a) Nine of the numbers are missing from the table.
Copy it out and fill in the missing numbers.

(b) Work out the value of W + D + L for Six Stars.
What information does the formula W + D + L give you?

(c) The *Avonford Star* article tells you that Avonford beat Shellbury 4–3
last night.
How many points did Avonford and Shellbury have before the match?

4 Jenny travels regularly on the motorway for her job.
She says

'I work out roughly how long a journey will take using this formula:
Every 100 km takes 1 hour and every stop for a meal takes 1 hour.'

How long does Jenny take on the following journeys?
(a) 400 km with 1 meal   **(b)** 600 km with 2 meals
(c) 150 km with no meals.

One journey takes Jenny $7\frac{1}{2}$ hours, including 2 meals.

(d) How many km is the journey?

Working with formulae

You can give a formula in words or
you can write it using letters.

A party of adults and children are going to
this aquarium.

The cost can be written

Avonford Aquarium

Entrance Fee:	Adults	£8.00
	Children	£5.00

AVONFORD
AA AQUARIUM

Last entrance 4.50pm

- **In words**
  *The cost in pounds is eight times the number
  of adults added to five times the number of
  children.*

- **In letters** $P = 8 \times a + 5 \times c$

  *c stands for the number
  of children.*

  *P is the cost in
  pounds.*

  *a stands for the number
  of adults.*

  *An expression has
  letters and usually some
  numbers too.*

It is common to leave the $\times$ signs out when you use letters.
So the formula is $P = 8a + 5c$. $8a + 5c$ is called an **expression**.

EXAMPLE　　Find the value of $8a + 5c$ when $a = 3$ and $c = 6$.

Solution
$$8a + 5c$$
$$= 8 \times 3 + 5 \times 6$$
$$= 24 + 30$$
$$= 54$$

*Notice that you have to
put the $\times$ signs in to work
this out.*

When you write a formula in letters you are using **algebra**.
The letters stand for the numbers.
The numbers are not always the same.
In the example above, $a = 3$, $c = 6$ is a party of 3 adults and 6 children.

Task

1 Work out the value of $8a + 5c$ when:

　(a) $a = 7$ and $c = 5$　**(b)** $a = 9$ and $c = 8$
　(c) $a = 0$ and $c = 3$　**(d)** $a = 4$ and $c = 30$

2 The cost of a party is £40.

　Work out how many different combinations of adults and children could go to the
　aquarium for £40 using the prices given above.

  How do you work out $8 \times 3 + 5 \times 6$ on your calculator?

You must make sure you know how to get the right answer on your calculator.
The order for pressing the keys can be different for different calculators.

Exercise

1 Find the value of $p + q + r$ when
(a) $p = 2$, $q = 3$ and $r = 1$ (b) $p = 5$, $q = 3$ and $r = 2$
(c) $p = 99$, $q = 101$ and $r = 100$ (d) $p = 0$, $q = 0$ and $r = 0$
(e) $p = 5$, $q = 19$ and $r = 1$ (f) $p = 59$, $q = 99$ and $r = -99$

2 Find the value of $x + y - z$ when
(a) $x = 3$, $y = 4$ and $z = 5$ (b) $x = 10$, $y = 10$ and $z = 10$
(c) $x = 6$, $y = 12$ and $z = 0$ (d) $x = 8$, $y = 2$ and $z = 10$
(e) $x = 23$, $y = 17$ and $z = 30$ (f) $x = 0$, $y = 73$ and $z = 73$

3 Find the value of $8a + 5c$ when
(a) $a = 2$, $c = 5$ (b) $a = 1$, $c = 6$
(c) $a = 2$, $c = 2$ (d) $a = 5$, $c = 0$
(e) $a = 5$, $c = 8$ (f) $a = 8$, $c = 5$
(g) $a = 0$, $c = 0$ (h) $a = 10$, $c = 10$
(i) $a = 100$, $c = 100$ (j) $a = 5$, $c = -8$

4 Use the formula
$$C = 5b - 2$$
to find the value of C when
(a) $b = 2$ (b) $b = 8$
(c) $b = 12$ (d) $b = 20$
(e) The formula refers to the notice about paperback books.
   (i) What does b stand for?
   (ii) What does C stand for?
(f) Jane spends £43 on books.
   How many books does she buy?

BOOKWORM

Paperback Books
£5.00 each

Discount of £2
for all customers

5 Use the formula
$$P = 2f + c$$
to find the value of P when
(a) $f = 4$, $c = 4$ (b) $f = 3$, $c = 2$
(c) $f = 5$, $c = 8$ (d) $f = 1$, $c = 0$
(e) The formula refers to the notice about fish and chips.
What do the letters f, c and P stand for?

—TODAYS SPECIAL—
FISH £2.00
CHIPS £1.00

Investigation   Four people try to work out the value of $2x + 4y$ when $x = 3$ and $y = 5$. Here are their answers.

Ali 68   Sam 70   Mel 50   Fran 26

Who is right?

What mistakes do you think the others made?

Finishing off

Now that you have finished this chapter you should be able to:

- understand what a formula is
- be able to write a formula
- be able to use a formula.

Review exercise

1 The price of cinema tickets is given by

$$P = 4A + 3C$$

The formula refers to the cinema advert.

(a) What does A stand for?
What does C stand for?
What does P stand for?

Avonford Cinema

Prices :   ADULTS   £4.00
           CHILDREN   £3.00

(b) Find the cost of
  (i) 2 adults and 2 children   **(ii)** 2 children
  (iii) 5 adults and 3 children.

(c) How many children can go to the cinema for £12?

(d) How many adults can go to the cinema for £12?

The cinema has a special offer on:

(e) Write a new formula for the price of the tickets.

(f) How many children can now go to the cinema for £12?
How many adults can now go to the cinema for £12?

Avonford Cinema

SPECIAL OFFER   ALL TICKETS
                £1.00 OFF!

2 Find the value of $a + b - c$ when:
  (a) $a = 1$, $b = 2$ and $c = 1$ **(b)** $a = 4$, $b = 2$ and $c = 6$
  (c) $a = 12$, $b = 10$ and $c = 0$ **(d)** $a = 50$, $b = 60$ and $c = 10$
  (e) $a = 11$, $b = 10$ and $c = 20$ **(f)** $a = 111$, $b = 110$ and $c = 120$

3 Find the value of $2x + 3y$ when:
  (a) $x = 7$, $y = 2$ **(b)** $x = 1$, $y = 1$
  (c) $x = 2$, $y = 3$ **(d)** $x = 0$, $y = 10$
  (e) $x = 5$, $y = 5$ **(f)** $x = 3$, $y = 2$
  (g) $x = 7$, $y = 2$ **(h)** $x = 9$, $y = 1$
  (i) $x = 1000$, $y = 1000$ **(j)** $x = 3$, $y = -2$

4 A pet shop is selling hamsters for £3 and gerbils for £4.

(a) Show how you would work out the cost of 2 hamsters and 4 gerbils.

(b) Write down a formula for the cost of h hamsters and g gerbils.

(c) Use your formula to calculate the cost of 6 hamsters and 8 gerbils.

(d) How many hamsters and gerbils can you buy for £24? How many different answers are there?

5 Paul is organising a trip to Alton Towers with his local club.

Minibuses large (16 people) £25
small (10 people) £15

(a) Show how you would work out the cost of 5 large minibuses and 3 small minibuses.

(b) Write down a formula for the cost of taking l large coaches and s small coaches.

(c) How much does it cost to hire 4 large and 3 small coaches?

(d) There are 50 members at the club. What is the cheapest way for them to travel to Alton Towers?

(e) Paul spends £95 on minibus hire. How many large and small minibuses did he hire?

Investigation Karen is taking some members of her youth group to the zoo. Karen spends £17.00 on tickets for five people.

1 Karen uses the formula $P = 5a + 3s + 2c$ to work out the total price. What do P, a, s and c stand for?

Francistown City Zoo

Entrance fees:

Adults £5.00
Students (with I.D.) £3.00
Children £2.00

Enjoy your visit !

2 Find two different combinations of five people that Karen can take to the zoo for £17.

Chris is a keen golfer. He visits Hoebridge
Manor Golf Course for a game.
On every golf course there is a target score
for each hole.

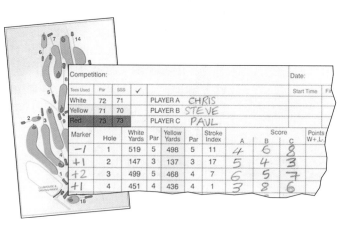

Par 5 means the target for the hole is 5.
Chris scores 4.
He is one less than the target score.
He could write this as (-1).

The next hole is par 3. He scores 5.
He could write this as $(+2)$.

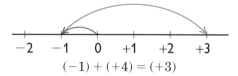 **Task**

Write these scores as $+$ or $-$ numbers:

(a) | par 5 score 3 | **(b)** | par 5 score 8 | **(c)** | par 5 score 4 | **(d)** | par 2 score 5 | **(e)** | par 4 score 1 | **(f)** | par 4 score 8

Plus $(+)$ can be used in many circumstances, and minus $(-)$ to mean the opposite.

? **Decide whether to call these numbers $+$ or $-$:**

(a) A present of £10 / A bill for £6 **(b)** 30 steps backwards / 10 steps forwards **(c)** A temperature of 20° above freezing / A temperature of 6° below freezing

Chris practises by playing consecutive holes. He scores as follows:

1 one below par then four above par
$(-1) + (+4) = (+3)$

2 two below par then three above par
$(-2) + (+3) = (+1)$

3 two above par then three below par
$(+2) + (-3) = (-1)$

4 one below par then two below par
$(-1) + (-2) = (-3)$

Numbers can be shown
on a *number line*.

Check the results above, starting at zero each time.

1

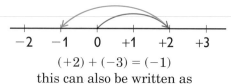

$(-1) + (+4) = (+3)$

2

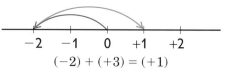

$(-2) + (+3) = (+1)$

3

$(+2) + (-3) = (-1)$
this can also be written as
$2 - 3 = -1$

4

$(-1) + (-2) = (-3)$
and this can also be written as
$-1 - 2 = -3$

? **How do you enter a negative number into your calculator?**

Exercise

1 Write these scores as + or − numbers.

(a)
| par 5 |
| score 4 |

(b)
| par 5 |
| score 7 |

(c)
| par 4 |
| score 2 |

(d)
| par 4 |
| score 3 |

(e)
| par 4 |
| score 5 |

(f)
| par 3 |
| score 5 |

2 Decide whether to call these numbers + or − numbers:
(a) a present of £50   **(b)** a speed of 10 mph over the speed limit
(c) a temperature of 4° below freezing
(d) climbing to a height of 1000 feet   **(e)** a National Lottery win of £10
(f) putting £1 on the lottery but not winning.

3 Choose a number to go with each statement.

A	The average winter temperature for Moscow	−36
B	The 'height' of the Dead Sea	+4 406 feet
C	The goal difference for Division 1 champions	−2 286 feet
D	Julius Caesar first arrived in Britain	−10°C
E	The goal difference for a relegated team	−55
F	The height of Ben Nevis	+42

4 Chris's aim is to score −2 after each pair of holes.
Which of these pairs give −2?
(a) $(-4) + (+2)$ **(b)** $(-1) + (-3)$ **(c)** $(+7) + (-2)$
(d) $(-1) + 0$ **(e)** $(-1) + (-1)$ **(f)** $(-2) + (+2)$

5 Copy the number line from the page opposite.
Mark the following numbers on it:
(a) -3 **(b)** $+1$ **(c)** -5 **(d)** -1 **(e)** $+2$

6 Work out the following:
(a) $(-4) + (+6)$ **(b)** $(-2) + (-3)$ **(c)** $(+1) + (-2)$
(d) $(+7) + (-5)$ **(e)** $(-3) + (+2)$ **(f)** $(-4) + (+4)$
(g) $(+4) + (+1)$ **(h)** $(+2) + (-7)$ **(i)** $(+11) + (-2)$
(j) $(+17) + (-15)$ **(k)** $(-13) + (+12)$ **(l)** $(-14) + (+14)$

7 Work out the following:
(a) $-5 + 7$ **(b)** $-3 - 2$ **(c)** $8 - 11$
(d) $6 + 4$ **(e)** $6 - 9$ **(f)** $-3 + 5$
(g) $-2 + 3 + 1$ **(h)** $4 - 6 - 3$ **(i)** $-5 - 2 + 3 + 1$

Do these questions again again using your calculator.
This checks that you can use your calculator with negative numbers.

Subtraction of negative numbers

F.A. Carling Premiership (up to and including 30 August 1998)

	Played	Won	Drawn	Lost	For	Against	Points
Liverpool	3	2	1	0	6	2	7
Aston Villa	3	2	1	0	4	1	7
Nottingham Forest	3	2	0	1	4	3	6
Charlton Athletic	3	1	2	0	5	0	5
Wimbledon	3	1	2	0	4	2	5
Middlesbrough	3	0	2	1	2	4	2
Newcastle United	3	0	2	1	2	5	2
Chelsea	2	0	1	1	2	3	1
Everton	3	0	1	2	0	3	1
Southampton	3	0	0	3	2	9	0

When two clubs have the same number of points, like Liverpool and Aston Villa above, their position in the table is decided by goal difference.

Goal difference = 'goals for' − 'goals against'

> So Liverpool are above Aston Villa.

Liverpool　　goal difference = $6 - 2 = 4$
Aston Villa　goal difference = $4 - 1 = 3$.

Middlesbrough's goal difference = $2 - 4 = -2$
Newcastle have the same number of points as
Middlesbrough *but* Newcastle's goal difference = $2 - 5 = -3$.

> -2 is greater than -3, so Middlesbrough go above Newcastle.

Task

Look at these patterns.

$5 - 3 = 2$
$5 - 4 = 1$
$5 - 5 = 0$
$5 - 6 = -1$
$5 - 7 = -2$
$5 -$

> **1** Continue this pattern as far as $5 - 12 = -7$

Now look at this pattern in the opposite way.

> **2** Continue this pattern as far as $5 - (-5) =$

$5 - 4　　= 1$
$5 - 3　　= 2$
$5 - 2　　= 3$
$5 - 1　　=$
$5 - 0　　=$
$5 - (-1) =$

?　What happens when you have a $- (-$number$)$?

Check that you have understood:

$4 - 2 = 2$　and　$2 - 9 = -7$
but $5 - (-3) = 5 + 3 = 8$.

Exercise

1 Simplify
(a) $-(+2)$ (b) $-(-3)$ (c) $-(-6)$ (d) $-(+1)$
(e) $-(-1)$ (f) $-(-4)$ (g) $-(+7)$ (h) $-(+11)$

2 Put in order of size, smallest first.
(a) $-1, +2, -2, 0, +1, -3$
(b) $+1, -5, -1, +4, -2$
(c) $3, -5, -3, 1, -2$

3 Put in order of size, largest first.
(a) $-2, 2, 4, 0, -4$
(b) $4, -2, 1, -1, -3, -6$
(c) $10, 0, -2, 3, -6, 7, 17$

4 Work out these questions.
(a) $(-5) - (+2)$ (b) $(-1) - (+3)$
(c) $(+6) - (+2)$ (d) $(+7) - (+6)$
(e) $(+7) - (+8)$ (f) $(+5) - (-1)$
(g) $(+3) - (-2)$ (h) $(-6) - (-3)$
(i) $(-2) - (-2)$ (j) $(-4) - (-1)$

5 Work out (evaluate)
(a) $6 - 2$ (b) $3 - 7$
(c) $1 - 5$ (d) $-4 - 9$
(e) $6 - (-1)$ (f) $3 - (-2)$
(g) $-4 - (-3)$ (h) $-1 - (-5)$
(i) $-6 - (-2)$ (j) $-10 - (-15)$

6 Work out (evaluate)
(a) $6 - 3$ (b) $6 - (-3)$
(c) $-6 + 2$ (d) $-4 - 4$
(e) $-1 - 7$ (f) $-2 - (-9)$
(g) $4 - (-1)$ (h) $3 - (-2)$
(i) $-8 - (-11)$ (j) $-8 - (-3)$

7 Find the value of
(a) $-2 - 3 + 1$ (b) $-6 - (-6) + 3$
(c) $-1 - 1 - 1$ (d) $-2 - 2 - 2 - 2$

Note 7(c) is the same as 3 lots of (-1)
$3 \times (-1) = -3$.

7(d) is the same as 4 lots of (-2)
$4 \times (-2) = -8$.

Multiplying and dividing negative numbers

Avonford School has a tuck shop.
Pupils can either pay cash or write their name
and the amount owed in a book and pay later.

Joanne treats herself to a chocolate bar every
school day for a week.
She writes her name in the book.
At the end of the week she *owes*   5 lots of 30 pence.
$$5 \times (-30) = -150 \text{ pence.}$$

Simon buys two Munchie bars for 25 pence each. He *owes*   2 lots of 25 pence.
$$2 \times (-25) = -50 \text{ pence.}$$

Task

There is a pattern for multiplying + and − numbers.
Look at the 5 times table starting with $5 \times 3 = 15$
$$Or \ (+5) \times (+3) = (+15).$$

I   Copy and complete this table.

$$5 \times 3 \quad = 15$$
$$5 \times 2 \quad =$$
$$5 \times 1 \quad =$$
$$5 \times 0 \quad =$$
$$5 \times (-1) =$$
$$5 \times (-2) =$$

Subtract five

Red number going down by 1

$$\frac{+}{number} \times \frac{+}{number} = \frac{+}{number}$$

$$\frac{+}{number} \times \frac{-}{number} = \frac{-}{number}$$

2   Now do the same for the 4 times table and the 3 times table.

Use the last result of each of your tables to start the negative 2 times table (i.e.,
the (-2) times table)
$$(-2) \times 5 = -10$$
$$(-2) \times 4 = -8$$
$$(-2) \times 3 = \qquad \text{and continue to } (-2) \times (-3)$$

? **What happens when you multiply a negative number by a negative number?**

Multiplication questions can be changed into division questions using the same numbers.

Example I $6 \times 7 = 42$ so $42 \div 6 = 7$
                                  and $42 \div 7 = 6.$

Example 2 $9 \times 8 = 72$ so $72 \div 9 = 8$
                                  and $72 \div 8 = 9.$

? $(-3) \times (-7) = +21$ **What is $(+21) \div (-3)$ and $(+21) \div (-7)$?**
   $(-4) \times (+5) = -20$ **What is $(-20) \div (-4)$ and $(-20) \div (+5)$?**

Exercise

1. Work out
   (a) $(+2) \times (-5)$
   (b) $(+3) \times (-7)$
   (c) $(-6) \times (5)$
   (d) $(-9) \times 4$
   (e) $(-3) \times (-2)$
   (f) $(-5) \times (-1)$
   (g) $(-8) \times (-9)$
   (h) $0 \times (-7)$
   (i) 6×0
   (j) $(-4) \times 3$
   (k) $5 \times (-6)$
   (l) $(-7) \times (-7)$
   (m) $(-1)^2$
   (n) $(-8) \times (-6)$
   (o) $(+2) \times (+6)$
   (p) $(+5) \times 7$
   (q) $0 \times (-3)$
   (r) $(-3) \times 4$
   (s) $6 \times (-2)$
   (t) $7 \times (-9)$
   (u) $(-2) \times (-2)$
   (v) $(-2)^3$
   (w) $(-3)^2$
   (x) $(-9) \times (-10)$
   (y) $25 \times (-4)$
   (z) $(-4)^2$

2. $(-4) \times (-6) = (+24)$

   Use this to work out
   (a) $(+24) \div (-6)$
   (b) $(+24) \div (-4)$

3. $(-5) \times (+6) = (-30)$

   Use this to work out
   (a) $(-30) \div (+6)$
   (b) $(-30) \div (-5)$

4. Evaluate
   (a) $(-8) \div 2$
   (b) $(-10) \div 5$
   (c) $(-6) \div (+3)$
   (d) $8 \div (-4)$
   (e) $16 \div (-8)$
   (f) $(-24) \div (-3)$
   (g) $(-30) \div (-6)$
   (h) $(-42) \div (-6)$
   (i) $42 \div (-3)$
   (j) $48 \div 3$
   (k) $(-26) \div (-13)$
   (l) $(+20) \div (+5)$
   (m) $36 \div 3$
   (n) $(-36) \div 12$
   (o) $(-28) \div (-7)$
   (p) $(+10) \div (+10)$
   (q) $(-26) \div 2$
   (r) $(-12) \div (-12)$
   (s) $52 \div (-4)$
   (t) $63 \div (-9)$
   (u) $(-72) \div (-9)$
   (v) $100 \div (-4)$
   (w) $(-100) \div 20$
   (x) $(-60) \div (-5)$
   (y) $(-1) \div (-1)$
   (z) $14 \div (-2)$

5. Evaluate
   (a) $(-3) \times (-2) \times (-1)$
   (b) $(-2) \times (+5) \times (+4)$
   (c) $(+72) \div (-8)$
   (d) $(-2) \times (-2) \times (-2)$
   (e) $(-2)^3$
   (f) $(-3)^3$
   (g) $(+32) \div (-8)$
   (h) $(-48) \div (-12)$
   (i) $(-48) \div 3$
   (j) $(-98) \div (-7)$
   (k) $(10) \times (-3) \times (-7)$
   (l) $(-91) \div 7$
   (m) $(+51) \div (-3)$
   (n) $75 \div 5$
   (o) $(-4)^2$
   (p) $(-5)^2$

Finishing off

Now that you have finished this chapter you should be able to:

● understand + (positive) and − (negative) numbers
● add + and − numbers
● subtract + and − numbers
● multiply + and − numbers
● divide + and − numbers.

Review exercise

1 Write these as + and − numbers.

(a) A gift worth £40.

(b) A diver 60 feet below the surface.

(c) A bill for £200.

	Bill of Sale	
Quantity	Description	Goods
1	282 L-G	£88.00
2	606 L-L	£112.00
	TOTAL	£200.00

(d) A temperature of 24° C.

(e) 3° below freezing.

(f) A mountaineer 2 000 feet up.

2 Copy this number line.

Mark these numbers on it
(a) −1 **(b)** −8 **(c)** 6 **(d)** +2 **(e)** −6 **(f)** 7

3 Put these numbers in order of size, starting with the smallest:
−1, 0, −6, +1, +5, −3.

4   Work out
(a) $(+3) + (-4)$ (b) $(-3) + (+2)$ (c) $(-1) + (-2)$
(d) $(-5) + (+8)$ (e) $0 + (-6)$ (f) $7 + (-8)$
(g) $(-5) + (-3)$ (h) $19 + (-12)$ (i) $23 + (-27)$
(j) $(-33) + (-3)$ (k) $(-42) + (+18)$ (l) $27 + (-19)$

5   Work out (evaluate)
(a) $7 - 9$ (b) $-6 - 1$ (c) $5 - 3$
(d) $-2 + 2$ (e) $-2 + 6$ (f) $-5 + 1$
(g) $-6 + 3$ (h) $4 + -2$ (i) $7 + -1$
(j) $-5 - 4$ (k) $-7 + 10$ (l) $-23 + 32$

6   Work out
(a) $(+6) - (-4)$ (b) $(-5) - (+3)$ (c) $(-4) - (+7)$
(d) $(+5) - (-2)$ (e) $(-9) - (-6)$ (f) $(-1) - (-8)$
(g) $(-7) - (-3)$ (h) $(-10) - (+5)$ (i) $(+7) - (+9)$
(j) $(+13) - (-20)$ (k) $(-17) - (+11)$ (l) $(-23) - (-45)$

7   Evaluate
(a) $(-2) \times (+4)$ (b) $(5) \times (-3)$ (c) $(-6) \times (-7)$
(d) $(-4) \times (-9)$ (e) $(-2) \times (+3) \times (-5)$ (f) $(-6) \times 0$
(g) $(-1)^2$ (h) $(-3)^2$ (i) $(-2)^3$
(j) $(-5)^4$ (k) $(-2)^4$ (l) $(-2)^2 \times (-3)^5$

8   Evaluate
(a) $(-24) \div (+4)$ (b) $(-12) \div (-3)$ (c) $(-30) \div (-6)$
(d) $(+42) \div (-6)$ (e) $12 \div 3$ (f) $(-64) \div (-4)$
(g) $(-54) \div (+9)$ (h) $(+63) \div (-7)$ (i) $38 \div (-2)$
(j) $(-56) \div (-8)$ (k) $(-64) \div 8$ (l) $100 \div (-4)$

Activity   Speed test.
How quickly can you do these correctly?

(a) $5 - 8$ (b) $-1 - 7$
(c) $6 - -3$ (d) $(-9) - (-1)$
(e) $(-2) + 5 + (-3)$ (f) $(-32) \div (-8)$
(g) $(-7) \times (-4)$ (h) $(-6) \times 5$
(i) $(-3) \times (-2) \times (-4)$ (j) $-20 \div 5$
(k) $56 \div (-8)$ (l) $(-7) \times 0$
(m) $(-4)^2$ (n) $(-3)^3$

Daniel is making a mobile.

He is using triangles, squares and rectangles.

The mobile is **balanced**.

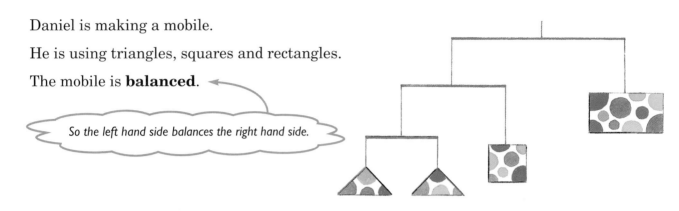

So the left hand side balances the right hand side.

  ? **How many triangles balance one square?**
How many squares balance one rectangle?
How many triangles balance one rectangle?

Task

Use your own shapes made up of triangles to design your own mobile.
Make sure that both sides balance.

April has made another mobile.

To make sure that both sides balance she has weighed some of her pieces.

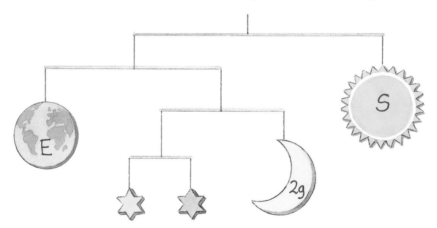

? **What does each *star* weigh?**

April has put letters on some of her pieces.
Each letter represents the mass of that piece.

E stands for the mass of the earth.

? **What is the value of E?**
What is the value of S? What does S stand for?

Exercise

1. Monica has made a mobile:

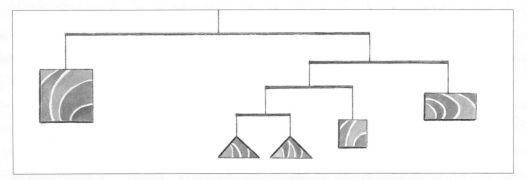

(a) How many triangles are needed to balance one small square?
(b) How many triangles are needed to balance one rectangle?
(c) How many triangles are needed to balance one large square?

2. How many triangles need to be added to each of these mobiles so that they balance?

(a)

(b)

(c)

(d)

3. How many grams are each of the lettered pieces in these mobiles?

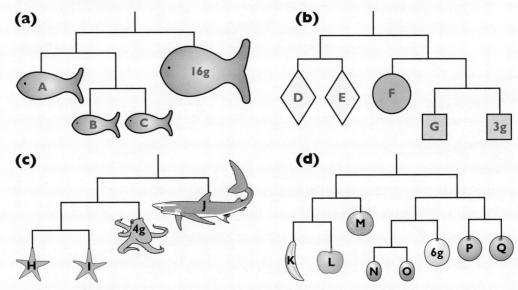

(a)

(b)

(c)

(d)

Solving equations

James's teacher sets him a problem.

His teacher has two identical packages which she puts on some old-fashioned weighing scales.

She wants to know how much each package weighs.

James writes down:

> The weight of two packages + 3 kg = 7 kg

James realises that it would be quicker to write:

$$2 \times p + 3 = 7$$
$$\text{so} \quad 2p + 3 = 7$$

This is called an **equation** – it only has one right answer.

? **What does 2p mean?**

James removes 3 kg from both sides of the scales.
The scales still balance.

? **Why did James take 3 kg from both sides of the scales?**

James now writes:

> Remove 3 kg from each side
>
> $2p + 3 = 7$
> $2p = 4$

? **How can you work out how much one package weighs?**
How much is this?

Task

Invent your own problems with scales which balance.
Get a friend to solve them.

? **How can you check that your answers are right?**
Why is it important that the scales balance at each stage?

Exercise

Write down equations for each of the following sets of scales. Use the same method that James did to work out how much each package weighs.

Draw the scales at each stage in your working.

Further solving equations

I think of a number and subtract 7. My answer is 4.

Alex thinks of a number.
Emma wants to find out Alex's number.
She writes down:

mystery number − 7 = 4
m − 7 = 4

 What does m stand for?

m − 7 + 7 = 4 + 7
m = 11

Emma then undoes what Alex did by adding 7 to both sides.

? **How can you check that Emma has found Alex's mystery number?**

Emma now thinks of a number:

I think of a number.
I double it and add 15.
My answer is 29.

Alex writes:

2 n + 15 = 29

Doubling is the same as multiplying by 2.

? **What should Alex do to undo 'add 15'?**
What should Alex do to undo 'multiply by 2'?

Alex writes:

	2 n + 15 = 29
Subtract 15 from both sides	2 n + 15 − 15 = 29 − 15
So	2 n = 14
Divide both sides by 2	2 n ÷ 2 = 14 ÷ 2
So	n = 7

? **Does it matter whether Alex undoes 'add 15' or 'multiply by 2' first?**

Task

1 With a partner take it in turns to think of a number.
2 Write down an equation for your partner's number.
3 Solve your equation to find the mystery number.

? **How can you check that you have found your partner's number correctly?**

Exercise

In this exercise make sure you set out your work in the same way Alex and Emma did.

Check in each case that you have found the correct answer.

1 Solve these equations by subtracting from both sides.
(a) $m + 4 = 11$ **(b)** $a + 11 = 15$ **(c)** $6 + b = 8$
(d) $x + 5 = 15$ **(e)** $y + 7 = 17$ **(f)** $z + 15 = 115$

2 Solve these equations by adding to both sides:
(a) $p - 6 = 10$ **(b)** $d - 7 = 13$ **(c)** $a - 4 = 4$
(d) $q - 5 = 15$ **(e)** $s - 9 = 15$ **(f)** $t - 25 = 975$

3 Solve these equations. (You will need to think carefully about whether to add or subtract in each case.)
(a) $c - 7 = 10$ **(b)** $5 + d = 7$ **(c)** $g - 5 = 5$
(d) $u + 5 = 19$ **(e)** $h - 8 = 42$ **(f)** $j + 125 = 1125$

4 Solve these equations.
(a) $2a = 6$ **(b)** $4b = 12$ **(c)** $3m = 15$

5 Solve the following equations.
(a) $3a + 4 = 10$ **(b)** $5d + 3 = 18$ **(c)** $2s - 6 = 4$
(d) $2n - 4 = 8$ **(e)** $6b + 5 = 17$ **(f)** $4c - 5 = 11$
(g) $2x + 5 = 45$ **(h)** $3y - 8 = 28$ **(i)** $9z + 35 = 125$
(j) $a + 5 = 5$ **(k)** $2b - 7 = 7$ **(i)** $100c + 500 = 1500$

6 Jenny and Simon are both thinking of mystery numbers.

*I think of a number.
I multiply by 4.
I add 5.
My answer is 25.*

Jenny

*I think of a number.
I double it.
I subtract 6.
My answer is 10.*

Simon

(a) Write down an equation for Jenny's mystery number.
(b) Solve your equation.
(c) Write down an equation for Simon's mystery number.
(d) What number was Simon thinking of?

Activity Make a poster of your own 'Think of a Number' question.

Explain clearly on your poster how to solve the problem.

Finishing off

Now that you have finished this chapter you should be able to:

- understand what an equation is
- be able to write an equation
- be able to use an equation.

Review exercise

1 Find the weights of each of the lettered pieces in the following two mobiles.

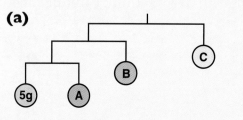

2 Write down an equation for each of the following sets of scales. Solve your equations making sure that the scales balance at each stage.

3 Solve the following equations.
(a) $5p = 20$ (b) $6 + f = 7$ (c) $8a = 32$
(d) $g - 2 = 8$ (e) $m - 11 = 21$ (f) $9h = 36$
(g) $12x = 72$ (h) $y - 8 = 22$ (i) $999z = 999$

4 Solve the following equations:
(a) $2a + 3 = 5$ (b) $4d + 1 = 9$ (c) $2 + 2c = 8$
(d) $6c + 2 = 20$ (e) $6m + 4 = 16$ (f) $3d + 2 = 5$
(g) $12x + 6 = 30$ (h) $5y - 18 = 22$ (i) $999z + 999 = 999$

5 Solve the following equations:

(a) $4b - 6 = 14$ **(b)** $4 + 6b = 10$ **(c)** $3f - 9 = 21$

(d) $4g - 1 = 7$ **(e)** $9b - 10 = 62$ **(f)** $7 + 3f = 37$

(g) $12x - 6 = 30$ **(h)** $15y - 8 = 22$ **(i)** $9z + 990 = 999$

6 Jenny thinks of a number.

I multiply my number by 4 and add 6. My answer is 30.

(a) Write down an equation for Jenny's number.

(b) Solve your equation to work out Jenny's mystery number.

7 Ben thinks of a number.

I multiply my number by 2 and subtract 4. My answer is 8.

(a) Write down an equation for Ben's number.

(b) Solve your equation to work out Ben's mystery number.

8 Steve buys 5 pens in a shop for 60p.

(a) Write down an equation for this information using p as the cost of one pen.

(b) Solve your equation to find the cost of one pen.

9 Kate buys 2 apples at 12p each and 4 bananas from her local shop. She spends 84p altogether.

(a) Write down an equation for this information, using b as the cost of one banana.

(b) Solve your equation to find the cost of one banana.

Investigation Leah and Ryan are making up equations for each other to solve.

Solve $5x + 2 = 17$

Solve $3x = 9$

What is the value of x in each case?

Write down five other equations which have a solution of $x = 3$.

Here is a piece of card before it is folded to make a fruit pastilles packet.

 Discuss the answers to the following questions with a partner.

- What will be the shape of the packet?
- What are all the different parts for?
- How many **faces** will the packet have?
- What shape will the faces be?
- Where the card is folded there will be an **edge** of the packet.
- How many folds have to be made?
- How many edges will the packet have?
- How many **vertices** (corners) will the packet have?

The card is a useful example of a **net**.

 Task

Here is an example of a mathematical net drawn on centimetre squared paper.
Copy it and add flaps for sticking.
Use the least number of flaps possible.

Before you make the solid shape answer these questions.

- How many flaps does your net have?
- How many folds will you need to make?

Compare your net with a friend's.

 Have you put your flaps in the same positions?
Can the arrangement of flaps be different?
Do you always need the same number of flaps for this net?

The net above should make this **cuboid**.

Its **dimensions** are 3 cm long by 2 cm wide by 2 cm high.

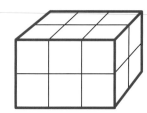

Exercise

1 Use centimetre squared paper to draw a net for a cuboid with these dimensions:

length 4 cm   width 2 cm   height 2 cm

Add flaps, cut out the net and construct the cuboid.

2 Use centimetre squared paper to construct a cuboid measuring 5 cm by 4 cm by 1 cm.

3 Use centimetre squared paper to draw a net and make a cuboid where all the faces are squares.

What name do we give to this special type of cuboid?

4 Use centimetre squared paper to draw a net and make a cube with edges of length 3 cm.

5 Use squared paper to construct a cuboid where none of the faces are squares.

6 Construct a cuboid where only two of the faces are squares.

7 Can you construct a cuboid where exactly four of the faces are squares?

Activity COMPETITION!

Each member of the class has the same sized piece of squared paper. Who can use it to construct the largest cuboid?

 What do we mean by largest?

Activity Draw the net on the opposite page on plain paper.
You should use a ruler and a set square.

To test how well you have done it, cut it out and see if the cuboid looks right.

Are your perpendicular lines really at right angles?

Prisms

triangular prism

When folded and glued it makes a triangular prism.

A prism is a polygon 'stretched' backwards to make
a solid shape.

A Toblerone packet is a triangle stretched backwards.

Task

? A triangular prism has 5 faces.
What shapes are they?

? A triangular prism has 9 edges and 6 vertices.
Can you think of a solid shape which has 8 faces, 18 edges and 12 vertices?

Copy and fill in this table.

Shape	Number of faces (F)	Number of vertices (V)	Number of edges (E)
Triangular prism	5	6	9
	8	12	18
Rectangular prism			
Pentagonal prism			

? Can you spot a **relationship** between the numbers for each shape?

Write down an **equation** connecting F, V and E.

The relationship you have found is called Euler's Rule.

Euler was a famous Swiss mathematician of the 18th century.

Exercise

1. Use squared paper to construct a triangular prism.

2. Ask your teacher for nets to make these prisms:

   Triangular prism
   Hexagonal prism
   Octagonal prism
   Cuboid
   L-shaped prism
   Pentagonal prism

   Cut out the nets and construct the prisms.
   Copy and fill in the table as you make each prism.
   Does each prism fit the relationship you found on the opposite page?

Shape	Number of faces (*F*)	Number of vertices (*V*)	Number of edges (*E*)

3. Glue together two prisms from Question 2 to make a new prism.
   Does it fit the relationship?

4. Glue two or more prisms together in any way you like.
   Does this new shape fit Euler's Rule?

5. Here are three **views** of a triangular prism.

Plan   End elevation   Side elevation

   Draw and label each view of the shapes in Questions 2, 3 and 4.
   You may find squared paper helpful for some of them.

Activity   Using a ruler and protractor, draw the net of a triangular prism on plain paper.

Check your work by making the prism.

Does it look right?

Further solid shapes

There are many other solid shapes besides prisms.

Here is a **tetrahedron** along with the net to make it.

Tetra means four, *hedron* means face.

On page 176 you should have discovered the relationship

Tetrahedron

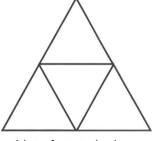

Net of a tetrahedron

$$F + V = E + 2$$

where F is the number of faces, V the number of vertices and E the number of edges.

 Does the tetrahedron obey this rule?

 Task

Ask your teacher for nets of the solids named in the table below. They are difficult to draw!

Cut out the nets and make the solid shapes.
Copy the table and fill it in as you make the shapes.

Shape	Faces (F)	Vertices (V)	Edges (E)
tetrahedron			
hexahedron (cube)			
octahedron			
dodecahedron			
icosahedron			

These shapes are called The Five Platonic Solids.

Plato was a Greek philosopher who was born in the fifth century B.C.

 What can you say about the faces of a Platonic solid? Do these solids obey the $F + V = E + 2$ rule?

The mathematical name for the shape of a soccer ball is a **sphere**.

How are leather soccer balls made like this one?

Activity

1. Use squared paper to draw a net for a **square based pyramid**.
   Construct the pyramid and check that it obeys $F + V = E + 2$.

2. Draw a net and construct a model of a house like this one.
   Does the model obey $F + V = E + 2$?

3. Draw a net and construct a model of a house with a different roof shape.

4. Use nets to make models of other objects.
   Check that each one obeys Euler's Rule.

Activity

Any solid shape where all the faces are flat is called a **polyhedron** (*Poly* means many.)
Euler's Rule works for any polyhedron.

A **cylinder** is not a polyhedron as it has a curved face.
Look at the two diagrams below.
One of them is a net for a cylinder.
One of them is *not* a net as it will not make any solid shape.

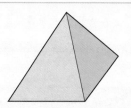

Decide which one is the net of a cylinder.
Trace it on to some thin card, cut it out and make the cylinder.
You will have to add some small flaps.
Why do they have to be small?

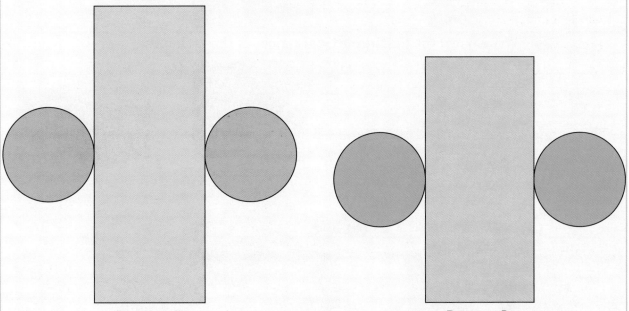

Diagram A   Diagram B

Explain why one diagram is a net and the other diagram is not.

Finishing off

Now that you have finished this chapter you should:

- be able to recognise a cuboid
- know that a cuboid has six rectangular faces, twelve edges and eight vertices
- know that a cube is a special cuboid where all the faces are squares
- know that a prism is any flat shape 'stretched' backwards
- be able to recognise a triangular prism, a cylinder, a sphere, a square based pyramid and a cone
- be able to construct solid shapes from nets.

Review exercise

1. Which of these solid shapes are (a) cuboids and (b) cubes?

A B C D

E F G

2. Write down the **mathematical** names of these shapes.

(a) (b) (c)

(d) (e)

3 Match the names to the shapes:

cuboid   cylinder   hexagonal prism   irregular prism
equilateral triangle prism   isosceles triangle prism

(a)

(b)

(c)

(d)

(e)

(f)

4 Imagine a loaf of bread which is cuboid shaped.

(a) What shape are the slices?
(b) What shape is the face of each slice where the cut has been made?

5 What shape are the pages of this book?

6 **(a)** Write the names of these spheres in order of size, smallest first:

cricket ball   football   marble   golf ball

(b) Which sport uses a ball which is *not* a sphere?

7 Using a pair of compasses, draw a net to make a prism in the shape of an equilateral triangle.

8 Here is the plan and elevation of a **cone**.

Plan

Elevation

Cone

Why is there only one elevation shown?

9 Draw and label the plan and two elevations of
(a) a cylinder   **(b)** a square based pyramid   **(c)** each of the Platonic Solids.

Activity   Make a die for playing board games, by first drawing a net on squared paper.
It can be as large as you like.
Draw the spots for the die *before* you fold the net. Make sure that the spots on opposite sides add up to seven.

The equation of a line

Sally, Joe, and Oliver are playing co-ordinate bingo.

They each draw a line on their co-ordinate grid connecting 4 points.

They take turns to pick cards from a pack with co-ordinates on them.

The winner is the person whose line is completed with crosses first.

The co-ordinates of the points on Joe's line are: (1, 1)
(1, 2)
(1, 3)
(1, 4)

> The first co-ordinate is the x co-ordinate.

? What is the x co-ordinate always equal to?

Joe's points are on the line called $x = 1$.

> The second co-ordinate is the y co-ordinate.

? What other points lie on the line $x = 1$?

> This is called the **equation** of the line.

The co-ordinates of the points on Sally's line are: (1, 3)
(2, 2)
(3, 1)
(4, 0)

? What patterns do you notice in these co-ordinates?

The equation of Sally's line is $x + y = 4$.

? What other points lie on the line $x + y = 4$?
What are the co-ordinates of the points on Oliver's line?

The equation of Oliver's line is $y = x$.

? What are the co-ordinates of some other points which lie on the line $y = x$?

Task

Play your own game of co-ordinate bingo in a group. Use the same size grid as above.

Write down the co-ordinates of each line you use.
Find the equation of each line in your group.

? Does every line have an equation?
All the co-ordinates in co-ordinate bingo are whole numbers.
Does the equation of a line apply to other points as well, like $(1\frac{1}{2}, 1\frac{1}{2})$ and (2.4, 1.6)?

Exercise

1 Write down the co-ordinates of four points on each of the following lines. Comment on the patterns that you notice in the co-ordinates for each line. Find the equation of each line.

(a)

(b)

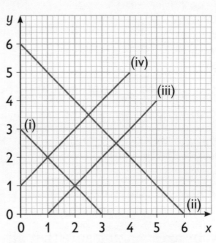

2 Write down the co-ordinates of four points which are on each of the following lines.

(a) $y = x$ **(b)** $x + y = 8$ **(c)** $y = x + 3$
(d) $y = x - 2$ **(e)** $y - x = 2$ **(f)** $x - y = 2$

Which two lines have the same points on them?

3 For each of the following sets of points;

     (i) plot them on graph paper
     (ii) draw a straight line through them
     (iii) write down the co-ordinates of 2 more points on the line
     (iv) find the equation of the line

(a) $(-5, -5)$ **(b)** $(9, 6)$ **(c)** $(4, 3)$
      $(-4, -4)$ $(8, 5)$ $(3, 4)$
      $(-3, -3)$ $(7, 4)$ $(2, 5)$
      $(-2, -2)$ $(6, 3)$ $(1, 6)$

Activity   Make a poster showing the pattern formed by the following lines.

         (a) $x = 2$ **(b)** $x = 5$
         (c) $y = 2$ **(d)** $y = 5$
         (e) $y = x$ **(f)** $x + y = 7$

     Find two more lines that will divide the four central triangles into eight.

?   How can you divide the eight triangles into sixteen?

Drawing lines

Follow these steps to draw the graph of $y = 3x$.

First of all make a table and choose some numbers for the x co-ordinates.

Multiply every x co-ordinate by 3.

x	−3	−2	−1	0	1	2	3
$y = 3x$			−3			6	

We chose the numbers −3, −2, −1, 0, 1, 2, 3 for x.

Then use the x co-ordinates to find the y co-ordinates.

 What are the rest of the y co-ordinates?

So, one of the points is (2, 6).

Look again at the table.

 How do you know how big you need to draw your axes?

Draw your axes making sure that all your points will fit on it.

Plot all the points that you have found.

Notice the lines are labelled not the squares

Join up all your points with a straight line using a sharp pencil and a ruler.

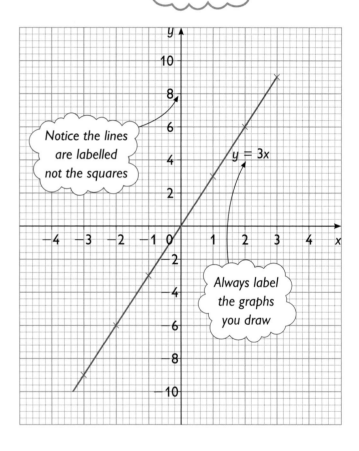

$y = 3x$

Always label the graphs you draw

⚠ Look at the scales on the x-axis and the y-axis. They are different.

However, you must have the same scale for $+x$ and $−x$, and the scale you use for $−y$ must be the same as for $+y$.

 What is the value of y when $x = 2.5$?
What is the value of x when $y = 4$?
How accurate are your answers?

 ## Task

Follow the steps above to draw the graphs of
$y = x$ $y = 2x$ and $y = 4x$ on the same axes.

Compare the three graphs. What do you notice?

 Which graph is the steepest?

Exercise

1 For each part of this question:

(i) copy and complete the table
(ii) write down the largest and smallest x and y co-ordinates
(iii) draw the graph

(a)

x	-4	-3	-2	-1	0	1	2	3	4
$y = x + 1$	-3			0				4	

(b)

x	-4	-3	-2	-1	0	1	2	3	4
$y = x + 5$		2		4			7		

(c)

x	-4	-3	-2	-1	0	1	2	3	4
$y = x - 2$	-6			-3			0		

(d)

x	-4	-3	-2	-1	0	1	2	3	4
$y = 5x$	-20			-5					20

2 Here is the graph of $y = 2x + 1$.

(a) What is the value of y when

    (i) $x = 3$
    (ii) $x = 0$
    (iii) $x = 3.5$?

(b) What is the value of x when

    (i) $y = 11$
    (ii) $y = 6$
    (iii) $y = 9$?

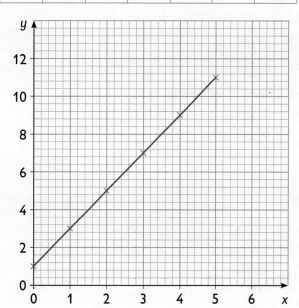

Investigation Draw the graphs of $y = x + 1$
$y = x + 2$
$y = x + 3$ on the same axes.

What do you notice?
What does the graph of $y = x - 1$ look like?

Interpreting graphs

THE AVONFORD STAR

What A Scorcher!!

Temperatures in Avonford reach a record high!

Avonford has just got in to the record books with having the hottest day since records began. The temperature soared to a sizzling 40°C and only fell to 18°C last night.

Avonford compared with the coldest place yesterday in Britain, Bridgetown.

Look at the line graph in the newspaper article.
What is the temperature in both towns at 11 o'clock?
At which times is the temperature in Bridgetown 18°C?

 When is the temperature difference the greatest between the two towns?
What does each small square represent on each axes?
When is the temperature in both towns the same?

This is a conversion graph.
You can use it to convert between
Fahrenheit and Celsius temperatures.

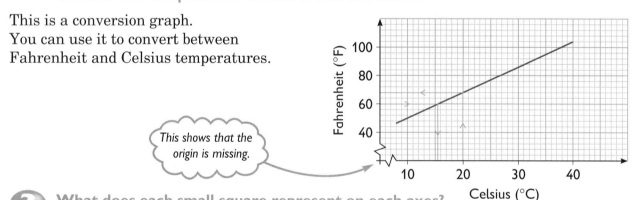

This shows that the origin is missing.

 What does each small square represent on each axes?
What is 20°C in Fahrenheit? What is 60°F in Celsius?

Task

Look again at the newspaper article above. Write down the temperature in each town for every hour. Use the conversion graph to convert the temperatures to Fahrenheit.

Make your own newspaper article and line graphs using the Fahrenheit temperatures.

Comment on the shape of your line graphs and the line graphs in the newspaper article.

 Can you convert exactly between Celsius and Fahrenheit by using the conversion graph?

Exercise

1 Look at the conversion chart on the page opposite.

 (a) Convert the following temperatures to celsius:

 (i) 100°F **(ii)** 80°F **(iii)** 50°F

 (b) Convert the following temperatures to Fahrenheit:

 (i) 15°C **(ii)** 30°C **(iii)** 35°C

2 This graph shows the temperatures of two hospital patients during one day.

 (a) When do the two first have the same temperature?
 (b) When is Carole's temperature the highest?
 (c) What are their temperatures at 12 noon?
 (d) Between what times is Sunny's temperature falling?

3 The graph shows the temperature of a cup of coffee at different times.

 (a) What is the temperature at time
  (i) 10 minutes **(ii)** 20 minutes
  (iii) 30 minutes?

 (b) At what time is its temperature
  (i) 60° **(ii)** 40°?

 (c) What is the temperature when it is made?

 (d) When is it cooling fastest?

4 Mark walks to his local shop to buy some sweets and then returns home. Here is a distance-time graph for his journey.

 (a) Explain the shape of this graph.
 (b) How far is the shop from Mark's home?
 (c) How long does Mark spend in the shop?
 (d) How long does it take Mark to walk home?

Finishing off

Now that you have finished this chapter you should be able to:

- interpret a line graph
- use a conversion graph
- find an equation of a line
- understand what an equation of a line is
- draw a graph.

Review exercise

1 Below is a conversion graph used to convert between miles and kilometres.

(a) The distance between Norwich and Cambridge is 100 kilometres.
How far is this in miles?
(b) The distance between Birmingham and Manchester is 84 miles.
How far is this in kilometres?
(c) Susan travels from Edinburgh to Newcastle – a distance of 170 kilometres.
How far is this in miles?
(d) James travels from London to Brighton – a distance of 52 miles.
How far is this in kilometres?

2 A telephone company called *In Touch* makes the following charges for calls:

> **Stay 'In Touch'**
>
> | Calls only | 6p per minute |
> |---|---|
> | plus | 10p connection charge |

(a) Copy and complete the following table showing the company's phone charges:

Length of call (in minutes)	1	2	3	4	5	6	7	8
Cost of call (in pence)	16			34				

(b) Draw a graph to show this information.

3 Write down the co-ordinates of four points marked on each of the following lines:

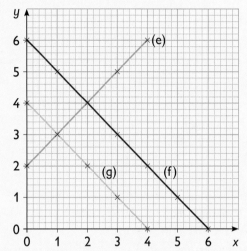

(a) Write down any patterns you notice in each set of co-ordinates.
(b) Find the equation of each of the lines.

4 Complete the following tables for $y = x + 6$ and $y = 2x$.

(i)

x	-4	-3	-2	-1	0	1	2	3	4
$y = x + 6$		3		5			8		

(ii)

x	-4	-3	-2	-1	0	1	2	3	4
$y = 2x$	-8				0			6	

Draw the graphs of $y = 2x$ and $y = x + 6$ on the same axes.

5 **(a)** Draw the graphs of the following lines on the same piece of graph paper. Use the same scales for x and y.
　　(i) $x = 4$ 　**(ii)** $x = -2$ 　**(iii)** $y = 0$ 　**(iv)** $y = 3$

(b) Write down four co-ordinates that are on
　　(i) the x axis 　　　　**(ii)** the y axis

Find the equations of the x axis and y axis.

(c) Draw the lines
　　(i) $y = x$ 　　　　**(ii)** $y = -x$.
At what angle do these two lines cross?

Carmen is a keen gardener.
She is making a herb bed in the shape of a
rectangle.
The length is 8 feet, the width is 6 feet.
She is going to mark the edges with wire edging.

Each piece is 1 foot long.

←1 foot→

 How many pieces will she need to go all the way round the herb bed?

There are two lengths needing 8 pieces each $2 \times 8 = 16$
There are two widths needing 6 pieces each $2 \times 6 = 12+$

The total number of pieces needed is 28.   Total $\underline{28}$

The distance round the outside of a shape is called the **perimeter**.
The perimeter of Carmen's herb bed is 28 feet.

Task

Work out the perimeter of these polygons.
Sometimes there is more than one way to do this.
See if you can find the *quickest* way to calculate each one.

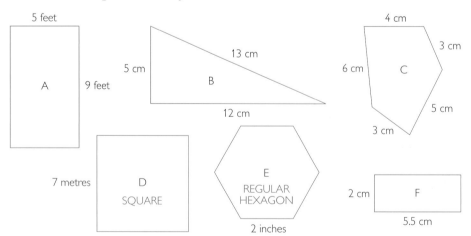

For each type of shape see if you can write down a **formula** for the perimeter.

EXAMPLE   Perimeter of a square = 4 × length

The perimeter of a polygon is found by adding the lengths of the sides together.

 What sort of polygons have formulae for their perimeter?

Exercise

1. Measure the lengths of the sides of these shapes to work out the perimeter.

(a)   **(b)**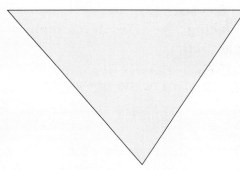

2. Calculate the perimeters of these shapes. (Do not draw them.)

(a) 9 cm, 3 cm

(b) 3.4 cm, 7.3 cm

(c) 3.1 cm, 8.1 cm, 7.5 cm

(d) 3.2 cm, 5.9 cm, 3.6 cm, 6.1 cm, 4.2 cm

(e) 6 cm, 14 cm

3. Carmen is making an ornamental pond. She is going to put safety railing around its perimeter. Railing costs £15 per metre. How much will she have to pay for the railing she needs?

5 m, 2 m, 0.5 m

Activity Imagine you have 60 pieces of edging to surround a flower bed. Draw as many different designs as you can, using all 60 pieces. You may find squared paper helpful. Decide which of your designs would hold the most flowers.

Area and volume

Area

Owain is a builder.
He has to cover the roof of a building with sheets of plywood.

Each sheet is a square 1 metre wide and 1 metre long.
There are 36 sheets on the roof.
The **area** of the roof is 36 square metres.

Area is an amount of flat space.

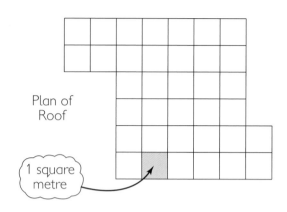

Plan of Roof

1 square metre

 What is the formula for the area of a rectangle? How does it work?

Volume

Here is a sugar cube.
It is 1 cm long, 1 cm wide and 1 cm high.
Its **volume** is 1 cubic centimetre.

Volume is an amount of solid space.

A factory shop sells souvenir boxes of sugar cubes.
A box is 5 cm long, 4 cm wide and 3 cm high.

The box is a cuboid.
Use the correct formula to calculate its volume.

1 cm, 1 cm, 1 cm

3 cm, 4 cm, 5 cm

 Can you explain why the formula for the volume of a cuboid works?

Area of a rectangle = length × width.
Area is measured in square units e.g. m².

Volume of a cuboid = length × width × height.
Volume is measured in cubic units e.g. cm³.

 Task

Another cuboid souvenir box which holds 60 sugar cubes is 6 cm long, 5 cm wide and 2 cm high.

6 cm × 5 cm × 2 cm = 60 cm³

1 Find other cuboids which could hold 60 sugar cubes. Write down the calculation of their volumes like the one above.
How many *different* cuboids are there which hold 60 sugar cubes?

2 Decide which would be the best and which would be the least practical souvenir box design. Write down your reasons.
Make a drawing of the best and the least practical designs.

Exercise

1. Find the area of each of these shapes. Each square represents 1 square cm.

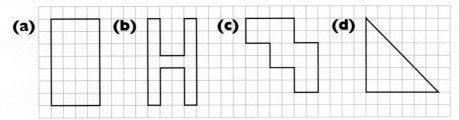

(a) (b) (c) (d)

2. Calculate the volume of these cuboids.

(a) 4 m, 5 m, 2 m

(b) 8 cm, 4 cm, 4 cm

3. Calculate the areas of these rectangles.
   (a) length = 4 cm, width = 10 cm   (b) length = 9 cm, width = 3 cm
   (c) length = 7 m, width = 11 m   (d) length = 8 cm, width = 3.5 cm
   (e) length = 70 yards, width = 30 yards (f) length = 6 inches,
                                                width = $4\frac{1}{2}$ inches

4. Calculate the volumes of cuboids with these dimensions.
   (a) length 10 cm, width 3 cm, height 2 cm
   (b) length 4 inches, width 5 inches, height $2\frac{1}{2}$ inches
   (c) length 1 m, width 1 m, height 12 m
   (d) length 12 cm, width $2\frac{1}{2}$ cm, height 4 cm

5. Find the volume of this shape.
   Each cube is a cubic cm.

6. Calculate the volume of these objects.

(a) 1 foot, 3 feet, 5 feet, 5 feet, 2 feet

(b) 100 m, 40 m, 70 m, 20 m, 20 m, 20 m

More areas

Here is a rectangle with a triangle drawn inside it.

The area of the rectangle is

$8\ cm \times 5\ cm = 40\ cm^2$.

 How can you *calculate* the area of the triangle without counting squares?

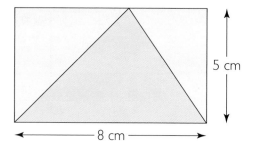

5 cm

8 cm

Task

Draw a rough copy of this shape. Write on it the measurements as shown. Calculate the area of the shape. Show on your diagram how you do this.

Compare your working with other people in your class.
Has everyone done it the same way?

4 cm

2 cm

6 cm

3 cm

10 cm

 How many different ways are there of calculating the area of this shape?

Here is a cuboid souvenir box with the lid closed.
Its **surface area** is the total area of cardboard surrounding the volume.

Area of top plus bottom $= 2 \times 5\ cm \times 4\ cm = 40\ cm^2$
Area of front plus back $\ = 2 \times 5\ cm \times 3\ cm = 30\ cm^2$
Area of sides $\qquad\quad = 2 \times 3\ cm \times 4\ cm = 24\ cm^2\ +$

Total surface area $\qquad\qquad\qquad\quad\ \underline{94\ cm^2}$

3 cm

4 cm

5 cm

Task

Find the surface area of the other cuboids which hold 60 centimetre cubes.
Which ones use the most and least cardboard?

 Can you think of a *formula* for the surface area of a cuboid?

Area of a triangle $= \frac{1}{2} \times$ base $\times$ height.

Some shapes can be split into rectangles to find their area.

Exercise

1 Calculate the areas of these triangles.

(a) 5 cm / 6 cm

(b) 4 cm / 9 cm

(c) 8 m / 5 m

(d) 5 cm / 7 cm

(e) 10 cm / 8 cm

(f) 7 feet / 8 feet

2 Calculate the area of these shapes.

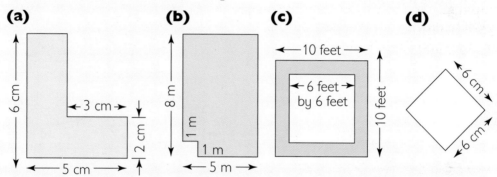

(a) 6 cm, 3 cm, 5 cm, 2 cm

(b) 8 m, 1 m, 1 m, 5 m

(c) 10 feet, 6 feet by 6 feet, 10 feet

(d) 6 cm, 6 cm

3 Liban is painting the end of his house.
Each tin of paint covers 25 m².
How much paint will he need to buy to
cover the wall?

13 m / 9 m / 8 m

4 Estimate the area of this pond.
The squares are square metres.

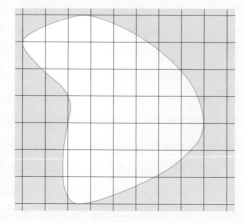

5 Estimate the area of the bottom of
this watch battery.
The squares
are square
millimetres.

1.5 V

Volumes of prisms

Task

I Here is a novelty box of sugar cubes.
It is an L shaped prism.

? **How many cubes touch the *bottom* of the box?**
What is the area of the bottom of the box?

Calculate the number of cm cubes in the box.

Write down your working out.

3 cm

2 This T shaped prism is filled with cm sugar cubes.
Calculate its volume.

Write down your working out.

3 cm

Volume of prism = area of cross section × length

EXAMPLE

Find the volume of this triangular prism.

Area of triangle = $\frac{1}{2}$ × base × height

Area of cross section ⟨ $= \frac{1}{2} \times 7$ cm × 4 cm ⟩

$= \frac{1}{2} \times 28$ cm^2
$= 14$ cm^2

Volume of prism $= 14$ cm$^2 \times 10$ cm
$= 140$ cm^3

4 cm

7 cm

10 cm

Exercise

1 Calculate the volume of these prisms.

(a)

2 cm
2 cm
8 cm

(b)

2 cm
2 cm
8 cm

(c)

3 m
6 m
4 m

(d)

3 inches
5 inches
4 inches

2 Calculate the volume of these wooden letters.

(a)

1 cm
5 cm
2 cm
2 cm
1 cm
1 cm
1 cm

(b)

3 cm
5 cm
2 cm
4 cm
3 cm

3 What is the volume of this house?

18 m
12 m
30 m
20 m

4 The area of the end of this tin is 150 cm². What is its volume?

Spaghetti Numbers
10 cm

Finishing off

Now that you have finished this chapter you should:

- be able to calculate the perimeter of a flat shape
- be able to find the area of a flat shape
- be able to use the formulae to calculate the area of a rectangle and a triangle
- be able to use the formulae to calculate the volume of a cuboid and other prisms
- be able to use a formula to find the surface area of a cuboid
- know that area is measured in square units e.g. cm^2
- know that volume is measured in cubic units e.g. cm^3.

Review exercise

1 Calculate the perimeter and area of these rectangles.
 (a) Length 4 cm, width 6 cm
 (b) Length 8 m, width 3 m
 (c) Length 6 inches, width $2\frac{1}{2}$ inches
 (d) Length 4 yards, width $5\frac{1}{2}$ yards
 (e) Length 1 mile, width 1 mile.

2 Estimate the area of
 this island.
 The squares are
 square miles.

3 Calculate the area of these rectangles.
 (a) Base 6 cm, height 10 cm
 (b) Base 4 m, height 3 m
 (c) Base 7 cm, height 9 cm.

4 Calculate the area of this
 triangle.

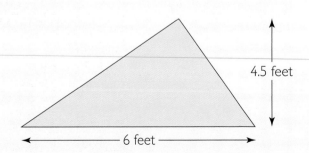

4.5 feet

6 feet

5 Calculate the volume of these solid shapes.

(a)

9 m

2 m

← 3 m →

(b)

3 cm

3 cm

← 3 cm →

Investigation The volume of liquid or gas that a container will hold is often called its **capacity**.

The metric unit of capacity is the **litre**.
1 litre is equal to 1000 millilitres.
Obtain a 1 litre carton in the shape of a cuboid.
Measure its dimensions and calculate its volume in cubic centimetres.
Litres and cubic centimetres are both metric units of volume.
What is the relationship between them?

  The sizes of car engines are often given in litres or cubic centimetres (cc).
Typical examples are 2.0 litres and 1800 cc.
What are these values referring to?

Investigation A fuel tank is to be made out of sheet aluminium in the shape of a closed cuboid.
Its capacity has to be 216 litres.

Design a suitable tank, giving its dimensions.

Sheet aluminium costs £24.50 per square metre.
What is the cheapest design you can come up with?

Activity Find the volumes of the following objects:

- a cassette case
- a compact disc case
- a house brick
- this book
- one page of this book.

Use cm^3, m^3, mm^3 or whatever units you think are most suitable.

Decision tree diagrams

Michael is visiting his local aquarium.

? **How many different types of fish are there in the tank?**
How many ways can you sort these fish?

Michael uses this **decision tree diagram** to sort the fish.

This is a diagram which asks questions to help you sort information.

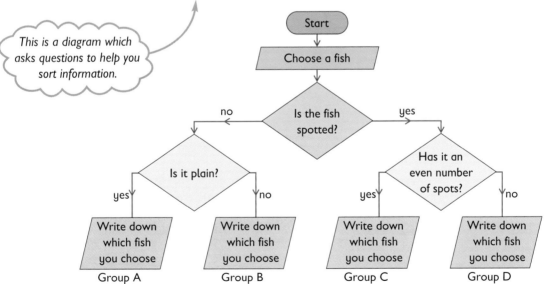

Task

Use the decision tree diagram to find out which fish go into which group.

? **How has Michael sorted the fish?**

Exercise

1   Look at the fish tank on the opposite page. This time use this decision
    tree diagram to sort the fish in a different way.

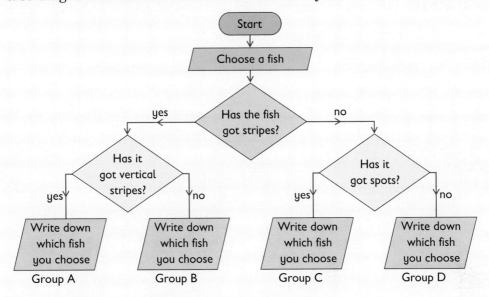

What groups have you sorted the fish into?

2   Design a decision tree diagram to sort the fish in the tank opposite into
    blue and red fish.

3   Design a decision tree diagram to sort the fish into:
    • blue with stripes   • red with stripes
    • blue without stripes   • red without stripes

4   Design your own decision tree diagram to sort the fish into different
    groups from those above.

Investigation

2	4	7	9	27

1	16	19	5	8	5

11	64	13	25	49

How many different ways can you sort these numbers?
Design two different decision tree diagrams to sort the numbers.

Flow charts and number patterns

A **flow chart** is a list of instructions and questions which help you carry out a task.

We can use flow charts to investigate number patterns.

Use the flow chart above to make a 'number chain'.
What are these numbers called?

Now use the same flow chart but at the first instruction write down the number 2 instead of 1.
What are these numbers called?

 What numbers would you get if the starting number was 3?

Draw your own flow chart to generate the first 20 odd numbers.

Draw another flow chart to produce the first 5 multiples of 5.

How do you know when to stop?

Exercise

1 Look at the fish tank on the opposite page. This time use this decision tree diagram to sort the fish in a different way.

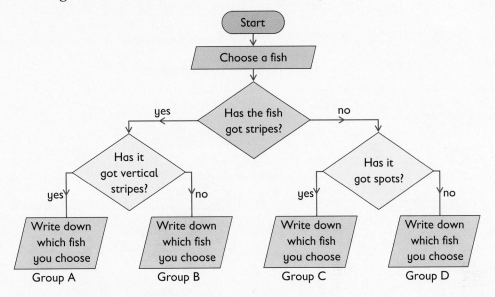

What groups have you sorted the fish into?

2 Design a decision tree diagram to sort the fish in the tank opposite into blue and red fish.

3 Design a decision tree diagram to sort the fish into:
- blue with stripes
- blue without stripes
- red with stripes
- red without stripes

4 Design your own decision tree diagram to sort the fish into different groups from those above.

Investigation

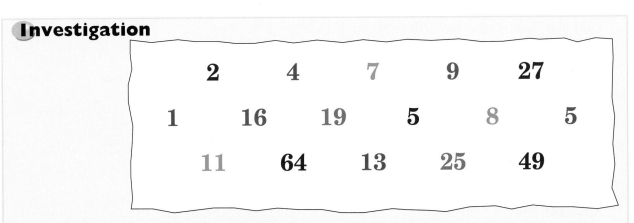

How many different ways can you sort these numbers?
Design two different decision tree diagrams to sort the numbers.

Flow charts and number patterns

A **flow chart** is a list of instructions and questions which help you carry out a task.

We can use flow charts to investigate number patterns.

Task

Use the flow chart above to make a 'number chain'.
What are these numbers called?

Now use the same flow chart but at the first instruction write down the number 2 instead of 1.
What are these numbers called?

 What numbers would you get if the starting number was 3?

Draw your own flow chart to generate the first 20 odd numbers.

Draw another flow chart to produce the first 5 multiples of 5.

How do you know when to stop?

Exercise

1 Follow this flow chart to make a number chain.
What types of number have you written down?

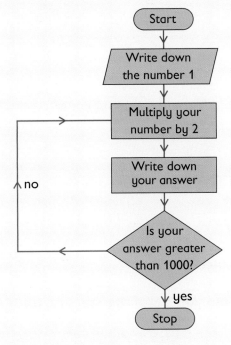

2 Design a flow chart to produce the answers to the seven times table.

3 Use the flow chart below to investigate a number pattern.

How many numbers do you think you will have to write down before you get to a number greater than 1000?

Use the flow chart to check your answer.

Activity Draw a flow chart to show how to make a cup of tea.
Draw a flow chart to show how to complete another activity.

Working systematically with patterns

Tanya is stacking cans at her local supermarket.
She has made a stack which is four layers high.

 How many cans are there in this stack?

Tanya wants to know how many cans would be in a
stack which is 12 layers high.

 How can she work this out?

Tanya decides to work systematically so that she will know that she has found the
right answer.

She starts by looking at one layer: Then two layers:

There is 1 can.

There are 3 cans.

Task

Draw the next three layers in Tanya's stack of cans.
How many cans are there in each?

Tanya makes a table to help her find a pattern.

Number of layers	Number of cans	
1	1	
2	3	goes up by 2
3	?	goes up by ?
4	?	goes up by ?
5		goes up by ?
6		

Task

Use Tanya's pattern to work out how many cans there are in 10 layers.
Now work out how to stack 100 cans.

 What are the advantages of working systematically?

Investigation Andy washes up on a Saturday morning in the local cafe.

He stacks the cups and saucers like this:

Andy can put as many saucers on top of each other as he likes.

However he can't put a cup on top of a cup else the pile will fall over.

Andy wants to work out how many different ways he can stack 10 items.

He starts by drawing three different ways:

Andy isn't working systematically.

(a) How will he know that he has found all the different ways possible?

(b) What should Andy do to help him find a pattern?

Andy starts again, this time working systematically.
He looks at stacking 1 item then 2 items and so on.

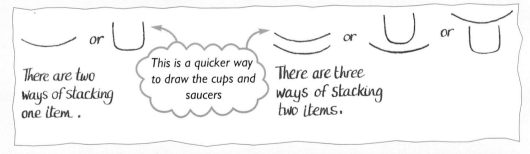

There are two ways of stacking one item.

This is a quicker way to draw the cups and saucers

There are three ways of stacking two items.

(c) Draw all the ways of stacking 3, 4 and 5 items making sure that you are working logically.

(d) How many ways are there of stacking 6 items?

(e) Predict how many ways there are of stacking 10 items.

(f) Why was it easier to work systematically to solve this problem?

(g) This number pattern has a special name.
Find out what they are called.

Growth patterns

Karen is making growth patterns using match sticks.

Here are the first three stages of the growth pattern:

Karen adds two more matches to make the second stage.

Task

1 What will the next stage in Karen's pattern look like?
 Draw the next four stages.

2 How many matches are added to make *each new stage*?

Karen counts how many matches she needs for the first three stages.

 How many matches are used for the next two stages?

Karen makes a table for her growth pattern.

You can write this as
$1 \rightarrow 3$, $2 \rightarrow 5$
This is called
a **mapping**.

Number of Stages	Number of Matches
1	3
2	5
3	?
4	?
5	?
6	?

Task

Complete Karen's table. What patterns do you notice?
How many matches will be used in **(a)** the next stage?
                                 (b) the 10th stage?

 How can you check that you are right?

Exercise

For each question
(a) draw the next three growth patterns
(b) copy and complete the table
(c) predict how many match sticks or squares are needed for the next two stages.

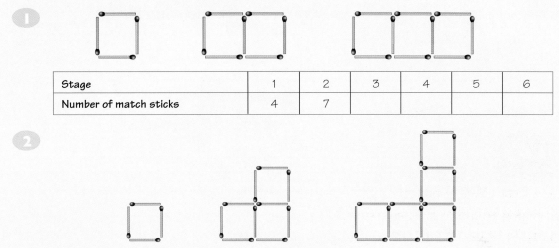

1

Stage	1	2	3	4	5	6
Number of match sticks	4	7				

2

Stage	1	2	3	4	5	6
Number of squares	1	3				
Number of match sticks	4	10				

3

Stage	1	2	3	4	5	6
Number of squares	1	4				
Number of match sticks	4	13				

4

Stage	1	2	3	4	5	6
Number of match sticks	6	11				

Investigation Invent your own growth patterns using match sticks or squares. Show the number of match sticks or squares at each stage in a table.

Number patterns – making predictions

Ted is building a fence.
To make one section Ted needs

> 2 upright posts
> and 2 horizontal bars.

Ted now adds another section of fencing.
He now uses

> 3 upright posts
> and 4 horizontal bars.

 What will three sections of fencing look like?
How many posts and bars will Ted need for three sections?

Ted wants to make a fence using 20 sections.
He wants to find a pattern so that he can work out how many posts and bars he will need.
Ted makes two mappings to help him.

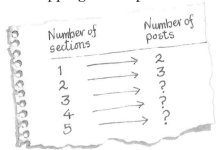

Number of sections	Number of posts
1	→ 2
2	→ 3
3	→ ?
4	→ ?
5	→ ?

Number of sections	Number of bars
1	→ 2
2	→ 4
3	→ ?
4	→ ?
5	→ ?

Task

1 Draw the next three stages in Ted's fencing pattern.

2 How many bars and posts does Ted need for:
  (a) 4 sections   **(b)** 5 sections   **(c)** 6 sections?
  What patterns do you notice?

3 Make a prediction for 8 sections and check it.

Ted writes down the rules:

> Number of posts = number of sections + 1
>   So $p = s + 1$
>
> Number of bars = 2 × the number of sections
>   So $b = 2s$

What do p, s and b stand for?
How many bars and posts are needed for (a) 20 sections? (b) 100 sections?

Exercise

1 Mark wants to build a fence around his garden.
This is one section.

He adds on another section.

(a) Draw what up to five sections would look like.
(b) How many bars and posts need to be added for each section?
(c) Make two mappings like Ted did on the opposite page to show how many posts and bars Mark will need for up to five sections.
(d) Predict how many posts and cross bars Mark will need for
   (i) 10   (ii) 20   (iii) 50   sections.
(e) Explain how you worked out your answers to part (c).
(f) Write down the rule you are using.

2 Penny is making patterns using hoops.

?
1   2   3   4

(a) Draw the first pattern.
(b) Draw patterns five and six.
(c) Complete Penny's table for the first 6 patterns.

Pattern	Number of hoops
1	?
2	6
3	?

(d) How many hoops are needed for the
   (i) 7th   (ii) 10th   (iii) 20th   pattern?
(e) Explain how you worked out your answers to part (d).
(f) Write down the rule you are using.

Finishing off

Now that you have finished this chapter you should be able to:

- continue with a pattern
- work systematically
- use and design a flow chart
- spot patterns
- use and design decision tree diagrams
- draw a table to organise your results
- make predictions and check them
- write down a rule.

Review exercise

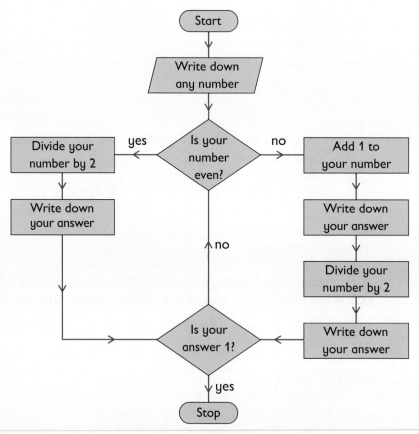

(a) Write down the number chains for 5 different starting numbers.
(b) Why does the flow diagram stop at 1?
(c) Do large numbers have the longest chains?
(d) Which numbers have the shortest chains?

Investigate the number of chains for different starting numbers.

2 Sarah is building a fence.
These are the first two sections:

(a) Draw the next three stages.
(b) Copy and complete the tables.

Number of sections	1	2	3	4	5
Number of diagonal bars					

Number of sections	1	2	3	4	5
Number of horizontal bars					

(c) How many diagonal bars and horizontal bars are needed for ten sections?
Write down the rules you used to make your predictions.

3 Joe is building four footpaths at a cross-roads in the local park.
He needs to know how many paving stones he will need.

Stage 1

Stage 2

Stage 3

(a) Draw the next three stages. **(b)** Copy and complete the table.

Number of stages	1	2	3	4	5	6	7
Number of paving stones	1	5					

(c) Predict how many paving stones Joe will need for the 10th section.
(d) What pattern do you notice? Write down the rule in words.

Handshakes

If everyone in the class shook hands with everyone
else how many handshakes would there be?

Find out by working systematically and looking for
the pattern in your results.

Start by imagining that there are only two people in the class,
then three, and so on.

Division (dealing with remainders)

Look at the above.
When 23 is divided by 4 there is a remainder.

Now look carefully at the rope puzzle.
When a remainder can be cut up, the sensible answer is a decimal or fraction.

Sometimes a sensible answer is found by rounding down, sometimes by rounding up.

? **Which of these numbers is the most appropriate answer to each of the puzzles above?**

5 6 $5\frac{3}{4}$ 5.75

Task

Make up four questions where the answer is obtained by dividing 37 by 5.

One question should be written so that to get a sensible answer, you round up.

For the second question you will round down, and for the other two questions the sensible answer should be a fraction and a decimal.

When the sensible answer is not a whole number we need to turn the remainder into a decimal or a fraction.

EXAMPLE 1   The remainder as a fraction

$$23 \div 4 = 5\frac{3}{4}$$

The divisor

When 23 is divided by 4 the remainder is 3

Take the remainder into the next column.

EXAMPLE 2   The remainder as a decimal

$$4 \overline{)\, 23.^30^20}$$
$$5.\,7\,5$$

Keep dividing after the decimal point.

Add as many noughts as you need.

Exercise

1 Give a sensible answer to the following questions.

(a)
> I need 15 eggs.
> How many boxes should I buy?

(b) 4.2 lb
> How many 5lb bags of potatoes can be filled?

(c)
> The Cola is to be shared between 4 glasses. How much Cola in each glass?

2 A school has 1332 pupils and 92 members of staff. How many buses would be needed to take the whole school on an outing?
(A bus can carry 45 people.)

3 Neeta needs 478 tiles to tile her bathroom.
How many boxes should Neeta buy?
How many spare tiles will there be?

ECONOMY BATHROOM TILES
12 Tiles per pack

4 For each of the following division sums give the answer with the remainder expressed
(i) as a decimal   **(ii)** as a fraction.

(a) $57 \div 8$ **(b)** $679 \div 25$ **(c)** $532 \div 10$ **(d)** $235 \div 16$

5 For each of the following
(i) work out the remainder for each of the divisions
(ii) write the remainder as a fraction.

(a) $35 \div 4$ **(b)** $17 \div 5$ **(c)** $102 \div 20$ **(d)** $47 \div 9$ **(e)** $112 \div 7$

(f) $78 \div 15$ **(g)** $265 \div 27$ **(h)** $352 \div 19$

6 Give a suitable answer to the following
(a) £3 $\div$ 6   **(b)** £2.50 $\div$ 3   **(c)** £4.99 $\div$ 5   **(d)** £6.99 $\div$ 12

Activity It would be easier to use a calculator for parts (f), (g) and (h) of Question 5.

How can you use a calculator to find the remainder from a division sum?
Write a set of instructions for a friend.

Rounding (giving numbers to a sensible degree of accuracy)

Record Numbers Head for the Coast as Temperatures Soar

The AA reported that 4312 people per hour were heading into the coastal resort of Scarborough

> Welcome to Harrisville
> Population 253 892

? **Why are you unlikely to see information like this displayed so accurately?**

4312 lies between 4300 and 4400.

Which number is 4312 nearest to?
4312 = 4300 (correct to the nearest 100)

253 892 lies between 253 000 and 254 000

Which number is 253 892 nearest to?
253 892 = 254 000 (correct to the nearest 1000)

? **Why has the larger number been chosen in the second example?**

Task

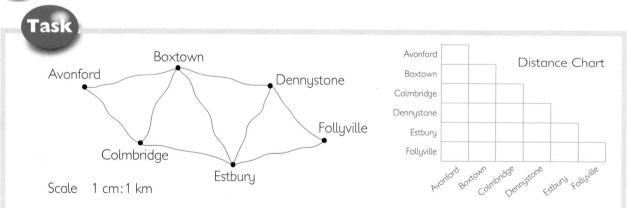

Scale   1 cm : 1 km

1 Measure the distances between the towns on the map as accurately as possible.
How accurate are your measurements?
2 Copy and complete the measurements on the distance chart.
How accurate are the measurements between towns Avonford and Dennystone and Boxtown and Follyville?

The number 23 000 is accurate to the nearest 1000.

23 000 to the nearest 1000 includes the numbers *from 22 500 to 23 500.*
This is known as the **range**.

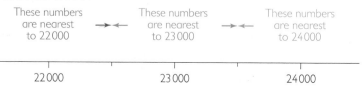

| These numbers are nearest to 22 000 | These numbers are nearest to 23 000 | These numbers are nearest to 24 000 |

22 000   23 000   24 000

Exercise

1 Give a sensible approximation to the numbers in each of the following statements.

(a) The number of bacteria in 1 litre of water is 43 659.

(b) There are 262 pencils in this box.

(c) I walk 789 metres to school.

(d) This box of apples weighs 9635 grams.

In each case, state the degree of accuracy you are using.

2 The population of Appleby village is given to the nearest 100.
What is the largest number that this could be?
What is the smallest?

3 The following statements are wrong.
Rewrite them correctly.

(a) 8346 = 835 (correct to the nearest 10).

(b) 7895 = 7900 (correct to the nearest 1000).

(c) 354 = 350.

4 What is the highest and lowest possible number of sweets in the jar?

5 Give the range of possible numbers in each of the following.

(a) 6750 (to the nearest 10)

(b) 3670 (to the nearest 10)

(c) 800 (to the nearest 100)

(d) 2000 (to the nearest 100)

(e) 2000 (to the nearest 1000).

Activity Look through an atlas or encyclopaedia until you find some numbers that have been rounded.
Record these numbers in a table like this.

Number	Information given	Degree of accuracy
2 175 000 km^2	area of Greenland	to the nearest 1000 km^2

Activity Collect some packets or boxes that display the number of average contents on the side (e.g. the number of matches in a box).

How accurate are the numbers you have found?
Explain your answers.

To the nearest whole number or whole unit

1

> 2.4 cm = 2 cm
> (correct to the nearest whole number)

2

> 12.7 kg = 13 kg
> (correct to the nearest whole number)

3

> 10.46 m = 10 m
> (correct to the nearest whole number)

Task

1 Make a copy of this number line

Use arrows to place 8.2, 5.6, 3.41 and 1.72 on the line.
Write each number to the nearest whole number.

2 Draw number lines to help you write these to the nearest whole number:

35.2   11.7   21.34   12.73

3 Write down a rule to explain when to round up to the next whole number and when to round down.
Give your rule to a friend and ask them to use it to write the following numbers to the nearest whole number.

8.75   12.12   29.8   312.49

 A length given as 5 m has been measured to the nearest metre.
What is the lowest possible value for the true measurement? What is the highest?

To the nearest penny

When a division sum involves an amount of money, the answer is not always an exact number of pennies.

The answer must then be rounded to the nearest penny.

34p ÷ 5   = 6.8p

> This equals 7p to the nearest penny.

£12.50 ÷ 8   = £1.5625

> This equals £1.56 to the nearest penny.

 Give your answers to the following correct to the nearest penny.
(a) 69p ÷ 7   (b) £2.95 ÷ 6

Exercise

1 Write the following numbers to the nearest whole number.
   (a) 67.2 **(b)** 345.9 **(c)** 2.95 **(d)** 9.36 **(e)** 9.78
   (f) 12.47 **(g)** 127.37 **(h)** 1.568 **(i)** 10.365 **(j)** 654.931

2 Give the answers to the following to the nearest penny.
   (a) 37p ÷ 4 **(b)** £1.32 ÷ 5 **(c)** 89p ÷ 7 **(d)** £4.80 ÷ 9
   (e) £12.60 ÷ 3 **(f)** £38 ÷ 6 **(g)** £115 ÷ 7 **(h)** £2.75 ÷ 15

3 Round the following to the required accuracy
   (a) 35.4 cm (nearest cm) **(b)** 15.47 kg (nearest kg)
   (c) 6.98 litres (nearest litre)

4 The following measurements have been taken to the accuracy stated.
   In each case give the highest and lowest possible value for
   that measurement.
   (a) 12 m (to the nearest m) **(b)** 78 cm (to the nearest cm)
   (c) 23 kg (to the nearest kg) **(d)** 4.56 m (to the nearest cm)
   (e) 560 g (to the nearest 10 g)

5 How many minutes is this for
   each question?
   Give your answer to the
   nearest minute.
   How long will it take to answer all
   7 questions?

> **MATHS EXAM**
>
> **Time allowed: 40 minutes**
>
> **This paper contains 7 questions**

6 £20 is to be shared equally between 9 children.
   (a) How much would each child receive?
   (b) How much of the £20 will be left?

7 Jane's aunt wishes to give her £500.
   She wants to pay this by giving her an equal amount each month
   for a year.
   Explain why this is not possible.

Investigation Numbers can also be rounded to a number of decimal places.
   Example 1 56.734 = 56.7 to one decimal place

   One number after the decimal point.

   No need to round up as this is nearer to 56.7 than 56.8.

   Example 2 8.4583 = 8.46 to two decimal places

   Two numbers after the decimal point.

   This number is rounded up because it is nearer to 8.46 than 8.45.

   Write the following numbers (a) correct to one decimal place and
   (b) correct to two decimal places?

   2.3647   35.431   456.945   0.1763

Checking your answers

$$81 - 54 = 37 \qquad 27 \times 93 = 6411$$

 The Calculations above are wrong.
How can you tell?

Answers can be checked by:

I Finding an approximate answer

> *Make these numbers as simple as possible so that you can do the calculation in your head.*

> *This means 'approximately equal to'.*

$$322 \times 8.9$$
$$\approx 300 \times 10 = 3\,000$$

> *Rounded to the nearest 100.*

> *Rounded to the nearest 10.*

 Find an approximate answer to $\dfrac{42 \times 112}{2.3}$

2 Using an inverse operation

> *Adding 34 is the inverse (opposite) of subtracting 34.*

$$72 - 34 = 38 \qquad \text{because} \qquad 38 + 34 = 72$$

 What is the inverse of divide by 6?
Use this to check if 480 ÷ 6 = 70 is correct.

Task

Use an approximation or an inverse operation to find which of the following calculations contain a mistake.
For each of the other calculations say whether they are (i) definitely correct
or (ii) could be correct

I $27 \times 82 = 2\,214$ **2** $85 - 47 = 22$ **3** $720 \div 12 = 60$

4 $\dfrac{87 \times 236}{15} = 13\,688$ **5** $\sqrt{74} = 8.062$ **6** $\sqrt{112} = 13.6$

Look at numbers 5 and 6 in the task.

The inverse of 'find the square root of' is 'square'.

 Between which two square numbers does 89 lie?

Explain why it is possible to say that $9 < \sqrt{89} < 10$
Explain why $\sqrt{45} = 5.71$ must be wrong.

Exercise

1   State the inverse operation for each of the following:
    (a) add 7   **(b)** subtract 4   **(c)** divide by 9
    (d) multiply by 8   **(e)** square   **(f)** halve
    (g) treble   **(h)** add 2 and then multiply by 4

2   Work out the following and then use an inverse operation to check
    your answers
    (a) $13 + 7$ **(b)** $67 - 45$ **(c)** $84 \div 7$
    (d) $\sqrt{64}$ **(e)** $8 \times 4 - 2$

3   For each of the calculations below there is a choice of possible answers.
    Use an approximation to help you select the correct answer.
    (a) $3.2 \times 8.9 =$ **(i)** 284.8   **(ii)** 28.48   **(iii)** 54.8

    (b) $72 \div 12.5 =$ **(i)** 9.45   **(ii)** 3.76   **(iii)** 5.76

    (c) $\frac{110 \times 94}{88} =$ **(i)** 117.5   **(ii)** 1 175   **(iii)** 11.75

    (d) $\sqrt{(37 \times 26)} =$ **(i)** 3.1016   **(ii)** 310.16   **(iii)** 31.016

4   $6 < \sqrt{40} < 7$ because $36 < 40 < 49$
    Write similar statements to show the approximate size of the following
    square roots.
    (a) $\sqrt{22}$ **(b)** $\sqrt{5}$ **(c)** $\sqrt{104}$ **(d)** $\sqrt{390}$

5   Jane has asked her friend to check her homework.

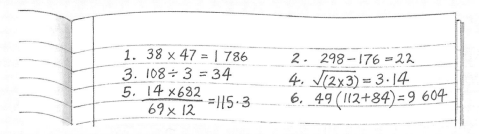

1. $38 \times 47 = 1\,786$ 2. $298 - 176 = 22$
3. $108 \div 3 = 34$ 4. $\sqrt{(2 \times 3)} = 3.14$
5. $\dfrac{14 \times 682}{69 \times 12} = 115.3$ 6. $49(112 + 84) = 9\,604$

Which of the calculations has Jane got wrong?
In each case explain Jane's mistake.

Investigation   Only one of the following four numbers is the correct answer to
59×122.

An approximate answer is $60 \times 120 = 7\,200$.

Choose the correct answer and explain your choice.

7 205   7 187   7 198   7 216

Finishing off

Now that you have finished this chapter you should be able to:

- give a sensible answer when a division sum gives a remainder
- round numbers to the nearest 1000, 100, 10
- give a range of values for a number given to a degree of accuracy
- round to the nearest whole number
- round to the nearest penny, centimetre, kilogram or any other unit of measure
- use an approximation or inverse operation to check your calculations
- place the square root of a number between two consecutive whole numbers.

Review exercise

1 Round the following numbers
   (i) to the nearest whole number   **(ii)** to the nearest 10.

   (a) 23.45   **(b)** 14.76   **(c)** 35.346   **(d)** 19.6
   (e) 135.4678   **(f)** 235   **(g)** 9.7   **(h)** 8.62

2 Give the following numbers
   (i) to the nearest 100   **(ii)** to the nearest 1000.

   (a) 2135   **(b)** 4697   **(c)** 8052   **(d)** 7049
   (e) 872   **(f)** 432   **(g)** 456   **(h)** 1456

3 The map shows the area, in square kilometres, of some countries in Europe. Give each one correct to the nearest thousand square km.

NORWAY 324220
FINLAND 337050
SWEDEN 449800
DENMARK 43075
BELGIUM 30513
SWITZERLAND 41288
FRANCE 552553
PORTUGAL 91631
AUSTRIA 83850
SPAIN 504879
ITALY 91631

4 By rounding the following numbers to a suitable degree of accuracy find an approximate answer to each of the following:
(a) 436×84 **(b)** $1095 \div 540$ **(c)** 8.36×12.7 **(d)** $42(87 + 94)$

5 Calculate to the nearest penny
(a) £7.83 ÷ 5 **(b)** £25.63 ÷ 4 **(c)** £143 ÷ 6 **(d)** £2.56 ÷ 7.3.

6 Round the following numbers
(i) to one decimal place **(ii)** to two decimal places.
(a) 4.734 **(b)** 35.683 **(c)** 0.1579 **(d)** 0.076

7 4 m to the nearest m covers a range of possible measurements.
This can be shown on a number line.

Use a number line to describe the range of the following quantities
(a) 7 m to the nearest m **(b)** £7 to the nearest £
(c) 250 cm to the nearest cm **(d)** 89 gm to the nearest gm
(e) 110 degrees to the nearest degree.

8 Find the remainder when
(a) 59 is divided by 7 **(b)** 247 is divided by 15
(c) 658 is divided by 39.

9 Between which two consecutive whole numbers do the following lie?
(a) $\sqrt{72}$ **(b)** $\sqrt{128}$ **(c)** $\sqrt{889}$

10 Rewrite the following sentences giving the numbers to a sensible degree of accuracy.
(a) There were 23 679 people at the match.
(b) The rope is 56.72 cm long.
(c) This week's lottery prize was worth £3 458 216.82.
(d) It takes 3 hr 17 min 45 secs to fly from London to Rome.
(e) The elephant weighs 972.5 kg.

11 The photograph shows part of a crowd of people attending a pop concert.
Estimate the number of people in the crowd in the photograph. Use the square grid to help you.

How accurate is your estimate?

It is very likely to rain again tomorrow.

It is unlikely that England will win the next World Cup.

My piano teacher says that I will probably pass my exam.

People often use words like 'probable', 'likely' and 'unlikely'.

You can use a **probability scale** to show how likely different events are.

Events with a probability of 0 are **impossible**.

0 $\frac{1}{2}$ 1

Events with a probability of 1 are **certain**.

? Think of some events with probability 0.
Think of some events with probability 1.

When you toss a coin, you have a 50-50 chance of getting a head.
This is sometimes called **evens**.
Getting a head when you toss a coin has a probability of $\frac{1}{2}$.

? Think of some more events with probability $\frac{1}{2}$.

You can put events on a probability scale to show how likely they are.
Very unlikely events go near the end marked 0.
Very likely events go near the end marked 1.
Other events might go nearer the middle.

Very unlikely

Very likely

0 $\frac{1}{2}$ 1

You will live to be 100 years old.

You will get a head when you toss a coin.

You will get married one day.

Task

In pairs, make a list of about 8 more events like the examples above.
Draw a probability scale and put each event on the scale.

Make a probability scale using the examples from the whole class.

Exercise

1 Choose one of these words or phrases to describe each of the events below.

certain   very likely   likely   evens   unlikely   very unlikely   impossible

(a) It will snow on Christmas Day.
(b) You will eat chips sometime this week.
(c) The day after Tuesday will be Wednesday.
(d) It will rain tomorrow.
(e) The next baby born in the local hospital will be a girl.
(f) You will get a 7 when you throw an ordinary die.
(g) There will be news on the TV tonight.
(h) You will visit the moon someday.

2 Copy this probability scale and mark each of the events in Question 1 on the scale.

0                     $\frac{1}{2}$ 1

3 Think of an event that is
(a) certain
(b) impossible
(c) very likely
(d) likely
(e) very unlikely
(f) likely
(g) evens

Draw a probability scale and mark each of your events on it.

4 **(a)** What do you think the weather is most likely to be tomorrow?

(b) Write these possible weathers in order of probability.
Put the most likely one first.
You can add some other types of weather if you like.

sunny   wet   cloudy   snowy   sunshine and showers

(c) Draw a probability scale and mark the different weathers on it.

Finding probabilities

Michael and Alistair are playing a board game.
They toss a coin to decide who will go first.
Michael calls 'heads'.

When you toss a coin, there are two
possible outcomes.
The coin could land on 'heads' or on 'tails'.
These two outcomes are equally likely.

*The probability of getting a
Head is 1 in 2, or $\frac{1}{2}$.*

Michael and Alistair need to throw a six to start.

When you throw a die, there are six possible outcomes.
The die could show any of the numbers 1, 2, 3, 4, 5 or 6.
These six outcomes are all equally likely.

*The probability of getting a
6 is 1 in 6, or $\frac{1}{6}$.*

 What is the probability of getting a 1 when throwing a die?
Is it harder to get a six than any other number?
What is the probability of *not* getting a 1?

If an event has *n* equally likely outcomes, the probability of each outcome is $\frac{1}{n}$.

 Task

Throw a die 60 times. Record the number of times each number comes up.

 How many times would you expect each number to come up?

Collect the whole class's results together.

 **How many times would you expect each number to come up in the
whole class?**
How close are your results?
**What would you expect to happen if you put the results from
5 classes together?**

Later in the game, Alistair has almost won.
He needs to get a 5 or a 6 on his next turn to win.

*The probability that Alistair will
win on this turn is 2 in 6, or $\frac{2}{6}$.*

There are six possible outcomes when Alistair throws the die.
There are two possible outcomes which mean that he will win.

 What is a simpler way of writing the fraction $\frac{2}{6}$?
What is the probability that Alistair will not win on this turn?

Exercise

1 Jason is using this six-sided spinner in a game.
What is the probability of getting
(a) 2
(b) red
(c) green
(d) blue
(e) an odd number
(f) yellow?

2 Amy picks a card at random from a normal pack of 52 cards.
What is the probability that Amy picks
(a) the Ace of Spades   **(b)** a card which is not the Ace of Spades
(c) a King   **(d)** a Heart
(e) a card which is not a Heart
(f) a picture card (a King, a Queen or a Jack)
(g) a red card
(h) a card with an even number on it?

3 Marie has a box of sweets. The sweets are different shapes and are
wrapped in different coloured papers.

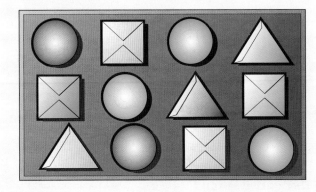

Marie chooses a sweet at random. What is the probability that she chooses
(a) a round sweet   **(b)** a sweet which is not round
(c) a square sweet   **(d)** a yellow sweet
(e) a green sweet   **(f)** a sweet which is not green
(g) a red triangular sweet   **(h)** a blue round sweet
(i) a green triangular sweet   **(j)** a round yellow sweet?

Investigation Toss a coin 20 times and record your results.
How many heads would you expect to get?

Repeat the experiment several times.
Were your results the same each time?

Fair games

Samir and Helen are playing a game with a 10 sided die.
Samir says

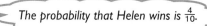

You win for numbers less than 5,
I win for numbers 5 or more.

 Is the game fair?
Explain your answer.

Helen wins if the number that
comes up is 1, 2, 3 or 4.

The probability that Helen wins is $\frac{4}{10}$.

Samir wins if the number that
comes up is 5, 6, 7, 8, 9 or 10.

The probability that Samir wins is $\frac{6}{10}$.

Samir is more likely to win the game, so the game is not fair.

 Do you think that Samir will win every time?
How many times do you think Samir will win if they play 10 times?

 Task

With a partner, play Samir and Helen's game 20 times.
(If you don't have a 10 sided die, you can use a set of playing cards.)

Think of a different rule that will make the game fair. Now play your game 20 times.

 Does a fair game mean that each player will always win the same number
of times?

Estimating probabilities

Helen thinks of a different game.
She says

Let's take it in turns to toss a
drawing pin. I win if it lands point up,
and you win if it lands point down.

 Do you think *this* game is fair?
Who do you think is more likely to win?

When you toss a coin, it is equally likely to land on heads or tails.
When you toss a drawing pin, it is not equally likely to
land point up or point down.
So you cannot write down a probability that a drawing
pin will land point down.

You can only carry out an experiment
to estimate the probability.

 Task

Toss a drawing pin 50 times. Keep a tally of the results.
Is it more likely to land point up or point down?

 Compare your results with the rest of the class.
How could you use your results to estimate the probability that the
drawing pin lands point up?

Exercise

1   Jamie and Joe are playing a game with an ordinary six-sided die.
Jamie has thought of some different rules which they could use.

For each rule, write down whether the game is fair or unfair.
(a) Jamie wins if an even number comes up.
(b) Jamie wins if a number in the 3 times table comes up.
(c) Jamie wins if a number less than 4 comes up.
(d) Jamie wins if a prime number comes up.
(e) Jamie wins if a number 3 or more comes up.

2   Michelle says

> *Tomorrow it could be sunny, wet or cloudy. That's three different possibilities. So the probability that it will be sunny is $\frac{1}{3}$.*

Is Michelle right?
Explain your answer.

3   Emma and Mark have a bag of coloured balls.
These are the balls that they have.

They take turns to pick a ball out of the bag without looking.
Emma says

> *I win if I pick out a red or blue ball. You win if you pick out a green or a yellow ball.*

(a) What is the probability that Emma wins?
(b) What is the probability that Mark wins?
(c) Is the game fair?
(d) Think of a different rule that would make the game fair.

4   A bag is filled with coloured tickets.
Janice shakes the bag, takes one out, records its colour and puts it back.
She does this several times. Here are her results.

Red	Green	Blue
6	15	4

(a) Use Janice's data to **estimate** the probability of getting each colour.

Later the bag is emptied and the tickets are counted:

Red 50,   Green 150,   Blue 50.

(b) Use these figures to **calculate** the probability of getting each colour.

Finishing off

| When you have finished this chapter you should be able to: |

- describe events using words such as certain, impossible, likely, unlikely and evens
- put events in order of probability
- mark events on a probability scale
- find the probability of an event using equally likely outcomes
- say whether a game is fair or unfair.

Review exercise

1   Choose one of these words or phrases to describe each of the events below.

certain   very likely   likely   evens   unlikely   very unlikely   impossible

  (a) Someone you know will win the lottery jackpot this week.
  (b) You will watch television tonight.
  (c) You will get a tail when you toss a coin.
  (d) You will get a six when you throw a die.
  (e) The sun will rise tomorrow.
  (f) You will live to be 200 years old.
  (g) You will see a red car on your way home from school.

2   Copy this probability scale and mark each of the events in Question 1 on the scale.

$$0 \qquad\qquad\qquad \tfrac{1}{2} \qquad\qquad\qquad 1$$

3   James is playing a game with an 8-sided die.
  The die has the numbers 1 to 8 on it.
  What is the probability that James scores
  (a) 5
  (b) an even number
  (c) 10
  (d) a number less than 4
  (e) a prime number
  (f) a number in the 3 times table.

4   50 tickets are sold for a raffle.
The main prize is a bicycle.

(a) Claire has bought 1 ticket. What is the probability that she wins the bicycle?

(b) John has bought 5 tickets. What is the probability that he wins the bicycle?

A ticket is drawn for the bicycle. Neither Claire nor John win.

(c) How many tickets are left in the draw?

The second prize is a bottle of wine.

(d) What is the probability that Claire wins the bottle of wine?

(e) What is the probability that John wins the bottle of wine?

5   Natalie and Liam are playing a game with this spinner.

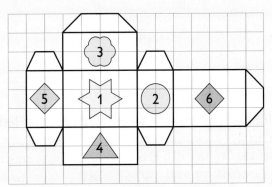

Which of these games is fair?

(a) Natalie wins if she gets red, otherwise Liam wins.

(b) Natalie wins if she gets a 1, otherwise Liam wins.

(c) Liam wins if he gets 2 or 3, otherwise Natalie wins.

(d) Natalie wins if she gets a 2, Liam wins if he gets a 3, otherwise it is a draw.

Think of another fair game they could play with the spinner.

Investigation   Copy this net onto centimetre squared paper or square dotty paper. Cut out the net and use it to make a die.

(a) Suppose you play a game with the die. You win if you score 1 or 6, and you lose if you score 2, 3, 4 or 5.
Do you think this is a fair game? Why?

(b) Play the game 50 times and keep a tally of your results.
Is the game fair?

(c) Can you find a fairer way of playing the game?

26 Transformations

This photograph of the night sky was taken by a camera with the shutter left open. Each line is the trail of a star as it moves round the sky during the hour.

? **What shape is the path of each star?**
Which stars move the most?

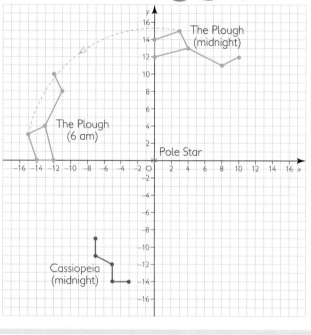

This kind of movement is called **rotation**.
Each trail you can see is part of a circle, called an **arc**.
All the circles have the same centre – the **centre of rotation**.

> The bright star near the centre of the picture is the Pole Star. It has hardly moved at all because it is almost at the centre of rotation.

You can plot the movement of the stars on a co-ordinate grid.
Here we can see how the Plough rotates in six hours.
The centre of rotation is the origin.
Each shape rotates a **quarter of a turn** (90°) in an **anticlockwise** direction.

 Task

1 Ask your teacher for a copy of the diagram above or copy it on to squared paper.
2 Copy and complete this table to show how the co-ordinates of the Plough have rotated.

The Plough		
midnight	→	6 am
(10, 12)		(−12, 10)
(8, 11)		
(6, 12)		
(4, 11)		
(3, 15)		(−15, 3)
(0, 12)		
(0, 14)		(−14, 0)

3 Make a similar table for Cassiopeia and draw its position at 6 am.
4 Place some tracing paper over the grid and stick a pin through the centre of rotation.

5 Trace the Plough and Cassiopeia at midnight then rotate them a ¼ of a turn anticlockwise.

? **Have you plotted Cassiopeia's 6 am position correctly?**

To describe a rotation accurately you must give the centre of rotation, the angle *and* the direction of turning.

Although the constellations have moved their *size* and *shape* have not changed. We say that the two outlines of the Plough are **congruent**.

Exercise

1 Draw and label a set of axes like the ones opposite.
Plot the following co-ordinates joining them *as you go along*.

$$(-16, 4) \quad (-13, 4) \quad (-10, 3) \quad (-7, 0) \quad (-10, 0) \quad (-13, -2)$$

You have drawn the constellation called *Camelopardalis* at 6 pm.
Plot and label the Pole Star at the origin.

(a) Draw and label the position of *Camelopardalis* at midnight when it
has rotated a quarter of a turn in an anticlockwise direction.
Use tracing paper if you wish.

(b) Draw and label the position of *Camelopardalis* after another six hours.
Describe fully the transformation which takes *Camelopardalis* from
its 6 pm position to its 6 am position. What do you notice about the
co-ordinates of *Camelopardalis* at 6 pm and 6 am?

2 Copy these grids and shapes on to squared paper.

 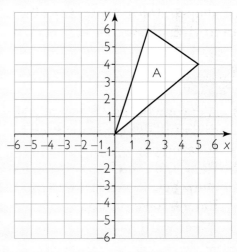

(a) For each one, rotate Shape A by a $\frac{1}{4}$ of a turn *in a clockwise direction*,
centre (0, 0). Label the resulting image B.

(b) For each one rotate Shape A by $\frac{1}{2}$ a turn around the origin.
Label the resulting image C.
Why does the direction not matter for this rotation?

3 Draw a pair of axes like those in Question 2.
Plot the following points and join them to form a letter L.

$$(0, 0) \quad (-5, 0) \quad (-5, 6) \quad (-3, 6) \quad (-3, 2) \quad (0, 2)$$

Rotate the L by $\frac{1}{4}$ of a turn *clockwise* and also by $\frac{1}{4}$ of a turn *anticlockwise*
about the origin. Label each image.
Describe *fully* the movement which would take one image to the other.

4 Why do the stars appear to move?
How long was the shutter open for the photograph opposite?

Translation

The movement of a shape in mathematics is called a **transformation**.
Rotation is one kind of transformation.
In the puzzle below the letter tiles slide to new positions in a different kind of way.

Task

Ask your teacher for a copy of the puzzle or copy it on to squared paper.

The S has been moved 4 to the right and 2 up.

I Draw the remaining tiles after you have followed these instructions:

  M   1 to the right and 2 up
  I   1 to the left and 2 up
  L   3 to the left and 2 up
  E   1 to the left and 2 up

What word have you made?

2 Write down the instructions which move the letters in LIMES to make SLIME on the bottom row.

3 Apply these instructions to the letters in SLIME.

  S   4 to the right and 6 up
  L   1 to the right and 6 up
  I   1 to the left and 6 up
  M   3 to the left and 6 up
  E   1 to the left and 6 up

What word have you made this time?

 What instruction moves the S in SMILE to the S in SLIME?
Write down the instructions which move the letters in SMILE to make SLIME on the bottom row.

The letter tiles in the puzzle move *without* turning.
This type of transformation is called **translation**.

When an **object** is translated, every point moves the *same distance* in a *parallel direction*.

Object ABC is translated 5 squares to the right and 1 square up to become **image** A' B' C'.
A maps to A', B maps to B' and C maps to C'.

 What translation takes A' B' C' to A" B" C"?
What translation takes A' B' C' to ABC?

What can you say about the shapes of these triangles regarding their shape and size?

Exercise

1. Describe the following transformations.
In each case say how many along and how many up or down

   (a) from C to B

   (b) from A to B

   (c) from D to A

   (d) from C to D

   (e) from D to C

   (f) from B to D

   (g) from B to C.

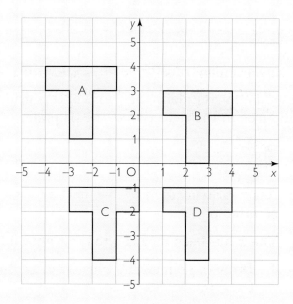

2. Draw x and y axes from -5 to $+5$ on centimetre squared paper.
Plot the following co-ordinates and join them to make a rectangle.

   $(1, 2)$ $(1, 5)$ $(3, 5)$ $(3, 2)$

   Label this rectangle P.

   (a) Translate rectangle P 5 to the left and 3 down. Label the new rectangle Q.

   (b) Translate rectangle P 1 to the left and 5 down. Label the new rectangle R.

   (c) Translate rectangle R 2 to the right and 4 up. Label the new rectangle S.

   (d) Describe the translation which takes P to S.

   (e) Translate rectangle Q 0 along and 3 up. Label the new rectangle T.

   (f) Describe the translation which takes T to P.

3. Draw and label x and y axes from -9 to $+9$.
Plot the following points and join them to make a triangle.

   $(-8, 2)$ $(-6, 7)$ $(-3, 2)$

   Label this triangle W.

   (a) Translate triangle W 11 to the right and 2 up. Label the new triangle X.

   (b) Rotate triangle X by $\frac{1}{2}$ a turn about the origin. Label the new triangle Y.

   (c) Rotate triangle W by $\frac{1}{2}$ a turn about the origin. Label the new triangle Z.

   (d) What transformation takes Y to Z? What do you notice about this transformation?

Reflection

Shapes can be transformed by **reflection** in a mirror.

Stand a mirror along the *y* axis of this grid
and look at the reflection of the triangle.   You will see this:

 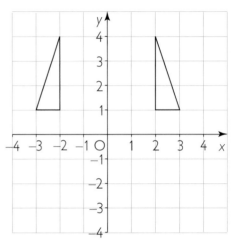

The shape on the left has been reflected in the *y* axis to form the shape on the right.

 Are the two triangles congruent?
What happens to writing when you read it in a mirror?

Task

I Copy the grid above with the single triangle on
to squared paper.
Draw where the triangle would be if you
reflected it in the *x* axis.
Check with a mirror.

2 Copy this grid including Shape A.
  (a) Reflect Shape A in the *y* axis.
      Label the result B.
  (b) Reflect B in the *x* axis.
      Label the result C.
  (c) Describe two transformations, one after the other, which would take C back to A.
      Does it matter what order the transformations are in?
  (d) Can you think of a *single* transformation which would take C to A?

 What happens to points on the mirror line in a reflection?

Shapes A, B and C are congruent.
Are they identical? Explain your answer.

To describe a reflection you *must* say where the mirror line is.

Exercise

1 **(a)** Copy this letter Y on to a co-ordinate grid as shown.

(b) Reflect the shape in the *y* axis. What can you say about the image?

(c) Reflect the new image in the *x* axis. Look carefully at the result. Is it 'back to front'?

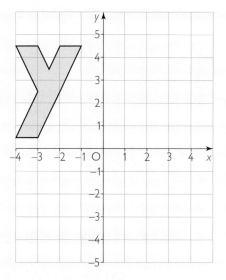

2 **(a)** Copy this letter A on to a co-ordinate grid as shown.

(b) Reflect the shape in the *y* axis. What can you say about the image?

(c) Reflect the new image in the *x* axis. Look carefully at the result. Is it 'back to front'?

(d) Why is the letter A always the 'right way round' but not the Y?

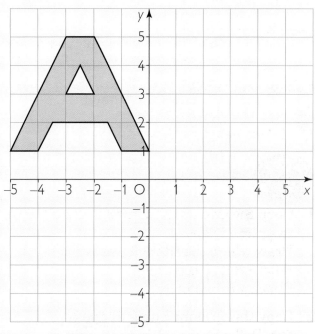

3 Draw *x* and *y* axes from −8 to +8. Plot the following points and join them to form a triangle labelled A.

$$(-7, -2) \quad (-2, -3) \quad (-5, -6)$$

Reflect triangle A in the *x* axis and label the image B.
Reflect triangle B in the *y* axis and label the new image C.
What single transformation would take A to C?

Activity Make a banner which says AMBULANCE when read in a mirror.

? Why do you see this sort of writing on the front of emergency vehicles?

Finishing off

Now that you have finished this chapter you should:

- be able to rotate, translate and reflect shapes on a co-ordinate grid
- know that these are types of transformation
- know that shapes which are the same size and shape as each other are congruent
- know that rotation, translation and reflection all produce images which are congruent with the original shape.

Review exercise

1. **(a)** Draw and label axes from -8 to $+8$ on centimetre squared paper.

   (b) Plot the following points and join them to form a triangle.

   $$(1, 2) \quad (3, 7) \quad (6, 1)$$

   Label the triangle A.

   (c) Reflect triangle A in the x axis and label the image B.

   (d) Rotate triangle B $\frac{1}{4}$ of a turn clockwise about centre of rotation $(0, 0)$.
   Label the image C.

   (e) Rotate triangle C $\frac{3}{4}$ of a turn anticlockwise about the origin.

   Label this image D.

   (f) What single transformation would have taken B straight to D?

   (g) Reflect D in the y axis.
   Where has D landed?

2. **(a)** Draw and label axes from -10 to $+10$.

   (b) Draw a shape on the grid which is not symmetrical.

   (c) Reflect the shape in the x axis.

   (d) Transform the image using a translation.

   (e) Is it possible to move the final image back to the original shape using a single transformation?

   If it is, can you describe the transformation which would do this?

3 All the shapes on this grid are congruent.

(a) For each of the following describe *fully* the transformation which takes the first shape on to the second.

(i) C to D

(ii) G to C

(iii) D to G

(iv) E to G.

(b) Think of a different transformation which takes C to D besides your answer to (a) part (i).

Why can both transformations work?

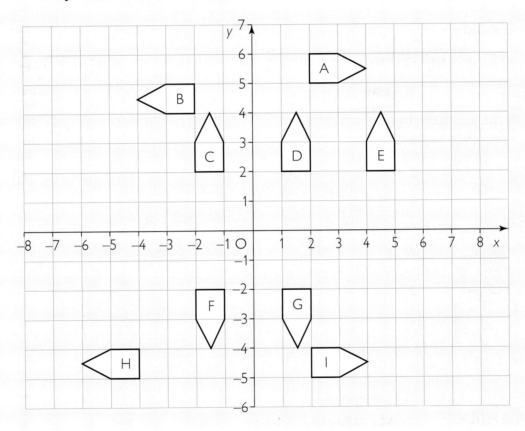

Investigation Find as many new transformations between pairs of shapes on the grid above as you can.

Beware – some of them are not easy to describe!

Investigation Draw this shape and reflect it in the *y* axis.

(a) What sort of triangle have you drawn?

(b) What can you say about its base angles?

(c) What happens if angle *A* is 60°?

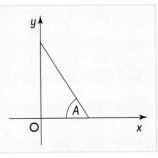

27 Operations in algebra

Brackets

Amber and Rhodri both enter $2 + 3 \times 5$ into their calculators.

The answer is 17.

No it's not. The answer is 25. My calculator says so, and calculators are never wrong.

Amber   Rhodri

Different calculators will give different answers.
How did the two calculators come up with 17 and 25?

$+$ and $\times$ are **operations**. The two calculators did the operations in different orders.

 What other operations are there?

You can use **brackets** to make the right order clear. You work out inside the brackets first.

Start by working out $6 + 8$ inside the brackets.

$(6 + 8) \div 2$
$14 \div 2$
7

$6 + (8 \div 2)$
$6 + 4$
10

Start by working out $8 \div 2$ inside the brackets.

⚠️ Brackets always come in pairs: (opening and closing).
You can never have one on its own.

Task

Look at this sum: $7 + 2 \times 3 - 1$
How many different answers can you find by using brackets in different places?
You may use more than one pair of brackets.

You also use brackets in algebra.

EXAMPLE   Find the value of $2 \times (x + y)$ when $x = 3$ and $y = 4$.

$2 \times (3 + 4)$
2×7
14

You would usually leave out the $\times$ sign in algebra and write this $2(x + y)$.

Another way of writing $2(x + y)$ is $2x + 2y$.

When $x = 3$ and $y = 4$
$2x + 2y = 6 + 8$
$= 14.$

This is the same answer as you got for $2(x + y)$.

 Choose different values for x and y. Use them to work out $2(x + y)$ and $2x + 2y$. Are the answers always the same? Is $2x - 2y$ the same as $2(x - y)$?

 How can you write $12x + 12y$ using brackets?

 How can you work out $2 \times (3 + 4)$ on your calculator?

Exercise

1 Work out the following

(a) $(2 + 3) \times 5$ **(b)** $(3 - 2) \times 100$ **(c)** $(2 + 1) \times 10$

(d) $(9 + 1) \times 10$ **(e)** $(12 - 2) \times 4$ **(f)** $(6 + 6) \times 3$

(g) $5 \times (8 - 4)$ **(h)** $(10 + 2) \div 3$ **(i)** $(7 + 3) \div 2$

(j) $9 \times (11 - 10)$ **(k)** $(5 + 2) \div 7$ **(l)** $(16 - 2) \div 7$

(m) $(4 - 1) \div 3$ **(n)** $(10 + 10) \times 5$ **(o)** $(6 \div 3) \times 5$

2 Work out the following

(a) $(5 + 4) \times (9 - 7)$ **(b)** $(9 - 1) \times (8 - 1)$ **(c)** $(100 - 10) \div (2 + 1)$

(d) $(3 + 2) \times (2 + 3)$ **(e)** $(5 - 4) \times (9 - 8)$ **(f)** $(6 + 6) \times (5 + 5)$

(g) $(3 - 2) \times (4 + 1)$ **(h)** $(6 - 2) \times (8 - 3)$ **(i)** $(9 - 4) \times (8 - 6)$

(j) $(7 - 1) - (8 - 6)$ **(k)** $(36 \div 3) \div (18 \div 9)$ **(l)** $(17 + 3) \div (8 - 3)$

(m) $(12 - 6) - (6 - 4)$ **(n)** $(12 \div 6) \div (6 \div 3)$ **(o)** $(9 \div 3) \times (5 - 2)$

3 Find the values of the following

(a) $3(x + y)$ when   **(i)** $x = 2$ and $y = 8$ **(ii)** $x = 4$ and $y = 1$

                    (iii) $x = 2$ and $y = 0$ **(iv)** $x = 5$ and $y = -1$

(b) $5(x - y)$ when   **(i)** $x = 10$ and $y = 8$ **(ii)** $x = 10$ and $y = 9$

                    (iii) $x = 10$ and $y = 0$ **(iv)** $x = 5$ and $y = 5$

(c) $(x + y) \times (x - y)$ when **(i)** $x = 5$ and $y = 2$ **(ii)** $x = 4$ and $y = 3$

                    (iii) $x = 6$ and $y = 0$ **(iv)** $x = 4$ and $y = 1$

(d) $(a + b + c) \div 3$ when **(i)** $a = 5, b = 6$ and   **(ii)** $a = 1, b = 1$ and

                        $c = 7$ $c = 1$

                    (iii) $a = 2, b = 1$ and   **(iv)** $a = 9, b = 6$ and

                        $c = 0$ $c = -6.$

4 Write the following without brackets

(a) $4(x + y)$ **(b)** $3(p + 2q)$ **(c)** $2(x + 2y + 3z)$

(d) $7(2a + 3b)$ **(e)** $4(5l - 2m)$ **(f)** $3(4a - 3b - 2c + d)$

5 Write the following using brackets

(a) $2x + 2y$ **(b)** $5a + 5b$ **(c)** $6c + 6d$

(d) $4p + 4q$ **(e)** $99l - 99m$ **(f)** $9x + 9y - 9z$

6 Check that you can use brackets on your calculator. Use it to check your answers to Question 1.

Investigation Sometimes you meet brackets inside brackets.

Work through

$$(2 + (4 - 3) \times 5) \times 6 - 1$$

to get the answer 41.

Copy and complete this rule:

    'Start with the ... brackets and work ...'.

BIDMAS

Look at this picture.

It contains squares of various sizes.

 How does the picture show you that
$4 \times 3^2 + 5 \times 2^2 + 8 \times 1^2 = 64$?

In the last lesson you learnt about brackets.
You always work out inside brackets first.

There are 3 operations in $4 \times 3^2 + 5 \times 2^2 + 8 \times 1^2$.
They are $\times$, $+$ and square.

Square can also be called 'to the power 2' or 'Index 2'.
To get the answer 64, you must carry out the operations in the right order.

	4×3^2	$+$	5×2^2	$+$	8×1^2
Index (square)	4×9	$+$	5×4	$+$	8×1
Multiply	36	$+$	20	$+$	8
Add			$= 64$		

You will find the word BIDMAS helpful.
It tells you the right order to carry out the operations.

B rackets
I ndex
D ivide
M ultiply
A dd
S ubtract

 Task

Copy and complete this cross-number:

Across
1 $120 \times 2 + 14$
4 $3 \times (11 \times 1000 + 1)$
6 3×2^2
7 $(2 + 2)^3$
8 $(21 \times 10 - 9)^2$
10 $1000 \div 5 - 9$

Down
1 $2 \times 10^4 + 3 \times 10^3 + 2 \times 10^2 + 1$
2 $(50 + 50) \div 2$
3 $200^2 + 3 \times 200 + 1$
4 $(1000 - 58) \div 3$
5 $(3 \times 10 + 1) \times (12 - 1)$
9 $(4 + 3 \times 2) \times 5 - 1$

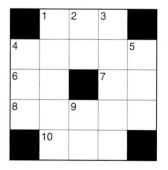

Now make a cross-number of your own with clues like these.
Ask a friend to test it. Then write it on a poster.

 How do you write (a) $x \times x \times x$
(b) $x + x + x$
(c) $x \times x + x$?

Exercise

1 Work out the following
    (a) $3 \times 10 + 4$ **(b)** $5 \times 10 + 9$ **(c)** $8 + 10 + 1$
    (d) 4×10^2 **(e)** 5×10^3 **(f)** 2×10^4
    (g) $4 \times 10^2 + 5 \times 10 + 1$ **(h)** $4 \times 10^2 + 5 \times 10$ **(i)** $4 + 10^2 + 1$
    (j) $3 \times 10^3 + 4 \times 10^2 + 6 \times 10 + 9$ **(k)** $3 \times 10^3 + 6 \times 10 + 9$
    (l) $3 \times 10^3 + 4 \times 10^2 + 9$ **(m)** $3 \times 10^3 + 9$
    (n) $3 \times 10^3 + 4 \times 10^2 + 6 \times 10$ **(o)** $3 \times 10^3 + 4 \times 10^2$

2 Write out the following
    (a) $1 + 3 \times 5$ **(b)** $12 + 8 \div 4$ **(c)** $(17 - 2) \div 3$
    (d) $6 + 2^3$ **(e)** $10^3 - 1$ **(f)** $2^3 + 3^2$
    (g) $3^2 - 2^3$ **(h)** $10^3 + 10^2 + 10 + 1$ **(i)** $(2 \times 8 + 4)^2$
    (j) $(29 - 4) \div 5$ **(k)** $3 \times 2^2 + 8$ **(l)** $(7 + 2 \times 2 - 1)^2$

3 Find the values of the following
    (a) $x^2 + y$ when   **(i)** $x = 2$ and $y = 3$ **(ii)** $x = 4$ and $y = 3$
                            (iii) $x = 1$ and $y = 1$ **(iv)** $x = 5$ and $y = 2$
    (b) $x + y^2$ when   **(i)** $x = 2$ and $y = 3$ **(ii)** $x = 4$ and $y = 3$
                            (iii) $x = 1$ and $y = 1$ **(iv)** $x = 5$ and $y = 2$
    (c) $(x + y)^2$ when   **(i)** $x = 2$ and $y = 3$ **(ii)** $x = 4$ and $y = 3$
                            (iii) $x = 1$ and $y = 1$ **(iv)** $x = 5$ and $y = 2$
    (d) $(x + y) \times 2$ when   **(i)** $x = 2$ and $y = 3$ **(ii)** $x = 4$ and $y = 3$
                            (iii) $x = 1$ and $y = 1$ **(iv)** $x = 5$ and $y = 2$

Activity   Here is a message in code. You will need to work out the code.
What does it say?

    $3 + 5 \times 4$ $(5 + 5) \div 2$ $(2 + 1) \times (2 + 2)$

    $2^2 \times 3$ $3 \times 2 - 6$ $2^4 \div 4$

    $3 \times (4 + 1)$ $(4 + 3) \times (14 \div 7)$ $3^2 - 2^2$

Investigation   Prime Factors

    1 Show that $2^2 \times 3^2 \times 5 = 180$.
        2, 3 and 5 are all prime numbers.

        They are also factors of 180.

    2 Find the prime factors of the following numbers.
        (Write your answers like the factors for 180 above.)
        (a) 10 **(b)** 20 **(c)** 100 **(d)** 200 **(e)** 1000 **(f)** 1 million
        (g) 3 million

    3 Write down rules for finding the prime factors of a number.

Collecting like terms

Liz is organising an evening at the Spotted Dragon for people at work.
She has written the cost of tickets as £*f* and £*d*.

 Why does Liz not know the values of *f* and *d*?

	Cutting Room	Sewing room	Despatch	Office
The total cost, in £, is	$2f + 4d$	$+\quad 3f + 5d$	$+\quad 2f + 3d$	$+\quad 6f + d$

Tidy this up. Collect all
like items together:
$$2f + 3f + 2f + 6f + 4d + 5d + 3d + d$$
$$= 13f \quad + \quad 13d$$
$$= 13(f + d)$$

*This is called
an expression*

*In this case you can
use brackets.*

*All the f terms are **like** each
other. All the d terms are **like**
each other. The f terms are
unlike the d terms*

Task

The Spotted Dragon say the costs will be £15 (full evening) and £5 (disco only).
What is the total cost?

How many different ways can you find to work out the total cost?

Which is the easiest to work out? Which is the hardest?

Sometimes there are numbers and minus terms.

EXAMPLE   Tidy up $3x - 4 - 8x + 5 + 12x - 3 - 2x + 11$

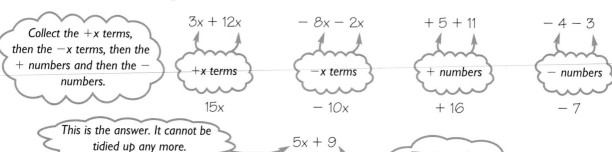

*Collect the +x terms,
then the −x terms, then the
+ numbers and then the −
numbers.*

$3x + 12x$	$- 8x - 2x$	$+ 5 + 11$	$- 4 - 3$
+x terms	*−x terms*	*+ numbers*	*− numbers*
$15x$	$- 10x$	$+ 16$	$- 7$

*This is the answer. It cannot be
tidied up any more.*

$5x + 9$

*This is another
expression.*

Exercise

1 Group the like terms together in these lists. The answer to part (a) is already there.
   (a) $+3x, +4y, +2x, -2y$ Answer $+3x, +2x$ and $+4y, -2y$
   (b) $+5x, +6y, -7x, -7y$
   (c) $+8x, +5, -7, -2x, +3x, -5$
   (d) $+8, -6, -2x, -3, +2y, -8$
   (e) $+a, +2a, +3b, +4, +5, +6b, +7a$

2 Tidy up the following
   (a) $5a + 3a$ **(b)** $4b + 7b$ **(c)** $3c - 2c + 4c$
   (d) $4d - 3d + d$ **(e)** $4e - 3e - e$ **(f)** $2f - f - f + 3f$
   (g) $3g - 2g - 8g + 11g$ **(h)** $6h + 2h - 9h + 11h$ **(i)** $i + 2i - 3i - 4i + 6i$
   (j) $2x + y + 3x + 2y$ **(k)** $5x + 2y + 6x + 9y$ **(l)** $5x - 4y - 4x + 6y$
   (m) $2x - 4y + 3x + 5x - 8y + 15y$
   (n) $3a + 2b - 4c + 5a - 3b - 2a + 5c - 2b + c$
   (o) $p - q - r + 2p + 3q - 3r + 4q - 5r + 6p - 7r + 2q$

3 Miranda keeps a record of the first and second class letters leaving her office. A first class letter cost fp to send. A second class letter cost sp.

	First Class	Second Class
	$f\,p$	$s\,p$
Monday	3	5
Tuesday	2	11
Wednesday	5	1
Thursday	20	12
Friday	10	11

   (a) What is the cost of the letters on each day of the week? Your answers will include the letters f and s.
   (b) What is the total cost?
   (c) At the time, $f = 29$ and $s = 21$. What is the total cost?

4 Tidy up the following. Use brackets in your answers where you can.
   (a) $2x + 3x + 10y - 5y$ **(b)** $3a + 5 + 4a + 2$
   (c) $2x + 6y + 8x - 3y$ **(d)** $7p - q + 3p - 1$
   (e) $8l + 6m - l + m$ **(f)** $8m + 25n + 7m - 15n - 5n$
   (g) $5x + 8 + 2x - 7$ **(h)** $5p + 7q + 5p - 7q$
   (i) $2(x + y) + x + 5y$ **(j)** $3(2x + y) + x + 10y$
   (k) $2(p + q) + 4p + q - 3p$ **(l)** $5(a + 2b) + 2(a + 2b) - 7b$
   (m) $2(x + 2y) + 3(x + 3y) + 2 (x - 3y)$ **(n)** $3(x - y) + 2(x + y) + 5(x + 2y)$

Inverse operations

Look at Kwame's game.
Try it with several different numbers.

 **Does Kwame's game always work?
Try starting with a minus number,
or a fraction.**

Kwame's Game

Think of a number
• **Multiply it by 2**
• **Add 5**
• **Subtract 5**
• **Divide your answer by 2**
  **You are back to the number
  you first thought of**

Take any starting number. Call it x.

* Multiply by 2 $2 \times x$ or $2x$
* Add 5 $2x + 5$
* Subtract 5 $2x + 5 - 5 = 2x$
* Divide by 2 $2 \times x \div 2 = x$

> These two cancel each other out.

> These two steps cancel each other out as well.

> This is the number you first thought of. So, yes, it always works.

You can see that -5 cancelled out $+5$
                      $\div 2$ cancelled out $\times 2$.

We say that $-$ is the **inverse** operation of $+$
                      $\div$ is the **inverse** operation of $\times$.

operation	Inverse operation
$+$	$-$
$-$	$+$
$\times$	$\div$
$\div$	$\times$

 What is the inverse operation of 'square'?

 Task

Make up a 'Think of a number' game of your own and try it with a friend.

You use inverse operations when you solve equations.
Look at this balance.

> Each coin weighs x grams.

 How does it give the equation $4x + 20 = x + 80$?

To solve the equation
1 Take away 20 from $4x + 20 - 20 = x + 80 - 20$ > $-$ is the inverse of $+$
   each side $4x$ $= x + 60$
2 Take away x from $4x - x$ $= +x - x + 60$ > $-$ is the inverse of $+$
   each side $3x$ $= 60$
3 Divide each side $3x \div 3$ $= 60 \div 3$
   by 3 x $= 20$ > $3x$ means $3 \times x$.
                                                       > $\div$ is the inverse of $\times$
So each coin weighs 20 grams.

Exercise

1 The diagram shows a journey made by a beetle. It starts at O and ends at O.

(a) Describe each stage of the journey. For example OA is 4 metres right.

(b) State which stages are the inverses of each other.

(c) What is the inverse of Left? What is the inverse of Down?

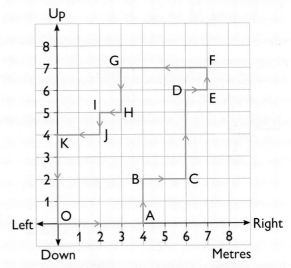

2 A soldier is on parade doing drill. He can be ordered 'Left Turn', 'Right Turn' or 'About Turn'.

(a) What is the inverse of the order 'Left Turn'?

(b) What is the inverse of the order 'Right Turn'?

(c) What is the inverse of the order 'About Turn'?

"About turn"

After about turn they face the other way.

3 Solve the following equations. Set out the various steps in full.

(a) $x + 5 = 7$

(b) $x - 6 = 1$

(c) $3x + 2 = 8$

(d) $5x + 8 = 18$

(e) $2x - 6 = 4$

(f) $2x - 2 = 12$

(g) $8x - 3 = 5$

(h) $5x - 2 = 18$

(i) $3x + 1 = 16$

(j) $4x + 2 = 14$

(k) $2 + 6x = 14$

(l) $7 + 2x = 17$

4 Solve the following equations. Set out the various steps in full.

(a) $12x + 5 = 10x + 9$

(b) $8x - 7 = 3x + 8$

(c) $4x + 2 = x + 8$

(d) $11x - 4 = 9x + 4$

(e) $16x - 7 = 9x + 42$

(f) $3x - 2 = 2x - 1$

(g) $4x + 1 = 2x + 21$

(h) $6x - 2 = 2x + 14$

(i) $3x + 8 = 19 - 8x$

(j) $16 - 7x = 18 - 9x$

(k) $3x + 2 + 2x - 3 = x + 7$

(l) $9x + 5 = 2x + 40 + 2x - 20$

5 Kwame thinks that solving $5x + 3 = 3x + 9$ gives $x = 3$.
He checks this by substituting $x = 3$ into both sides of the equation.

Left hand side: $5 \times 3 + 3 = 18$ Right hand side $3 \times 3 + 9 = 18$

The answers are the same so he is right.
Use this method to check all your answers to Question 3.

Finishing off

- work with brackets
- carry out operations in the correct order (BIDMAS)
- tidy up in algebra
- use inverse operations to help you solve equations.

Review exercise

1 Work out the following.
(a) $(2 + 3) \times 5$ (b) $(9 - 1) \div 4$ (c) $2 \times (4 - 1)$
(d) $(5 + 4) \times (5 - 4)$ (e) $(10 + 2) \times (14 - 2)$ (f) $(6 \times 2) \div (4 - 1)$

2 Find the values of the following.
(a) $5(x + y)$ when $x = 2$ and $y = 4$
(b) $3(x + 2y)$ when $x = 4$ and $y = 1$
(c) $(x + y) \times (x - y)$ when $x = 5$ and $y = 1$
(d) $(x + 1) \times (y + 1)$ when $x = 1$ and $y = 3$

3 Write the following using brackets.
(a) $2x + 2y$ (b) $4x + 4y$ (c) $6f + 6g$
(d) $12p + 12q$ (e) $6l - 6m$ (f) $6s - 6t$

4 Work out the following.
(a) $10^3 + 10^2 + 10 + 1$ (b) $2 \times 10^3 + 3 \times 10^2 + 4 \times 10 + 5$
(c) $2 + 3 \times 6$ (d) $(2 + 3) \times 4 + 1$
(e) $(2 + 3) \times (4 + 1)$ (f) $2 + 3 \times (4 + 1)$

5 Work out the following.
(a) $2^2 \times 3 \times 5$ (b) $2 \times 3^2 \times 5$ (c) $2 \times 3 \times 5^2$
(d) $2^2 \times 3^2 \times 5$ (e) $2 \times 3^2 \times 5^2$ (f) $2^2 \times 3^2 \times 5^2$

6 Tidy up the following. Use brackets in your answers where you can.
(a) $5a + b + 3a + 2b$ (b) $4c + 5d + 3c + 2d$
(c) $6x + 5 + 5x + 6$ (d) $12x + 6y - 10x - 4y$
(e) $6p + 3q + 4q + 2p + 10p + 11q$ (f) $3x - 4 - 2 - x + 6x + 8 + x$
(g) $5x + 4 + 2y - 2x - 6y - 3 + 6x + 8 + 9y - 3x$

7 Solve the following equations.
(a) $3x + 1 = 7$ (b) $4x + 5 = 25$ (c) $5x + 6 = 16$
(d) $3x - 2 = 4$ (e) $4x + 2 = 2x + 6$ (f) $11x - 1 = 10x + 5$
(g) $7x + 2 = 5x + 8$ (h) $12x + 8 = 9x + 11$ (i) $3x - 2 = 2 - x$
(j) $2 - x = 8 - 2x$

8 Check your answers to Question 7. Substitute the answers in both sides of the equation. You should get the same numbers.

9   Explain why this 'Think of a number' game works.
Start by calling your number x.

> Think of a number
> Multiply it by 3
> Add 4
> Add 2
> Subtract 6
> Divide by 3
> You are left with the
> number you first thought of.

10   Use your calculator to find $\sqrt{2}$.
Now find $(\sqrt{2})^2$ on your calculator. Explain your answer.

Investigation   Magic squares

In a magic square you get the same answer when you add up the numbers in each of the rows, in each of the columns *and* in each diagonal.

1   Show that Square 1 is a magic square.

13	8	9
6	10	14
11	12	7

Square 1

2   Now look at Square 2. It is given in algebra.
Show that Square 2 is a magic square.

$m + a$	$m - a + b$	$m - b$
$m - a - b$	m	$m + a + b$
$m + b$	$m + a - b$	$m - a$

Square 2

3   Find the values of m, a and b in Square 2 which give
   (a)   Square 1 values
   (b)   a magic square containing the numbers
         1, 2, 3, 4, 5, 6, 7, 8 and 9.

Answers

Here are the answers to the Review Exercises to enable you to check your progress. All other answers are supplied in the Teacher's Resource accompanying this book.

1 How our numbers work (pages 8–9)

1 (a) Twenty five thousand four hundred and sixty seven
   (b) Seven million, six hundred and forty nine thousand, three hundred and twenty five
   (c) Five hundred and sixty four million, seven hundred and forty four thousand, eight hundred and fifty three
   (d) One billion, thirty two million, four hundred thousand, six hundred and fifty seven

2 10^4, 40 × 1000, 45 678, 54 678, 10^5, 1 million

3 (a) Seven hundred and seventy eight million, three hundred thousand
   (b) Two million, one hundred and seventy five thousand
   (c) Eight thousand, eight hundred and forty eight
   (d) One hundred and sixty seven million
   (e) Thirty one million, five hundred and thirty six thousand
   (f) Two hundred and ninety nine million, seven hundred and ninety two thousand, five hundred

4 (a) 1 250 726   (b) 10 353 705 024

5 (a) 85 371   (b) 704 205
   (c) 6 003 205

6 (a) 60 000   (b) 6 400 000
   (c) 72 000   (d) 20
   (e) 30   (f) 30 000

7 £500

8 (a) 100 (b) 10 000 (c) 1 000 000

2 Position (pages 14–15)

1 (a) Trainers (b) Chair (c) A1, A2 (d) D2, D3

2 (a) 12 (b) 9 (c) 4 (d) 3 (e) 4 (f) G1, G14, F1, F13
   (g) C1 & C2, D1 & D2, E1 & E2, C11 & C12, D12 & D13, E13 & E14, H1& H2, H3 & H4

3 (a) 2C is the grid reference, 146 is the page number
   (b) Piccadilly Circus 1A 146, St James' Park 6A 146, Embankment 2D 146, Westminster 5D 146
   (c) (i) 4C (ii) 2A, 2B (iii) 6D, 5D

4 (a) 25 (b) 34 (c) A8 (d) Because cell D8 is highlighted
   (e) Means find the sum of cells D1 to D6 (f) 10 175
   (g) B2, B6, D2, D5, D6, D8, F4, F8

3 Basic number (pages 26–27)

1 (a) 85 (b) 396 (c) 678 (d) 187 (e) 623 (f) 701

2 (a) 47 (b) 90 (c) 108 (d) 77 (e) 224 (f) 636

3 (a) 117 (b) 91 (c) 100

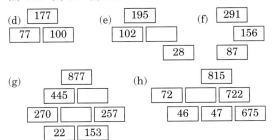

4 (a) 68 (b) 6 800 (c) 1 912 (d) 1 912 000 (e) 483
   (f) 4 830

5 (a) 1 505 (b) 48 438 (c) 47 151 (d) 10 971 (e) 45 496
   (f) 973 658

6 (a) 205 (b) 239 (c) 125 (d) 3 600 (e) 114 400
   (f) 2 060

7 (a) 612 804 (b) 405 612 804 (c) 405 612

8 (a) 72 (b) 36 (c) 74 (d) 296 (e) 2 664 (f) 1 332
   (g) 13 320 (h) 666 000

9 (a) 32 (b) 130 (c) 2 080 (d) 4 160 (e) 325 (f) 32 500

Activity

1 103 2 282 3 1 087 4 941 5 11 6 33 7 39 8 362
9 2 418 10 4 123 11 20 601 12 45 408 13 35 14 413
15 104 16 52 17 216 18 432 19 196 20 49

4 Angles (pages 38–39)

1 (a) F, B, D, A, E, C
   (b) (i) A (ii) B, D, F (iii) C

2 A = 113°, B = 49°, C = 343°

3 Ask your teacher to check your angles.

4 (a) 2 (b) 90° (c) 360° (d) 3 (e) 4

5 3°, 53°, right angle, obtuse angle, straight line, 240°, 300°

6 A = 34°, B = 146°, C = 120°, D = 133°, E = 121°, opposite sides of the quadrilateral are parallel

5 Displaying data (pages 48–49)

1 (a) 24 (b) 14 (c) 9
   (d) Ask your teacher to check your graph.

2 (a)

Grade	A	B	C	D	E
7T	4	10	8	5	3
7X	3	8	7	7	4

   (b) 30 (c) 29 (d) 7T

3 (a)

Drink	Tally	Frequency
Cola	卌 卌	10
Lemon	卌	5
Coffee	|||	3
Orange	||||	4
Tea	卌		6
	Total	28

   (b) 28 (c) Ask you teacher to check your pictogram

4 (a) $\frac{1}{4}$ (b) Dog (c) Dog, cat, guinea pig, rabbit, hamster

5 (a) People are less likely to be at work or school
   (b) 22nd July

(c)

Number of visitors	Tally	Frequency
0–49	||	2
50–99	卌 |||	8
100–149	卌	5
150–199		0
200–249	|||	3
250–299	卌 |||	8
300–349	||||	4
350–399			1
	Total	31

(d) Ask your teacher to check your bar chart.

6 Symmetry (pages 56–57)

1 (a) yes (b) no (c) yes (d) yes (e) no (f) yes (g) no (h) no (i) yes
2 (a) Denmark (1), Jamaica (2), Japan (2), Norway (1), Bangladesh (1), Botswana (2)
   (b) Jamaica (2), Japan (2), Trinidad and Tobago (2), Botswana (2)
3 Ask your teacher to check your answers.
4 Statues above entrance, window blinds, weathervane

7 Decimal notation (pages 64–65)

1 (a) $\frac{1}{4}$ (b) $\frac{3}{4}$ (c) $\frac{3}{8}$ (d) $\frac{5}{8}$ (e) $\frac{5}{8}$
2 (a) $\frac{1}{10}$ or $\frac{10}{100}$ (b) $\frac{3}{10}$ or $\frac{30}{100}$ (c) $\frac{13}{100}$ (d) $\frac{21}{100}$ (e) $\frac{37}{100}$
   (f) 0.1, 0.3, 0.13, 0.21, 0.37
3 4.6, 15.03, 0.009, 301.207, 0.059
4 (a) £0.11 (b) £0.23 (c) £0.08 (d) £0.02 (e) £1.95
   (f) £2.63
5 (a) A = 10.2, B = 11.4, C = 12.8, D = 13.6
   (b) W = 50, X = 58, Y = 64, Z = 76
   (c) L = 16.3, M = 16.8, N = 17.5
   (d) F = 88, G = 72, H = 52
6 (a) £3.92 (b) £1.08
7 (a) £27.32 (b) £2.68
8 (a) £17.03 (b) £8.53 (c) £4.55
9 (a) (i) Altogether £179.97 (ii) He has £20.03 left
   (b) £16.96

8 Co-ordinates (pages 72–73)

1 (a) (i) (0, 10) (ii) (20, 15)
   (b) (i) 15 km (ii) 25 km
   (c) (i) 15 km (ii) 20 km
2 (a) Ask you teacher to check your graph.
   (b) Hexagon (c) yes (d) no
3 Ask your teacher to check your graph.
   Add point (−3.5, −3.5) to make shape symmetrical
4 (a) A (−0.5, 0.5), B (0.5, 0.5), C (1.5, −0.5), D (−1.5, −0.5)
   (b) P(−1.4, 0.6), Q (0, 1.8), R (1.2, 0.4), S (−0.2, −0.8)
5 Because it is 4 away from his first guess.

9 Fractions (pages 84–85)

1 (a) $\frac{1}{4}$ (b) $\frac{1}{3}$ (c) $\frac{5}{7}$ (d) $\frac{3}{4}$ (e) $\frac{5}{8}$ (f) $\frac{3}{10}$
2 (a) $\frac{3}{4}$ (b) $\frac{4}{5}$ (c) $\frac{5}{6}$ (d) $\frac{3}{4}$ (e) $\frac{3}{5}$ (f) $\frac{3}{4}$ (g) $\frac{3}{5}$ (h) $\frac{2}{3}$ (i) $\frac{8}{9}$ (j) $\frac{1}{2}$
3 (a) $\frac{11}{100}$ (b) $\frac{3}{100}$ (c) $\frac{79}{100}$ (d) $\frac{91}{100}$
4 (a) $\frac{3}{25}$ (b) $\frac{1}{25}$ (c) $\frac{4}{5}$ (d) $\frac{23}{25}$ (e) $\frac{9}{20}$ (f) $\frac{9}{50}$ (g) $\frac{8}{25}$ (h) $\frac{3}{4}$
5 (a) £8 (b) 440 yards (c) 10 oz (d) £12
6 (a) £28 (b) £32 (c) £36 (d) £20 (e) £12 (f) £4
7 (a) £195 (b) $2 (c) 27 Euros (d) 36 kg (e) 2 m (f) 44 km
8 (a) $\frac{1}{12}$ (b) $\frac{2}{21}$ (c) $\frac{4}{13}$ (d) $\frac{1}{4}$ (e) $\frac{5}{55}$ (f) $\frac{2}{33}$
9 (a) $\frac{3}{5}$ (b) $\frac{1}{2}$ (c) $\frac{5}{14}$ (d) $\frac{12}{187}$ (e) $\frac{1}{63}$ (f) $\frac{7}{18}$
10 (a) 4 : 5 (b) 5 : 1 (c) 4 : 3 (d) 4 : 2 : 3 (e) 3 : 5 : 6
    (f) 8 : 5 : 6
11 (a) 3 kg lime and $1\frac{1}{2}$ kg potash
    (b) 8 kg hoof and horn, 8 kg lime, and 4 kg potash
12 (a) (3, 1), (6, 2), (9, 3)
    (b) $\frac{1}{3}, \frac{2}{6}, \frac{3}{9}$

Activity

(a) (i) $\frac{1}{36}$ (ii) $\frac{5}{36}$ (iii) $\frac{6}{36} = \frac{1}{6}$ (iv) $\frac{6}{36} = \frac{1}{6}$
(b) (ii) $\frac{4}{6} = \frac{2}{3}$ (c) $\frac{2}{6} = \frac{1}{3}$

10 Number patterns (pages 96–97)

1 (a) 3,6,9,12,15 (b) 7,14,21,28,35 (c) 12,24,36,48,60
   (d) 11,22,33,44,55 (e) 9,18,27,36,45 (f) 30,60,90,120,150
2 (a) 1,3,5,15 (b) 1,2,3,4,6,8,12,24 (c) 1,19 (d) 1,3,9,27
   (e) 1,2,4,8,16 (f) 1,13
   13 and 19 are prime
3 Ask you teacher to check your answers.
   (i) 9,16 and 64 can go into square trays
   (ii) 8,27 and 64 can go into cube shaped boxes
4 (a) 21,42,63 (b) 7,9,13,17,21,25,27,29,63
   (c) 9,16,25,64,100 (d) 8,27,64 (e) 7,13,17,29 (f) 8,16,64
5 (a) (i) 3 pcks hats, 2 pcks balloons, 3 pcks chocolates
   (ii) 8 balloons (iii) 3 hats
   (b) 20 friends
6 (a) 1, 2, 3, 6, 9, 18 pence
   (b) 18 pence

11 Everyday measures (pages 104–105)

1 86 400
2 Elephant – 1 ton
   Feather – 3 gm
   Baby – 4.5 kg
   Potatoes – 5 lb
   Sweets – 8 oz
3 (a) Longest river: Nile 6 669 km
   (b) tallest woman: 2.48 m (8 ft $1\frac{3}{4}$ in), a Zeng Jinlian
   (c) record for 100 metres: 9.79 sec (set in 1999 by Maurice Greene)
   (d) 5 litres in an average human man
   (e) heaviest man: 635 kg (100 stone), a Jon Minnoch
4 (a) 20 mins
   (b) 3 buses per hour
   (c) (i) 19:25 (ii) 10 mins
   (d) no – the last bus leaves at 8.39 p.m.
5 (a) 2 000 ml (b) 18 ft (c) 48 ounces
6 170 cm
7 (a) Monday and Thursday (b) No (c) 40 hrs
   (d) Friday – $6\frac{1}{2}$ hrs
8 15 people

12 Flat shapes (pages 116–117)

1 (a) isosceles triangle (b) regular pentagon
   (c) irregular hexagon (d) rectangle (e) scalene triangle
   (f) square (g) trapezium (h) irregular pentagon
   (i) rectangle (j) parallelogram (k) kite (l) rhombus
   (m) equilateral triangle
2 Ask your teacher to check your drawing.
3 Ask your teacher to check your drawing.
4 Ask your teacher to check your drawings.
   (c) Corresponding angles are equal.
      Each triangle contains a right angle.
      Angles inside each triangle add up to 180°.
5 Ask your teacher to check your answer.
6 Ask your teacher to check your drawing.
   Other two angles are 77° each.
7 23.3 m
8 Ask your teacher to check your drawing.

13 Multiplying and dividing decimals (pages 126–127)

1 £17.85 2 £47.36 3 £112.50
4 (a) 0.06 (b) 0.006 (c) 0.021 (d) 0.01 (e) 0.72
   (f) 0.00018
5 (a) 7.04 (b) 6.1488 (c) 0.9614 (d) 1.3485 (e) 0.167778
   (f) 143.82
6 (a) 1.75 (b) 0.12 (c) 0.85 (d) 0.65 (e) 8.9 (f) 1.6̇3̇
7

Fraction	Decimal
$\frac{1}{2}$	0.5
$\frac{1}{4}$	0.25
$\frac{3}{4}$	0.75
$\frac{1}{3}$	0.3̇
$\frac{2}{3}$	0.6̇

8 (a) 20.5 (b) 0.6 (c) 12.2 (d) 215 (e) 720 (f) 6
9 (a) £0.12 (b) £0.11   Second set
10 No, 26 × 0.7 = 18.2 cm
11 (a) 17.28 (b) 0.137 62 (c) 219.342 (d) 0.017
    (e) 1 029.031 (f) 0.001 12 (g) 2.34 (h) 0.356 (i) 3.2
    (j) 0.0141
12 (a) 0.375 (b) 0.6 (c) 0.4 (d) 0.625 (e) 0.875 (f) 0.1̇6̇
    (g) 0.8̇3̇ (h) 0.583̇
13 (a) 4 180 (b) 167.3 (c) 0.9 (d) 3 (e) 1 300 (f) 1 300
    (g) 0.4 (h) 7 (i) 4 000
14 (a) 7.36 (b) 0.003 (c) 0.0416 (d) 0.289 (e) 0.5
    (f) 0.163 (g) 0.000 2 (h) 0.000 004 (i) 0.000 007
15 (a) 44% (b) 40% (c) $37\frac{1}{2}$% (d) 45% (e) 11% (f) 7%
    (g) 60% (h) 75%
    7%, 11%, $37\frac{1}{2}$%, 40%, 44%, 45%, 60%, 75%
16 (a) $\frac{3}{5}$ (b) $\frac{3}{20}$ (c) $\frac{7}{25}$ (d) $\frac{1}{50}$
17 (a) 0.9 (b) 0.12 (c) 0.85 (d) 0.5̇
18 (a) $\frac{17}{100}$ (b) $\frac{3}{50}$ (c) $\frac{3}{10}$ (d) $\frac{1}{8}$

14 Number machines (pages 134–135)

1 (a) 2 (b) 3 (c) 50 (d) 0

2 (a)

Micro Mobiles	time in mins $\rightarrow \times 4 \rightarrow +20 \rightarrow$ Cost of call
Lo-Calls	time in mins $\rightarrow \times 6 \rightarrow +10 \rightarrow$ Cost of call

(b) Micro Mobiles (c) Lo-Call
(d) Micro Mobiles – 11 mins, Lo-Calls – 9 mins

3 (a) 4 (b) 6 (c) 11 (d) 17

4 (a) 2 (b) 12 (c) 5 (d) 10

5 (a) e.g.

4	$\rightarrow$	$\times 6$	$\rightarrow$	-3	$\rightarrow$	21
4	$\rightarrow$	$\times 2$	$\rightarrow$	$+13$	$\rightarrow$	21
4	$\rightarrow$	$\div 4$	$\rightarrow$	$+20$	$\rightarrow$	21
4	$\rightarrow$	$\times 4$	$\rightarrow$	$+5$	$\rightarrow$	21

(b) (i) 6 (ii) 26 (iii) 36 (iv) 101
(c) input $\rightarrow \times 5 \rightarrow +1 \rightarrow$ output
(d) (i) 8 (ii) 10 (iii) 15 (iv) 25

6 (a) (i) £7 (ii) £11 (iii) £19
(b) $c = 2 \times h - 1$

15 Scale (pages 142–143)

1

Object	Real length	Model length
Engine	20 m	10 cm
Level crossing	20 m	10 cm
Signals	8 m	4 cm
Station	100 m	50 cm
Tree	5 m	2.5 cm
Suitcase	100 cm or 1 m	5 mm
Station cat	40 cm	2 mm

2 (a) 1 : 300 (b) 1 : 20 (c) 1 : 100 000 (d) 1 : 50 000
(e) 1 : 500 000 (f) 1 : 20 (g) 1 : 50 (h) 1 : 2.5

3 (a) 1 cm to 0.25 km (b) 1 cm to 0.5 km (c) 1 km to 1 km

4 (a) 1 cm to 5 m (b) 4 cm to 1 m or 1 cm to 0.25 m
(c) 2 cm to 1 m or 1 cm to 0.5 m

5 (a) 2 miles (b) 3.5 miles (c) 4.75 miles

6 1 to 25

7 Forward 6, Left 90, Forward 1
Right 90, Forward 3, Left 90, Forward 5
Left 90, Forward 3, Right 90, Forward 1
Right 90, Forward 4, Left 90, Forward 1
Left 90, Forward 2, Right 90, Forward 1
Left 90, Forward 7, Left 90, Forward 5
Left 90, Forward 3, Right 90, Forward 1
Left 90, Forward 1, Right 90, Forward 1
Left 90, Forward 3, Left 90, Forward 1
Left 90, Forward 2, Right 90, Forward 1

8 (a) 500 m (b) 1700 m

16 Averages (pages 150–151)

1 (a) 2 (b) 2.2 (c) 2 (d) 6

2 (a) Mean for boys = 6.5
Mean for girls = 5.4
(b) Median for boys = 3.5
Median for girls = 5
(c) Mean
(d) Range for boys = 41, Range for girls = 9
(e) The boys' data is more spread out than the girls'.

3 (a) £3.25 (b) £4.225 or £4.23 (c) Mean (d) £3.40

4 (a)

46	47	48	49	50	51	52	53
1	2	3	5	9	6	3	1

(b) Mode = 50 (c) Mean = 49.8 (d) Median = 50

5 (a) Batch A mean = 1.688 Batch B mean = 1.8
median = 1.7 median = 1.7
range = 2 range = 3.4

17 Formulae (pages 156–157)

1 (a) A – adults C – children P – price
(b) (i) £14 (ii) £6 (iii) £29
(c) 4 (d) 3 (e) P = 3A + 2C (f) 6 children, 4 adults

2 (a) 2 (b) 0 (c) 22 (d) 100 (e) 1 (f) 101

3 (a) 20 (b) 5 (c) 13 (d) 30 (e) 25 (f) 12 (g) 20
(h) 21 (i) 5000 (j) 0

4 (a) cost = 2 × £3 + 4 × £4 = £22 (b) $C = 3h + 4g$
(c) £50 (d) 0 hamsters and 6 gerbils, or 3 gerbils and
4 hamsters, or 8 hamsters and 0 gerbils 3 ways

5 (a) Cost = 5 × 25 + 3 × 15 = £170 (b) Cost = $25l + 15s$
(c) £145 (d) 5 small (e) 2 large and 3 small

18 Negative numbers (pages 164–165)

1 (a) +40 (b) −60 (c) −200 (d) +24 (e) −3 (f) 2000

2

−10	−8	−6 −5		−1	0	2		5	6 7		10

3 −6, −3, −1, 0, +1, +5

4 (a) −1 (b) −1 (c) −3 (d) +3 (e) −6 (f) −1 (g) −8
(h) +7 (i) −4 (j) −36 (k) −24 (l) +8

5 (a) −2 (b) −7 (c) 2 (d) 0 (e) 4 (f) −4 (g) −3 (h) 2
(i) 6 (j) −9 (k) 3 (l) 9

6 (a) +10 (b) −8 (c) −11 (d) +7 (e) −3 (f) +7
(g) −4 (h) −15 (i) −2 (j) +33 (k) −28 (l) +22

7 (a) −8 (b) −15 (c) +42 (d) +36 (e) +30 (f) 0
(g) +1 (h) +9 (i) −8 (j) +625 (k) +16
(l) 4 × (−243) = −972

8 (a) −6 (b) +4 (c) +5 (d) −7 (e) +4 (f) +16 (g) −6
(h) −9 (i) −19 (j) +7 (k) −8 (l) −25

Activity
(a) −3 (b) −8 (c) 9 (d) −8 (e) 0 (f) +4 (g) +28
(h) −30 (i) −24 (j) −4 (k) −7 (l) 0 (m) 16 (n) −27

19 Equations (pages 172–173)

1 (a) A-5 g B-10 g C-20 g (b) D-0.5 g E-0.5 g F-1 g G-1 g

2 (a) 4 (b) 2 (c) 4 (d) 3

3 (a) 4 (b) 1 (c) 4 (d) 10 (e) 32 (f) 4 (g) 6 (h) 30 (i) 1

4 (a) 1 (b) 2 (c) 3 (d) 3 (e) 2 (f) 1 (g) 2 (h) 8 (i) 0

5 (a) 5 (b) 1 (c) 10 (d) 2 (e) 8 (f) 10 (g) 3 (h) 2 (i) 1

6 (a) 4n + 6 = 30 (b) 6

7 (a) 2n − 4 = 8 (b) 6

8 (a) 5p = 60 (b) 12p

9 (a) 24 + 4b = 84 (b) 15p

20 Solid shapes (pages 180–181)

1 (a) A, C, D, F, G (b) A, G

2 (a) cylinder (b) triangular prism (c) cuboid
(d) hexagonal prism (e) cuboid

3 A Isosceles triangular prism
B Irregular prism
C Cylinder
D Hexagonal prism
E Cuboid
F Equilateral triangular prism

4 (a) cuboid (b) rectangle

5 Cuboid

6 (a) Marble, golf ball, cricket ball, football (b) rugby

7 Ask your teacher to check your drawing.

8 All elevations are identical.

9 Ask your teacher to check your drawing.

21 Graphs (pages 188–189)

1 (a) 62 miles (b) 134 km (c) 106 miles (d) 84 km

2 (a)

Length of call (in mins)	1	2	3	4	5	6	7	8
Cost (in pence)	16	22	28	34	40	46	52	58

(b) Ask your teacher to check your graph.

3 (a) (0, 5), (1, 5), (2, 5), (3, 5), (4, 5), (5, 5), (6, 5) $y = 5$
(b) (4, 0), (4, 1), (4, 2), (4, 3), (4, 4), (5, 4), (6, 4) $x = 4$
(c) (0, 0), (1, 1), (2, 2), (3, 3), (4, 4), (5, 5), (6, 6) $y = x$
(d) (2, 0), (3, 1), (4, 2), (5, 3), (6, 4) $y = x - 2$
(e) (0, 2), (1, 3), (2, 4), (3, 5), (4, 6) $y = x + 2$
(f) (0, 6), (1, 5), (2, 4), (3, 3), (4, 2), (5, 1), (6, 0) $x + y = 6$
(g) (0, 4), (1, 3), (2, 2), (3, 1), (4, 0) $x + y = 4$

4 (i)

x	-4	-3	-2	-1	0	1	2	3	4
$y = x + 6$	2	3	4	5	6	7	8	9	10

(ii)

x	-4	-3	-2	-1	0	1	2	3	4
$y = 2x$	-8	-6	-4	-2	0	2	4	6	8

Ask your teacher to check your graphs.
5 (a) Ask your teacher to check your graphs.
(b) (i) e.g. (1, 0), (2, 0), (3, 0), (4, 0)
(ii) e.g. (0, 1), (0, 2), (0, 3), (0, 4)
$y = 0$ $x = 0$
(c) Ask your teacher to check your graphs. 90˚.

22 Measuring (pages 198–199)
1 (a) 20 cm, 24 cm² (b) 22 m, 24 m²
(c) 17 inches, 15 inches² (d) 19 yards, 22 yards²
(e) 4 miles, 1 mile²
2 approx 19 miles²
3 (a) 60 cm² (b) 12 m² (c) 63 cm²
4 13.5 feet²
5 (a) 54 m³ (b) 13.5 cm³

Investigation
1000 cm³; 1 ml = 1 cm³; total volume of cylinders in which fuel is burnt.

Investigation
Cheapest design (cube) costs £52.92

Activity
Approximate volumes: cassette case 122 cm³; CD case 176 cm³; imperial house brick 118 inches³; metric house brick $1397\frac{1}{2}$ cm³; this book 648 cm³; one page of this book 2.57 cm³.

23 Flow diagrams and number patterns (pages 210–211)
1 (a) Ask your teacher to check your answers
(b) Because $(1 + 1) \div 2 = 1$
(c) Not necessarily
(d) Shortest chains are the powers of 2 i.e. 2, 4, 8, 16, 32 . . .
2 (a)

Stage	1	2	3	4	5
Number of diagonal bars	2	4	6	8	10

(b)

Stage	1	2	3	4	5
Number of horizontal bars	3	6	9	12	15

(c) 20 diagonal bars and 30 horizontal bars
diagonal bars = 2 × number of sections   or D = 2S
cross bars = 3 × number of sections   or B = 3S
3 (a) Ask your teacher to check your diagrams.
(b)

Stage	1	2	3	4	5	6	7
Number of paving stones	1	5	9	13	17	21	25

(c) 37
(d) Increases by 4 each time.
Number of stones = 4 × stage −3

24 Accuracy (pages 220–221)
1 (a) 23 (b) 15 (c) 35 (d) 20
     20   10   40   20
(e) 135 (f) 235 (g) 10 (h) 9
     140   240   10   10

2 (a) 2100 (b) 4700 (c) 8100 (d) 7000
     2000   5000   8000   7000
(e) 900 (f) 400 (g) 500 (h) 1500
     1000   0   0   1000

3

France	553 000	Spain	505 000	Portugal	92 000
Belgium	31 000	Switzerland	41 000	Italy	92 000
Denmark	43 000	Sweden	450 000	Austria	84 000
Norway	324 000	Finland	337 000		

4 (a) 400 × 80 = 32 000 (or 400 × 100 = 40 000)
(b) 1 000 ÷ 500 = 2 (c) 8 × 12 = 96 (or 8 × 10 = 80)
(d) 40 (90 + 90) ≈ 40 × 200 = 8 000
5 (a) £1.57 (b) £6.41 (c) £23.83 (d) 35p
6 (a) (i) 4.7 (ii) 4.73 (b) (i) 35.7 (ii) 35.68
(c) (i) 0.2 (ii) 0.16 (d) (i) 0.1 (ii) 0.08
7 Ask your teacher to check your number lines.
8 (a) 3 (b) 7 (c) 34
9 (a) 8 and 9 (b) 11 and 12 (c) 29 and 30
10 Possible answers are:
(a) 24 000 (to the nearest 1 000)
(b) 57 cm (to the nearest cm)
(c) £3 500 000 (to the nearest £100 000)
(d) 3 hr 20 min (to the nearest 10 min)
(e) 1 000 kg (to the nearest 100 kg)
If you have given a different degree of accuracy, ask your teacher to check your answers.
11 Ask your teacher to check your answer.

25 Probability (pages 228–229)
1 Ask your teacher to check your answers.
2 Ask your teacher to check your answers.
3 (a) $\frac{1}{8}$ (b) $\frac{4}{8}$ or $\frac{1}{2}$ (c) 0 (d) $\frac{3}{8}$ (e) $\frac{4}{8}$ or $\frac{1}{2}$ (f) $\frac{2}{8}$ or $\frac{1}{4}$
4 (a) $\frac{1}{50}$ (b) $\frac{5}{50}$ or $\frac{1}{10}$ (c) 49 (d) $\frac{1}{49}$ (e) $\frac{5}{49}$
5 (a) fair (b) unfair (c) fair (d) fair

26 Transformations (pages 236–237)
1 Ask your teacher to check your diagrams.
(f) Rotation of $\frac{1}{2}$ turn about the origin.
(g) On A.
2 Ask your teacher to check your diagrams.
(e) This may be done by a reflection in a horizontal line, but only if the translation in (d) involved no left or right movement.
3 (a) (i) Reflection in y axis.
(ii) Rotation by $\frac{1}{2}$ turn about the origin.
(iii) Reflection in x axis.
(iv) Rotation by $\frac{1}{2}$ turn about (3, 0).
(b) Translation 3 to right, 0 up. C and D are symmetrical.

Investigation
72 transformations in total, some of which can be done in more than one way, due to the symmetry of the shape.
E.g. A → F is a rotation by $\frac{1}{4}$ turn clockwise about $(-3\frac{1}{2}, 3\frac{1}{2})$.

Investigation
(a) Isosceles (b) Equal (c) The triangle is equilateral.

27 Operations in algebra (pages 246–247)
1 (a) 25 (b) 2 (c) 6 (d) 9 (e) 144 (f) 4
2 (a) 30 (b) 18 (c) 24 (d) 8
3 (a) $2(x + y)$ (b) $4(x + y)$ (c) $6(f + g)$ (d) $12(p + q)$
(e) $6(l - m)$ (f) $6(s - t)$
4 (a) 1 111 (b) 2 345 (c) 20 (d) 21 (e) 25 (g) 17
5 (a) 60 (b) 90 (c) 150 (d) 180 (e) 450 (f) 900
6 (a) $8a + 3b$ (b) $7(c + d)$ (c) $11(x + 1)$ (d) $2(x + y)$
(e) $18(p + q)$ (f) $9x + 2$ (g) $6x + 5y + 9$
7 (a) 2 (b) 5 (c) 2 (d) 2 (e) 2 (f) 6 (g) 3 (h) 1 (i) 1
(j) 6
8 (a) 7 = 7 (b) 25 = 25 (c) 16 = 16 (d) 4 = 4
(e) 10 = 10 (f) 65 = 65 (g) 23 = 23 (h) 20 = 20
(i) 1 = 1 (j) −4 = −4
9 Steps are: x; $3x$; $3x + 4$; $3x + 6$; $3x$; x
10 $(\sqrt{2})^2 = 2$ $\sqrt{}$ and square are inverse operations

Investigation
1 All rows, columns and diagonals add to 30
2 All rows, columns and diagonals add to $3m$
3 (a) $m = 10, a = 3, b = 1$
(b) $m = 5, a = 3, b = 1$ or $m = 5, a = 1, b = 3$